The Holy Spirit

and the

ENDTIMES

BOOKS BY JAMES WILSON

Living as Ambassadors of Relationships
The Holy Spirit and the Endtimes

Available From
DESTINY IMAGE PUBLISHERS

The *Holy* *Spirit*

and the

ENDTIMES

A Season of Unusual Miracles

JAMES A. WILSON

DESTINY IMAGE® PUBLISHERS, INC.
P.O. Box 310, Shippensburg, PA 17257-0310

"Speaking to the Purposes of God for this Generation and for the Generations to Come."

This book and all other Destiny Image, Revival Press, Mercy Place, Fresh Bread, Destiny Image Fiction, and Treasure House books are available at Christian bookstores and distributors worldwide.

For a U.S. bookstore nearest you, call 1-800-722-6774.
For more information on foreign distributors, call 717-532-3040.
Or reach us on the Internet: www.destinyimage.com.

ISBN 10: 0-7684-2695-2
ISBN 13: 978-0-7684-2695-3

For Worldwide Distribution, Printed in the U.S.A.
1 2 3 4 5 6 7 8 9 10 11 / 12 11 10 09 08

DEDICATION

This book is dedicated to the memory of Ed Peterson and to the Lord my God. Ed's friendship and vision laid the groundwork for my understanding of ministry—after I had been in the ministry for over a decade and thought I knew what it was—and his inherited mantle formed the conceptual seedbed of the prophetic community for me. And the Lord my God—He is all things, and we can do all things in Him who strengthens us.

ACKNOWLEDGMENTS

I want to acknowledge and thank Ronda Ranalli, Jonathan Nori, Dean Drawbaugh, and the rest of the wonderful staff at Destiny Image Publishers for their faithfulness and their willingness to take risks for what they believe God is saying and doing. Thanks go also to Dr. Andre Van Mol; he is merciless, but surgically spot on, when it comes to reviewing what I have written for both accuracy and interest. I deeply appreciate his friendship. I am again deeply grateful to Nick and Kristin Sorani, and to Ray Shelton and the staff and owners of the JH Ranch, for their encouragement and for the provision of a place to write that is free from telephones, television, and too many knocks on the door. These friends literally and figuratively prepare tables in the wilderness—under the hand of God.

I don't know how to express my appreciation to Bill Johnson and the staff and leaders of Bethel Church, Redding. They are always there when Diana or I need support of any kind, and their encouragement has sustained us in dark nights and bright mornings. Mike Flynn is a co-laborer in the denominational field in which God filled us with His Spirit and His vision for branch and vine stretching way beyond one field without ever forgetting where it is rooted. Mike has mentored me when it was easy and when it was hard. John-David Schofield is a bishop in that same branch who has never been shy about who he is in Christ inside and beyond it. He has been a spiritual father to me and to countless others—and a great encourager of my witness.

I am deeply grateful to the people of the prophetic community in these latter days still under construction —and especially those whose names are unknown beyond a limited circle but whose witness is a component in the composite beacon of revelation that is the 29th chapter of the Book of Acts. These are the obscure little ones who received miracles and could not stop telling the story—like Gina, whose legs God restored from the disintegration of a car crash. There is Larry, who said unity in the Body will come only when we are hungry enough for it; pray not for unity, but for a hunger for it. There is Sinner Fiend, a Christian band who worshiped the Lord and risked big by depending on the Lord to keep instruments dry, as they transported them to a practice site in an open truck. (It rained everywhere in town except on them that night.) Ken Greenlee, Pio Arce, Lolita and Amado Medina, Mike and Judy Phillips, Steven and Helen Anderson, Hakon and Marie

Enoksson, and Reggie and Kante Kumar are friends we have met around the world who teach and bless us by their presence in our lives. And last, but certainly not least, the core team of intercessors for our ministry—led by Diana—whose faithful prayers are answered each time the Lord makes a miracle on our mission trips inside California and around the world. Their faithfulness is the ground on which we stand, as we seek the face of the Lord.

Diana and my children are the ground on which I stand in another way. Without them I would have no idea who I am or who I am called to become.

Finally, there is the Lord Himself, who was and is and is to come. Come soon.

ENDORSEMENTS

Jim Wilson carries within him great vision and passion for the Kingdom of God to break out on earth bringing transformation of lives, communities and even nations.

Jim offers in *The Holy Spirit and the Endtimes* a solid biblical foundation alongside some wonderful present day testimonies of how this process of transformation can work out in our world.

This book gives a refreshing and hope-filled outlook on these latter days, encouraging us to participate with the purposes of God and showing that we all in the Body of Christ can be actively involved in the prophetic acts and outworking of the Kingdom in our time. The Church is called to be a prophetic community, and this book teaches us how we can become that in meaningful and powerful ways. Jim also brings to us a healthy, God-focused understanding of spiritual warfare that the Church so desperately needs to hear in this time.

I heartily recommend *The Holy Spirit and the Endtimes* to you.

Steven Anderson
National Director, Healing Rooms,
Scotland

Jim Wilson's honesty and humility are used to demystify the area of prophecy and make it available to all believers. His relationship with the Lord has enabled him to plumb the depths of Christian realities and present them with fresh meaning and applicability, and his well-told stories verify to the reader the usefulness of the lessons he shares.

Rev. Mike Flynn
Director of Fresh Wind Ministries
Author, *How to be Good Without
Really Trying* and others

"They are a prophetic community in the best sense of that word because they reflect the Word that establishes that community and—by its expression—leaves no room for a counterfeit substitute." As quoted in his preface of, *The Holy Spirit and the Endtimes: A Season of Unusual Miracles*, Jim Wilson, in this foundational teaching for walking in the emerging apostolic and prophetic journey, tells it truly like it is from past, present, and future. This is a "must have" source for anyone wanting to understand the evolving messengers—the fivefold ministry—as called upon to further establish the Kingdom of God in earth as it is in Heaven. Jim has heard from God to give us such a clarion guide.

John Mark Pool
Founder Word to the World Ministries
Author, *Path of a Prophet*

Jim Wilson calls readers to their destiny in what is becoming the greatest move of God of all time. *The Holy Spirit and the Endtimes* is both testimonial, describing what God has done, and prophetic, preparing us for what will be. This book is sure to stir your heart to believe God for more and enable you to make yourself ready for God's purposes in the latter days.

Bill Johnson
Pastor, Bethel Church, Redding, California
Author, *When Heaven Invades Earth* and others

Jim Wilson's book brings forth some wonderful and practical insights into applying God's Word to real life. I love the undercurrent of Christ's compassion running through the text. Jim reveals the Master's heart toward the lost and our communities. You will be blessed as you read this book.

Joe McIntyre
President, International Fellowship of Ministries
Author, *E.W. Kenyon* and
His Message of Faith: The True Story

This is a book to help awaken the Church and move toward new horizons—an awakening as only the Reverend

Jim Wilson can do. His heart for God's people comes alive on the page.

Cindy Martinusen
Author, *The Salt Garden, Eventide,*
and *Orchid House*

TABLE OF CONTENTS

and snippets of prophecy. These words were delivered by people who were, for the most part, not prophets at all but who shared with fear and trembling the components of the vision God was giving to the whole of our gathering. The same process was at work some years earlier when a group of pastors gathered in the little town of Anderson, California, to seek God's face for how He wanted the Church to respond to welfare reform in our region. The fruit was Faithworks Coalition—a ministry of the gathered churches that has taken many and taught them to fish (instead of giving them a fish), while at the same time giving them the Gospel. The ministry builds transitional housing complexes in their spare time although their budget is so tight they are challenged each month to keep their doors open.

The real challenge of this kind of revelation, by the way, is that God expects each of us to rise to the opportunity to be prophetic in word and deed that He provides. He says that when we show up, He will show off. But He also says that if we do not show up, there will be no show.

This book is written from my personal perspective as one who has been involved in the renewal movement for the past twenty years and the community transformation phenomenon for more than ten. It is about the prophetic people He is creating, even as He created the Jews in the very act of calling them out of bondage in Egypt and into freedom in the promised land of Israel. It indicates how we become the people who bear the fruit that comes from repentance, in the most practical ways—paving a straight highway in the desert for our God. It intends to encourage us to become who we are by supporting one another in becoming people of God. It refers always to the ones who take no offense at the King, as

He is revealed in the Kingdom. It reflects the pouring out upon all flesh of God's Holy Spirit that was promised for these latter days.

I bear witness to what I have personally seen as a participant observer: that is the meaning of the word *witness* ("martyr"), as the Bible expresses it, and the only credible path I know; that "outpouring" is a process—one which began on Pentecost and is still unfolding and escalating as we await the return of the King, who is Himself God's greatest gift. Participation in preparing His return is the greatest privilege in the history of the world.

Chapter 1

THE PLACE OF PROPHECY

In the fall of 2003 the southern region of California was swept by the most devastating wildfires in her history. Thousands of homes were destroyed, along with uncountable acres of watershed and wildlife habitat. Firefighters from all over the state risked their lives to fight the fires raging over multiple counties. They fought alongside homeowners who joined in the effort to save their own homes and those of their neighbors. In the meantime, 125 pastors and intercessors gathered at the southern gateway to Yosemite National Park to pray and praise the Lord for their state and for His vision of their state.

This retreat had been planned and committed for months prior to the outbreak of fire. When push came to shove, southland pastors made a gut-wrenching decision to keep a vow to the Lord, rather than yield to the clear dictation of their circumstances that they remain with their families through the crisis. In honor of their sacrifice, we decided to devote the entire retreat to prayer for dousing of the wildfires. Someone produced a written transcript of a prophecy released some 12 months earlier. The prophet, Chuck Pierce, had foretold just such an outbreak of fire. Pierce also stated that God would gain victory by sending a wind from the west to the fire lines, if His people would humble themselves and pray (see 2 Chron. 7:14).

The catch here is that Californians rightly fear rising winds from any direction in a fire zone. It is the wind that whips the fires and makes them unpredictably deadly to those who fight them. Taking our cue again from the courage of the southern pastors, we decided to obey the prophetic word and pray as one for that wind to come and be the vehicle of God's glory. Satellite technology confirmed that on the third night of prayer a rain front rolled down the California coast—on course to miss landfall altogether. Late that evening a west wind came up to blow the rainfall right over the fire lines. The resulting wash of water broke the back of the fires and enabled the firefighters to at last bring them under control.

Clearly God intervened in the situation. Just as clearly He telegraphed His intention and His plan for our participation in the prophetic word He released. (He even provided, through the satellite photos, the technological means to document what He had done and declared.) Some of us, gathered at Yosemite, saw in the fulfillment of prophecy a walking out of God's Isaiah 55 statement—that His ways and words are not our ways and words, but that we should seek Him while He wills to be found if we would see His glory (see Isa. 55:6,8). That He used the wind we feared was especially mind-blowing—it acted on the rain front instead of on the fire front, but act it did! Others saw the incarnation of Jeremiah 29:11-13 in the event—that God knows His plans for our benefit and that when we seek His face we cannot fail to find Him. All of us thought of His promise to lavish the Spirit of prophecy on His Body in the latter days.

In the spring of 2004 God offered a more localized manifestation of modern prophecy in the life of a friend of mine. Gerry was diagnosed with terminal cancer. He was so far advanced by the time of his diagnosis that his doctor told him treatment would be useless; there was nothing for him but to gather his family and friends, settle his affairs, and prepare to go home. Gerry had been a faithful pastor for half a century in a denomination that believed spiritual gifts, such as the working of miracles, had disappeared from the Church after the first century. Most of his life and ministry had been spent in Siskiyou County. The extended family assembled for an evening of dinner, rendering praise to the Lord for the life and ministry of their patriarch, and remembering. Diana and I happened to be on hand and were included in the evening as a courtesy.

Midway through one of my favorite praise songs the Lord spoke to me—I believed—saying, "Why don't you just cancel the cancer?" I have been ministering in the gifts of the Holy Spirit for more than two decades, and if I have learned one thing it is really three things: you test the spirits, by their fruit you shall know them, and when the Lord asks you a question, He is not seeking information (see 1 John 4:1; Matt. 7:16, 20; Matt. 6:8).

I tested the spirits by asking the group, very politely, if they were willing to pray for Gerry in the authority we were all given, as in the days when tongues of fire descended on the first Pentecost. "What did we have to lose if we, in the name of Jesus, just cancelled the cancer in Gerry," I wondered out loud. Everyone thought it was a good idea, and so we prayed the declaration that we, in the name of Jesus, cancelled that cancer. We prayed it again—just in case either God or the cancer didn't hear it the first time—and awaited the fruit. Nothing happened.

Gerry did not jump up yelling that he was healed. He didn't even feel better. We went back to praising the Lord and celebrating the life of our friend and relative. When the evening was over we all went home with our private thoughts and prayers.

About three weeks later the Lord spoke to me again. This time He said, "When word of Gerry's healing gets out there will be revival in Siskiyou County." I countered, "But Lord, Gerry hasn't been healed." He responded, "Really?" Another three weeks passed before I received the e-mail from Gerry. He was entirely cancer-free. The doctors had no explanation, and he was planning to share the good news of the miracle with anyone who would listen. I was marveling that God said to cancel the cancer and it was "by-God" cancelled! But God also said it was not the healing that would trigger revival; it was the word of it getting out. Could that fulfillment be far behind? God said it, and it is marvelous in our eyes, although that fullness remains as unfolding a process as Pentecost across the board continues to be.

Prophecy is alive and well in the world today. It has never been dead, but it is a gift that enjoys both a seminal and a summary career at this time in the Body of Christ. That is to say that the Spirit of prophecy is leading the Body down paths not previously walked, and at the same time it is gathering us at a terminus of all of the paths we have traveled for millennia. As we walk and gather, we are given a fresh opportunity to learn once again what it is—this thing we call *prophecy*.

A Terminus of History

The modern prophetic movement gained much of its energy from the emergence of a group of prophets in Kansas City in the early 1980s. Paul Cain, Bob Jones, and Mike Bickle are among the names most closely associated with this group; Bickle went on to found the Kansas City International House of Prayer in the early '90s. His model has been copied in many cities around the nation and the world. The prayer centers that spring up are often known by the acronym IHOP, followed or preceded by the first letter of their city's name. (SIHOP—for example—indicates the Sacramento International House of Prayer, located in my own region of Northern California.) The primary purpose of these houses is not prophecy per se, but rather, concerted prayer for the communities in which they are based and for the nation. If we think of the Church as an orchestra then prophecy is the percussion section that sets tone, keeps time, and begins each movement of the symphony. The gathering of these called-out ones has become a rallying point for all in the Body who seek a deeper knowledge and experience of the living God, other than what can be obtained through the Reformation traditions of piety, study, and service alone.

The IHOP folks simply put pedal-to-the-metal in a phenomenon unfolding within the charismatic renewal of the

'60s and '70s. That renewal was triggered when an Episcopalian priest named Dennis Bennett received the baptism in the Holy Spirit. Bennett popularized a spiritual style that has always been present in the Body and has known both fame and notoriety in our time through such ongoing events as the Azusa Street Revival of the early 20th century. (The Assemblies of God, International Church of the Foursquare Gospel, The Vineyard Fellowships, and the Christian and Missionary Alliance are examples of denominations founded over the last century, or so, on the strength of prophetic activity.) Bennett's baptism brought Pentecostal experience to mainline and classical evangelical expressions of Christianity and gave it a theological underpinning to the bargain. It also gave vent to the Lord's sense of humor: could a denomination so reputedly cold, as to be known to its own members as "God's frozen chosen," be the seat of a revival that would permanently transform the horizons of the whole Body of Christ? Could this come to pass, despite the decision of denominational leaders to reject this move of God? It could and it would and it did—by God's grace.

There is nothing happening in the modern prophetic movement that is not a fulfillment of what God promised in the Old Testament. Every Christian should be familiar with the words of Joel 2:28, "And afterward I will pour out my Spirit on all people. Your sons and daughters will prophesy, your old men will dream dreams, your young men will see visions." Peter quoted the passage on the first Pentecost to answer onlookers who thought the disciples were drunk at 9:00 in the morning! (See Acts 2:14-15.) But Joel is not the only Old Testament prophet to foretell the coming of a new prophetic outpouring in times that would include our own.

The promise of a general outpouring of the Holy Spirit unfolds as both component and confirmation of the coming of Messiah in Isaiah, Jeremiah, and Ezekiel—a trinity of the greatest prophets of Israel. It is a recurring theme in Isaiah, where God links the outpouring of His Spirit to the healing of the land—"I will pour water on the thirsty land, and streams on the dry ground; I will pour out My Spirit on your offspring, and My blessing on your descendants" (see Isa. 32:15; 44:3). In Isaiah 54:13, God is more directly interested in preparing the minds and hearts of the people when He says, "All your sons will be taught by the Lord," and in Isaiah 59:21, He speaks with even greater clarity: "'As for Me, this is My covenant with them,' says the Lord, 'My Spirit, who is on you, and My words that I have put in your mouth will not depart from your mouth, or from the mouths of your children, or from the mouths of their descendants from this time on and forever,' says the Lord." This statement is delivered to a people accustomed to centuries of hearing the prophetic Word only from representatives of a small and elite group set apart for that purpose. The people who urged Moses to go up the mountain alone, so that they would not have to deal with the fearsome intimacy of their God (see Exod. 20:18-19), have no frame of reference for a general outpouring of the Spirit of the living God. But God had been preparing these same people for what He would deliver to us in the wake of His Son's resurrection—when we give new meaning to becoming His Body on earth.

The theme is repeated in Jeremiah 31, when God promises a new covenant to His people and says:

> *"This is the covenant I will make with the house of Israel after that time," declares the Lord, "I will put My law in their minds and write it on their hearts. I will be*

29

*their God, and they will be My people. No longer will a
man teach his neighbor, or a man his brother, saying,
'Know the Lord,' because they will all know Me, from
the least of them to the greatest"* (Jeremiah 31:33-34).

Ezekiel takes it up in chapter 11—"I will give them an
undivided heart and put a new spirit in them; I will remove
from them their heart of stone and give them a heart of
flesh. Then they will follow My decrees and be careful to
keep My laws. They will be My people, and I will be their
God" (Ezek. 11:19-20).

God never intended the resurrection of Israel to be along
the old fault lines of surrogate prophets—as valuable as they
were in their time—standing between the Presence on the
mountain and the people in the valley. "Then they will know
that I am the Lord their God, for though I sent them into exile
among the nations, I will gather them to their own land, not
leaving any behind. I will no longer hide My face from them,
for I will pour out My Spirit on the house of Israel, declares the
Sovereign Lord," in Ezekiel 39:28-29, and this follows the famous prophecy of the dry bones in Ezekiel chapter 37. That
poured-out Spirit was the *bringer-of-life* to the dry bones; He
will have to remain with those He has called into life in order to
shepherd what He has birthed and resurrected.

If we must believe that all Old Covenant prophecy points
ultimately to the coming of the Son of God onto the earth—
and we must indeed—then we are equally obliged to believe
that His coming will be accompanied by the promised general
outpouring of the same Holy Spirit that has always animated
the prophetic voice. His coming brings about the Kingdom,
and that general outpouring of His Spirit is the Kingdom!

Zechariah makes the most explicit connect between the spirit of Prophecy and the coming of the Christ. Zechariah 12:10 says, "And I will pour out on the house of David and the inhabitants of Jerusalem a Spirit of grace and supplication. They will look on Me, the One they have pierced, and they will mourn for Him as one mourns for an only child." It is only the Spirit—moving on and within each human heart—that produces persons capable of hearing and receiving the voice of God and becoming grafted into His Holy people. Yet, that same Spirit has always been the One animating the prophets; His primary purpose in the New Covenant is enabling all to prophetically recognize the Son and make an appropriate response to His suffering and glorification. God declares it in so many words in Revelation 19:10 when He says, "For the testimony of Jesus is the spirit of prophecy."

In the New Covenant we are promised, not prophets, but membership in the prophetic community of His Body.

It cannot be said enough: The whole economy of prophecy is transformed between the Old and New Covenants. It is the same, because God never changes (see Mal. 3:6); yet, it is utterly different, because God says, "Behold! I am doing a new thing" (see Isa. 43:19). The gift of prophecy—once given only to individuals ordained or set apart for it—is now resting on the Body and shared out lavishly on many who are from time to time called to exercise it. That outpouring changes everything.

It brings us to the seminal and summary moment in which we stand. It raises issues, even as it amps up the glory for which God has always been preparing us. One of these issues is how we can even define prophecy. Another is what we must do in order to recognize and respond to it.

WHAT PROPHECY IS

Prophecy is nothing more and nothing less than the voice of God in our midst; it is the revelation of "His-self" and "His-will." In the Old Testament the prophets spent the vast majority of their time and energy on interpreting present and historical events in the light of God's perspective. Thus, a triumph of secular diplomacy—such as the alliances forged by Ahab and Jezebel—is revealed by Elijah as caving in to idolatry; and the efforts of Zedekiah to hold out against the Babylonians are translated by Jeremiah as resistance to dependency on God. On the other hand, Elisha upbraids his king for not expecting as much temporal protection from God as He intends to give, and Ezekiel tells the people in exile that God is blessing and strengthening them as never before in their very captivity.

The predictive prophecies are the most dramatic. We tend to focus on Daniel and the apocalyptic visions of Ezekiel and Revelation. They are just as true and just as truly originating in God Himself; but we know them as truth through the fulfillment of those prophetic visions that can be seen closer to home—like the people who fought and prayed over the fires in 2003 and the pastor named Gerry in 2004. And we need to remember that every word of Scripture is prophecy—because it is the Word of God. We know prophecy to be authentic by its fruit, and nowhere is that fruit more visible than in the book we call the Bible.

But above all, we need to recognize that the primary purpose of prophecy in the world of the Old Covenant—from Moses to John the Baptist—was always to prepare the people for the coming of Messiah and to empower them to recognize Him when He comes. What about prophecy in the New

Covenant world? Can its purpose ever be other than to prepare the Body of Christ for the Kingdom He has won on the cross and claimed in His resurrection and to establish His Church in the Pentecost event—a prophetic purpose which empowers the people of His Body and blood to live in the Kingdom we usher in with our testimony?

Should we be surprised to find God giving a wholesale offering of the Spirit that animated the prophets in a world defined by the resurrection of the Son as a promise coming to fulfillment before our eyes? Should we be skeptical as we are held to a higher level of accountability for the gift that is given to all of us, in the midst of us, just as the Kingdom itself is in the midst of us? Should we be astounded to discover that the role of the prophets in the New Covenant time is radically different than it was in the Old, but every bit as central to what God is doing?

Modern prophecy must be at all times consistent with Scripture and sometimes coterminous with it. At the same time, authentic prophecy—even when it is simply the repetition of a biblical text applied to a present reality—must draw us along the highway we are called to pave for God in the desert. It will never hold us in some place where God used to want us to stand, anymore than the disciples could get away with arguing with Jesus that they did not want to turn their faces toward Jerusalem. There is not a jot or a tittle of Scripture that we can set aside. Neither can we hide behind memorized verses to avoid our calling from the Author of Scripture. Until we can honestly say that the Kingdom has come on earth as it is in Heaven, we cannot remain in place with a sense of integrity. To this extent, nothing has really changed.

But if we can recognize prophecy due to the Holy Spirit leading us to recognize the Word of God, we can also distinguish prophetic revelation from false utterances that pass for the real thing, but are really substitutes for engagement with the Person of God.

There are very obvious instances of false prophecy that crop up from time to time. Prior to the Iraq War, one recognized prophetic figure said the Lord told him that one million commitments to daily prayer on a particular web site would move Saddam Hussein to leave Iraq. Some two million actually signed up, but the war came anyway. Another predicted that American tanks would be destroyed by weather, bogging down the tanks in Iraqi mud and tank traps. Instead, weather in the form of a days-long sandstorm revealed the traps and saved the tanks. Their statements did not come true, and the authors glibly moved on to the next dramatic prediction on their web sites. (Fortunately for these prophets the sacrificial death and resurrection of Jesus Christ pays for their sin, as well as for the rest of us; and the requirement of death by stoning in Deuteronomy 18:20 is fulfilled without shedding their blood.) But Scripture tells us just as plainly in Deuteronomy 18:22, "If what a prophet proclaims in the name of the Lord does not take place or come true, that is a message the Lord has not spoken. That prophet has spoken presumptuously. Do not be afraid of him."

Message received: We are each responsible for listening to the voice of God resonating in our hearts—all the more in the New Testament Church featuring the outpouring upon all flesh (see Acts 2:17). We cannot excuse our own error with a lame, "But the great man said...." There are no great people in the Kingdom, only redeemed men and women. But it is still hard to see where the role of prophets and prophecy has really changed.

The Deuteronomy text covers those who make false prophetic predictions, but what about the bulk of prophecy— then and now—that deals with present and past events, interpreting them in the light of the revelation of the living God?

Among the authentic interpreters of the times, we find many people masquerading as prophets. These "worthies" are often downright hostile to anyone claiming to have a fresh revelation from the Lord, but their stock in trade is careful and scholarly analysis of the prophecies contained in Scripture. They usually deal only with the material concerning the last days—that found in Old Testament books like Daniel and Ezekiel, and New Testament samples like Revelation and the apocalyptic chapters in Matthew, Mark, and Luke. Since the last days are not yet upon us—at least not in the way these teachers speak about them—there is no way to apply the Deuteronomy 18 test to their proclamations (see Deut. 18:21-22). On top of that, they refuse to utter statements claiming to be fresh revelation; they content themselves with analysis of what the prophets of the distant past have said. There is nothing wrong with this on the surface, but these men and women make a very prosperous living handing out apparently inside information to their devotees on when the Lord Jesus will return and how we can recognize the signs of His imminent arrival.

These people are not prophets at all; they function in the tradition of the scribes of Jesus' day. He had some specially uncomplimentary things to say about them—not because their calling was invalid, but because of their claim to inside information about what the Scriptures really mean, and their disdain for those who wanted to engage with God rather than with others who claim to have gotten into His company at some point in the past. Jesus called them "whitewashed grave houses" (see Matt. 23:26).

These scribes in prophetic trappings are well dressed, and they speak a persuasive message. But they are living in places God used to frequent, pouring the new wine of His ever fresh presence into the old wineskins of their analysis. They look feverishly for the ten-horned creature of Revelation, and when their politics are offended by the European Common Market (which is in many ways legitimately offensive to Christians) they decide that they have found it. When the Common Market grows beyond ten members they look elsewhere—perhaps to the European Union or multi-national corporations—with never a backward glance at their own convoluted trail and not a moment spared to recant their false predictions. They write best sellers about the late great planet and/or the rapture so that we can buy their books and take comfort in the knowledge that we won't be left behind when it comes because we bought the book. The implication is that because we know what this book says we can pride ourselves in our knowledge, and forget all about the Great Commission and the Great Commandment. Furthermore, if we tell people about Jesus at all, we will let them know that their time is short and forget the important message that God loves them more than life itself—the existence of the Body and our participation in it as the welcomed-home prodigals, which we are, are living proof of that love.

My wife, Diana, likes to say that the scribes are telling us how to set our alarm clocks for when the bridegroom is expected, though the groom Himself ordered us to throw our alarm clocks out the window; it is sleeping on the job at any time that is an inexcusable sin. Jesus tells us in Matthew 24—for starters—that no one knows the day or the hour of His return (see Matt. 24:36). He hammers that we are to watch and wait and prepare for the greatest party the world has ever seen. Those who sleep through the beginning will not survive to see the end.

But the biggest and most fundamental problem with these scribes is that they stand above the rest of us—telling us what to expect from God, instead of training and coaching and mentoring us to hear God's voice for ourselves. They are not accountable to the rest of the Body because they see themselves as individually indispensable to its operation. They set themselves up outside of the Body, coming periodically into town—or into the local Christian bookstore—to teach the elect by injection what they contend their pastors will not teach them. The New Covenant actually unfolds as a First Corinthians 12 world in which each has a piece of the revelation of the Kingdom, and the pieces come together to present a cumulative portrait.

A bottom line test for authentic prophecy is that it will be scripturally consistent. It will pave a straight highway in the desert for our God in a way that both summarizes where we have been and launches us toward where God is going. And it will envision a corporate revelation of Kingdom that honors the First Corinthians 12 model.

A PROPHETIC CULTURE EMERGING

Jesus Culture is an annual event involving from fifteen hundred to three thousand young people who recently unfolded themselves at the convention center in our city. The vision of a youth pastor named Banning Liebscher, this celebration of God's call for an "on-earth-as-it-is-in-heaven" culture has grown to eight locations worldwide in eight years. This year a local leader prophesied a paraphrase of Jesus' word to Herod, "Today and tomorrow I go my way and the third day in Jerusalem." The leader interpreted his own word as forecasting a rocky beginning that would end in great glory for the Lord on the third day of the gathering. He saw a vision of a spiritual nuclear explosion over the convention center at the *end* of the event that was housed there. In fact, the youth worshiped with abandon on the *first* night and returned to the center for teaching on street ministry and the exercise of spiritual gifts the next morning. In the afternoon they fanned out over the city—going to nearly 50 predetermined locations in which they would pray for the sick, feed the hungry, and bless the schools that many of them attend in town. The fruit was disappointing; none of the people for whom they offered to pray would permit it, and so the teens returned to the convention center and worshiped with even greater passion on the second night.

On the third day they were back for more teaching and then to their locations for ministry. This time *no one refused* an offer for prayer, and hundreds of dramatic healings were reported when they returned that evening. The roar of praise to God nearly took the roof off before leaders sent them back to their homes in Redding and across the nation, satisfied that they had seen their nuclear explosion. But most interesting was the composite nature of its fulfillment. The prophetic statement over the whole event was just one component of the revelation.

One team went to a small community just north of Redding. Before heading out they asked the Lord to show them the people for whom they were called to pray. A young lady saw a vision of a man driving a brown truck. A young man saw the word "yellow" and heard the Lord say that the man wearing it had pain in his back. When the team saw a man driving a brown truck and wearing a yellow bandana they asked if his back was hurt. It was, and with his permission they prayed. In the meantime, his brother—who had been mocking the praying people until his brother announced that he was healed—asked prayer for himself and had an encounter with the living God. In other cases the team reported a partially amputated finger grew back and several broken bones healed within their casts. The pattern of God sharing pieces of revelation within the team was typical of the day. The prophetic leaders of the event saw their primary task as training their teams to operate in this way.

Frankly, some legitimate prophets make the same error as the scribes—giving us fish instead of teaching us to fish. But God took this unfolding of His intention so seriously that when He invented the Hebrew language He omitted a past tense from the grammar. Where we translate verses like the beginning of Isaiah 42 in terms of the heavens and earth that God has laid out, He calls them the "heavens" and "earth" that He is presently laying out. Likewise, He calls our creation and calling an ongoing activity (see Isa. 42:5-7). Jesus simply carries it to the next level when He declares in Matthew 9:17 that our development in the Spirit is making a place for the Spirit to develop in us; that is why He compares it to the new wine of His own earthly days that was poured into new wineskins while still in the fermentation process (see Matt. 9:17). In a profound sense, the Holy Spirit and the Kingdom it establishes are not at full potency on arrival; they are bubbling and sizzling as fermenting grapes do before we can taste and see that the new wine has come, indeed, and it is very good.

The legitimate role of the oracles of God's revelation has morphed into a role as coaches and mentors and parents of the oracles of God's oncoming and unfolding revelation. This is a composite revelation expressively emerging from the prophetic community as it is downloaded by the Holy Spirit. It is why John the Baptist, whom Jesus calls the greatest of the prophets, says that He must decrease as the Son of God increases (see John 3:30). The fullness of biblical prophecy is not found in this or that cataclysmic event, although these are coming incidents and incidental to the story. It is found in the unfolding revelation of the mind and heart of God as He comes more and more to live in the minds and hearts of His gathered people. Jesus' summary description of the Kingdom—and of that fullness of prophecy—is found in Matthew 11:4-6.

> Jesus replied, "Go back and report to John what you hear and see: The blind receive sight, the lame walk, those who have leprosy are cured, the deaf hear, the dead are raised, and the good news is preached to the poor. Blessed is the man who does not fall away on account of me" (Matthew 11:4-6).

Tragically, for the scribes and for those prophets who exalt themselves, there is a magnificent missed opportunity to receive the greatest honor of all in the biblical economy—honor reserved for the patriarchs who usher many generations of sons and daughters into the Kingdom, like Abraham, Isaac, Jacob, and patriarchs before them. Prophets who exalt themselves are like the baseball fan who watches a home run leave the park by standing at the outfield wall, looking at the stands as it passes overhead, but misses the crack of the bat and the magnificent arc of the shot in its flight. They sin when they urge others to stand facing backward, as they do.

The good news is that many modern prophets take joy in their role as people who primarily empower others in the Body to minister in the prophetic. Mike Bickle of the Kansas City IHOP and Kris Vallotton of the Bethel School of Supernatural Ministry in Redding, California, are among many in the forefront of this movement. Apostolic leaders like Jack Hayford—who do not think of themselves as prophets—have used their influence to encourage prophets to take their managerial place in the emerging prophetic economy. They are right in line with the unfolding revelation of God in the life of the New Testament Church.

PROPHETS AND PROPHETIC PEOPLE: A REVELATION BOTH CORPORATE AND COMPOSITE

In the New Testament many partake of the prophetic gift without holding the office we call "prophet." Peter and John are not recognized as prophets anywhere in Scripture; yet they speak prophetically before the Sanhedrin when they are arrested on the charge of healing in the name of Jesus (see Acts 4:1-21). Peter speaks a predictive prophecy in Acts 5 when Ananias and Sapphira are about to drop dead after holding back on the proceeds of their real estate transaction (see Acts 5:1-10). Peter delivers the most amazing interpretive prophecy of all time on the day of Pentecost when he declares that what the people are seeing is nothing less than the fulfillment of Joel 2:28, about the latter day outpouring of the Spirit of the living God on all flesh (see Acts 2:16). His vision of the sheet coming down from Heaven, and his call to the home of the centurion in light of it, also surely qualify as prophetic (see Acts 10:11-48). And John prophesies the entire book of Revelation.

Stephen is not considered a prophet; yet he preaches a lengthy prophetic discourse on the whole history of God's progressive revelation of Himself and what the people have typically done to those who reveal God to them (see Acts 6). Philip, another leader who is never identified as a prophet, is called away from the revival in Samaria to minister prophetically to an Ethiopian eunuch on the road to Gaza before being transported. He is transported—in a way that would have done Elijah proud—to Azotus where he continues his prophetic ministry (see Acts 8:4-8;26-40). And Paul prophesies blindness to the sorcerer Elymas, a prediction whose accuracy leads a Roman proconsul to faith in Jesus (see Acts 11:27-28).

Ironically enough, there are men and women in the Book of Acts who make their predictive statements and then largely disappear from the narrative of the mighty acts of God: Ananias who ministers to Saul after his conversion, and Agabus who prophesies the famine in Acts 11 and the imprisonment of Paul in Acts 21 (see Acts 11:27-28; 21). It is not that their gifts or their ministry are no longer valued in the Kingdom economy; it is rather that this ministry is more and more a corporate one, and their role has changed to that of mentor and manager of the gift rather than principal practitioner. These prophets have no problem with the new dispensation; they glory in it.

The change in the prophetic role is not as explicitly or generally declared throughout the New Testament as it is for the apostolic band, but it is easily inferred—they say in so many words that from now on the deacons will do the pragmatic ministry so that the apostles can be free to teach and mentor.

Paul himself paints the picture of a corporate gifting in First Corinthians 14. "Follow the way of love and eagerly desire spiritual gifts, especially the gift of prophecy," he exhorts, for "everyone who prophesies speaks to men for their strengthening, encouragement and comfort....he who prophesies edifies the Church I would like every one of you to speak in tongues but I would rather have you prophesy" (1 Cor. 14:3-4). This gift of prophecy is just as clearly one that comes in components as each makes his or her contribution to the revelation that God is unfolding—if we pay attention to the Book of Acts. In Acts 15, for example, the Apostolic Council says that "it seemed good to the Holy Spirit and to us" (Acts 15:28) to send the message to the churches now birthing beyond Jerusalem of abstinence from idol worship, sexual immorality, and the eating of blood or strangled meat as the minimum standard of conformity with apostolic faith and practice.

For the New Testament Church it is necessary to differentiate between a prophetic resurgence that encompasses the five-fold ministry of prophets, apostles, pastors, evangelists, and teachers, and the office of prophet. In the Old Testament the prophets were the spokespersons and principal actors in delivering God's revelation to the community. In the New Testament this broader prophetic economy is the perfect vehicle for the composite and unfolding revelation that God is visiting on the whole community.

In Northern California, where I live and minister, Faith-works Coalition is a wonderful expression of the corporate nature of contemporary prophecy. The coalition of some 70 local Shasta County churches was birthed in 1997 and teamed with the county department of social services to cut welfare roles in half over an 18-month period—providing access to jobs for many, while sharing the Gospel and the support of church families at the same time. They recently built and opened a 12-unit complex of two and three bedroom apartments for families in need of transitional housing, funded by grants and furnished by the donations of member churches. The group was chosen as a national point of light during the Clinton Administration and has helped to launch several offspring ministries around the country. An organization's history does not get much more pragmatic than that; yet its conception was foretold in a prophetic gathering held in Anderson, California, in February 1997.

A dozen local pastors gathered for a half-day prayer retreat in the gymnasium of a local Christian school. They were drawn together out of a mutual desire to pray and seek God's face over how He wanted the Church to respond to the recently enacted federal Welfare Reform Law. One of the pastors said that Christians seeking a vision should not do what any secular outfit does—have a brainstorming session and then make a plan based on the goals and objectives established during the brainstorming session. This pastor said that they needed to seek a supernaturally-imparted vision, in the most literal sense, and then brainstorm how to implement what God had shown them. The gathering in the gymnasium was a prophetic act based on the pastor's prophetic exhortation.

They prayed and read the Word of God. They asked God to show them what He wanted to do and how He wanted to do it. They closed their eyes and waited; when they had seen, they shared with one another. Multiple visions emerged. In one of the visions trucks were seen driving produce in from the country to the city over a road that was under construction as they drove; in another, homes all over the city were showing a blue porch light in honor of the churches gathering together to bless the larger community. One had a vision of the old story of "Stone Soup" coming into being in their midst. There was no one coherent picture—or even puzzle—that emerged. But as they talked of what they had seen and continued to pray, the outline of the Faithworks Coalition emerged.

Later they would marvel at how some of the things they had seen were clearly meant to be fulfilled in their sight over the next few years. The trucking vision was a literal foretaste of the grant of seven hundred acres of land that would be made early in the new century to a local rescue mission. The blue porch lights have not literally happened to date—and not all visions come literally to pass; the image became a rally point as the pastors asked other leaders to sign on to what became a crusade in the county.

The ministry of PrayNorthState was conceived in the same way—as the sum and substance of a corporate vision that first emerged as a series of visionary images when a group of about 25 pastors and lay leaders gathered for lunch and worship at a church in Redding. One saw a vision like Ezekiel's wheel in flight over Northern California as the churches, looking like women in white party dresses, came together to form one Bride of Christ. Another saw a Saturn moon rocket with all five engines (for the five-fold ministry) firing simultaneously, rather than in sequence; it takes such cumulative thrust to reach escape velocity. There was the one who saw a rolling series of worship and reconciliation services along the principal east-west and north-south arteries of the region—Routes 5 and 299. These roads naturally form a great cross across the region. Still, another saw leaders from many denominations walking arm-in-arm across a desert land after having climbed together dripping from a pool of living water. Wherever they walked, the water dripped from their bodies and the desert burst into a lusciously vibrant garden place.

At the time, Diana and I thought our calling was only to the county in which we live. The vision casting opened up the mind of God to us for the whole Northstate region. Over the years, our ministry has developed a regional radio and television outreach that celebrates any ministries that are outside of the box and capable of cross-denominational blessing of their communities. We teach people how to deploy in their own communities to lay down a continuous carpet of prayer on specific issues of interest to the Kingdom—like crime, public health, and economic issues; and then we leave them in the hands of local leadership. We present ourselves as catalysts and networkers for anyone who wants to minister across the lines, like Outreach America, for instance, a ministry that brings Christian music and witness to county fairs. As another example, we also take the lead ourselves when Christians want to declare the whole Word of God over their city in a public reading of the Bible but are in need of leadership to make it happen. Whenever we consider a new ministry project, the first thing we ask in prayer is, "Is this part of the vision you gave in September 2000?"

PREPARING FOR THE KINGDOM

Our job and our joy is to prepare for the Kingdom, not for the cataclysms that must precede it. The honor of the prophets and their indispensable role is to midwife that preparation. There are a few principles that can help us to stay within the lines of that birthing canal. One is simple accountability on the part of the prophets themselves and the people of the prophetic community, which is the Body of Christ.

Whenever we bring an interdenominational team to bless a church, a school, or a business, we instruct the team members to listen to the Lord and share with the person in charge of the site, whatever He may be saying or impressing on their hearts—even at the risk of sounding foolish. (One of the principal ministries of PrayNorthState is a teaming called Prayer Vanguard.) The Lord might be reaching out to one who does not yet know Him through a prophetic word—like the time He showed me a gas leak at a high school in which we were praying. The principal was one who did not believe in prophecy, and I adjusted my language accordingly. I did not say, "The Lord is saying," but rather, "I seem to sense something down by the 300 building that might be worth checking...." There was no odor by the building, but when the staff checked there was indeed a gas leak. The next year when we visited that school the first question from the principal was, "What are you hearing from the Spirit this year?"

But the other side of the coin carries the accountability. We also instruct our prayer warriors that—having delivered what they believe is a prophetic word—they are to let it go. One of the principal areas of conflict in the Body of Christ is between prophetic types who resent that the pastors "won't mind the clear Word of God that I have spoken," and the pastors who see them coming and see only disruption to the flock in their wake. Reality is that if the Word is truly from the Lord, the pastor will not be able to shake it out of his mind until he does something with it; and if the prophet has gotten it wrong, surely the last thing we would want is to pressure the pastor into acting on it. We say that the prophet's task is to speak and God's office is to persuade. It is a simple matter of protocol—of doing the right thing in the right way—and God honors protocol.

At a Prayer Vanguard event, we place ourselves at the disposal of the person who has been set over that facility, whether pastor, principal, or business owner. We worship the way that community worships. If they have a pipe organ, we sing "A Mighty Fortress is Our God," and if they have a kazoo we sing "Kum Ba Yah, Lord." We ask the person in charge to tell us what we should be praying for, and we limit our prayers to what has been so authorized. When we have prayed, we debrief the person in charge, sharing whatever we believe the Lord has shared; and in departing we bless the staff of that place. This too is a matter of protocol and we find that God lavishly honors it.

Another principal is that of faithfulness and humility—two sides of the same coin and one that is frequently lost in the glitzy world we have created. So many Christians think that only an Isaiah or an Elijah can speak the Word of the

Lord, when in truth God is creating a prophetic community of His Body in these latter days. The office of prophet is more important than ever in these times, but in order that many may be enabled to speak their share of the prophetic word of the Kingdom, which God is establishing by right of crucifixion, resurrection, and Pentecost. All too often, I hear Christians say something like, "I wish that I could pray for healing but I don't have that gift," or "I wish that I could visit people who are sick but I don't have that gift." In my experience we do not have spiritual gifts so much as the gifts have us—and prophecy is no exception.

We have the Spirit of the living God; we received that Spirit when we were baptized in the name of the Father and of the Son and of the Holy Spirit. The Spirit gives gifts and those gifts that are needed for the specific ministries to which we are called become activated whenever we seek first His Kingdom and His Glory.

I will never forget the time we took Prayer Vanguard to a church that was seeking to build a worship center. They had been meeting in a small downtown theatre for years because they lacked the funds to build on the land they owned. As we met on their land to ask God's blessing for their life and ministry, we asked the pastor, as we always do, to tell us what we should be praying. After he delivered his list of priorities, one of the women, on her very first prayer vanguard, raised her hand rather sheepishly. When I called on her, she said that it seemed as though the Lord was revealing a division in that congregation. Was there a plan for a school that was meeting opposition, she asked?

The pastor lowered his head and admitted that she was right on. He had not wanted to display his people's dirty laundry in public, as he put it, but he gave his permission to pray over that too. We prayed blessings and healing for all concerned. A month later I spoke with the pastor on the phone; he was ecstatic.

First he told me that the leader of the opposition had been with us that day. When he heard the prayers for blessing and healing it broke his heart; within two weeks everyone was on the same page concerning the school. But more than that was afoot. A contractor came by to ask if they had money for the foundation of the building they planned, and would he be permitted to donate the foundation for their worship center? Days later, another contractor showed up just as spontaneously and asked if they would allow him to donate the sod for the soccer field their school would need? Right behind him came the man who noted that sod must be watered and inquired how would it be if he gave the sprinkler pipe for their system? Today the church is up and running, and that congregation is the most dynamic in its small city.

The woman in the back who gave that word sought first the Kingdom, and the Spirit was given for what she was called to do. I don't know if she ever prophesied again—or if she became a bubbling brook of prophetic words. I do know that if the Lord has need of her to prophesy, she will be just fine with it. We like to say that faithfulness trumps giftedness every time.

Still, another principle worth practicing is the sovereignty of God's call. I am not a prophet, and I come from a family and spiritual background that makes me anything but a likely candidate for the exercise of the prophetic gift. Yet, God has called me to speak a new name over my city—Abundant Springs—and a new purpose over the mall that straddles the downtown, from commercial venture to service center.

In the case of the naming, He chose me precisely because I am a transplant to the city of Redding; and so I could not know that Redding sits over a gigantic aquifer. In the early days of the city, the biggest problem for homeowners was the springs that kept bubbling through flooring to flood their basements. In the time of this prophetic word—in which intercessors have been repeating it every chance they get—Redding has been designated as the fastest appreciating market in the state for investment housing. Furthermore, timber sales have returned to the level of the early '90s, before the collapse of the timber market. When God gave me that word I feared to speak it, because I am not a prophet; but I have come to be more concerned about not speaking what God gives. He is, after all, a God who speaks things into being. Without the Word there is no being.

About that downtown mall...I had no idea before I spoke the word that the mall was located near the center of what had been the prostitution zone of Redding once upon a time. Prostitution is, of course, a perversion of the gift of service. The way to redeem a gift that has been abused is to exercise it authentically. Once again, God chose a newcomer—ignorant of the history of that district—to declare God's healing for what remains a type of bondage in the downtown area. Today, with the opening of a community college nursing school as its anchor tenant, the mall is at least three quarters devoted to service; and we see God's hand in its total restoration that is to come. We like to say that God does not call the qualified; He qualifies the called.

Once when Bob Jones was speaking at a Redding church, he was asked to imagine the members of the five-fold ministry described in Ephesians 4 as the crew of the Starship Enterprise. Where would he post the various ministers? Jones laughed, but he did not hesitate. The apostles would man the bridge; the pastors would handle security; the teachers would be in charge of life support, and the evangelists would comprise the teams for exploration and other missions away from the ship. The prophets he would place in the engine room. Theirs, he said, was the task of providing propulsion for the ship—but he would never permit them to come onto the bridge. Propulsion and navigation are two very different functions, he allowed.

The Kingdom of God—the object of the prophetic community—is about the Spirit of the living God poured out on all flesh. It is about gathering all flesh into the community of the living God. It is just as much about occupying the land that has been won by the King on His Cross. Gathering is the task of evangelism. Preparing the ground so that the Great Commission can succeed and the King can take possession of what He has won is the purpose of the prophetic community. The war is won, but it is far from over, and so we engage spiritual warfare in order to facilitate that end. The rest of this book will deal with how God is calling His people to do that.

John the Baptist described this preparation from the banks of the Jordan River. He called upon the people to make a straight highway in the desert for the Lord our God—bearing fruit in keeping with repentance. Our prayers and praises enthrone the King. They provide the roadway on which He walks His land. The prophetic community exists to propagate the harvest with prayer and worship, and then to bring in the harvest on the strength of our testimony. Escalating prayer, worship, and testimony—in word and act— is the process of repentance as a lifestyle. In John's day the people were called to prepare for the first coming; we prepare for the second. The dynamics of the task remain the same, but they are disbursed and dispersed over the whole of the Body of Christ.

The prophets have a very different function in the day of the New Covenant than they had in the Old. The newness was prophesied by the prophets of old in what they did, as much as in what they said. (Daniel and his companions formed a prophetic community; Shadrach, Meshach and Abednego were walking prophecies as they accepted a fiery furnace before they would abandon their God.) The prophets will always prophesy the Kingdom until it comes in all of its fullness with the return of the King. But their primary task is to prepare a community of the prophetic ones to populate that Kingdom. They must decrease while the community must increase. But the good news is that Psalm 133 gets it totally right. God's call to life, itself, is in the midst of the community of unity. Jesus says the Kingdom is in the midst of it as well.

Chapter 2

A KINGDOM UNFOLDING

Qaumaniq Suuqinna was one of the last people I expected to see on a Sunday morning as I worshiped in a Los Angeles church, to which we both have ties. I was in town to help friends prepare for their wedding. Qaumaniq had come out from her home in Nashville, Tennessee, seeking support as she grappled with a diagnosis of thyroid cancer that was as serious as it was sudden.

During a time of prayer, in the middle of the service, Qaumaniq came forward while her friends gathered around her to pray. We did not curse the disease, and we did not ask God to intervene *if* it might be His will. (We know His will is to heal our diseases because we have been sent to do that in His

Name.) We gave God thanks for all things, even the cancer—inasmuch as it had brought all of us to prayer for our sister. We told the cancer itself that—having completed its only legitimate function—it should run along in the name of Jesus. We praised God for Qaumaniq and continued the service.

I next heard from the Suuqinnas about four weeks later. Qaumaniq had been in for her scheduled surgery but the doctors, after opening her up, could find no sign of the cancer that had been so obvious a month before. Our God is an awesome God. His Kingdom is coming, and His will is being done in our day, on earth as it is in Heaven.

We should not be too surprised. In Mark 9:1 Jesus says, "I tell you the truth, some who are standing here will not taste death before they see the kingdom of God come with power." He is clearly speaking of the Pentecost event. On that Sunday morning the Body of Christ—all 120 members of the yet-unborn Church—gathered for worship in the same Upper Room in which they prepared for His death just weeks earlier. The Spirit of the living God fell on all of them—regardless of gender, generation, or level of achievement. They praised God with the freedom for which Christ had set them free, and then the real action began. They went out onto the balcony and into the streets.

Acts 2 reports, "Now there were staying in Jerusalem God-fearing Jews from every nation under heaven. When they heard this sound, a crowd came together in bewilderment, because each one heard them speaking in his own language" (Acts 2:5-6). When Peter speaks to them of the prophecy from Joel coming true, they want to know what they can do about it. When he reminds them that they have recently put to death the One who fulfills it, they really want to know what they can do. Three thousand ask for baptism, the Spirit falls on all of them, and the Body of Christ is born. Within a few days several thousand more are added to the Body, as people continue to share their testimony and exercise the gifts that come with the infilling of the Holy Spirit. (See Acts 2:16-21; 37-41.) But this is only the beginning of what God is unfolding.

The city of Jerusalem is not all flesh by a long shot. The Lord had prophesied, prior to His ascension, that the disciples would be His witnesses—first in Jerusalem, and then progressively throughout Judea, Samaria, and the rest of the world (see Acts 1:8). In our own time, the Spirit of God has fallen on more than two billion human beings, and the Church has grown more in the past half-century than in the first 19. But this still accounts for only about a third of the population of the planet. All flesh is yet to come.

The Kingdom of Heaven did come with power on that first Pentecost. Men and women who are frightened and confused a few days earlier are filled with a bold faithfulness that not even death can overcome. They know and can apply Scriptures that were a solid wall to them before. They are miraculously enabled to heal the sick and address the powers that be with an articulate message—not just when Jesus is standing over them, but wherever they go. They even speak to people of all nations in the language each of them can most easily understand, whenever the Spirit enables them. But this coming Kingdom is an unfolding reality. The New Testament Greek word is *prolepsis* and it means, in effect, "living and active right now, but not quite yet."

This procession of the unfolding Kingdom of God is called *transformation* by many worldwide leaders. The city-wide prayer movement of Kansas City offers a popular definition of the term on their website. It is "a condition of dramatic socio-political renewal that results from God's people entering into corporate vision, corporate repentance and corporate prayer. During these extraordinary seasons the Kingdom of God pervades every institution of human endeavor."

The goal of prophetic resurgence in our time—of the witness of the Body, the shed blood of the Messiah, and of the unfolding Kingdom of God—is the complete transformation of the world into that Kingdom. This process of transformation must take place in each and every community in which we live, each one becoming a nexus of the Kingdom and connecting to all of the others in the Spirit, as His will progressively done. Nothing less than all the abundant life *in* Christ that is *of* Christ will do. Nothing short of the model found in First Corinthians 12—in which every part of the Body is both a component and a unit of intrinsic value—can describe God's plan with clarity. It is here. It is coming. And God requires our participation in every step of bringing His will to pass.

NEW WINESKINS

This unfolding Kingdom is like the wine the disciples drank in the first century. It is 100 percent wine, but it has not yet reached full potency when it is placed in the skins that are designed to hold it. It is still fermenting and bubbling and expanding as it is coming into all that the Lord has planned for it—although there is nothing lacking in its composition. For this reason Jesus says in Matthew 9:17, Mark 2:22, and Luke 5:37 that His people must become new wineskins in order to accommodate the stretching that the ongoing fermentation of the Spirit will require.

Of course, Jesus is using wine as a metaphor for the Holy Spirit—a common enough practice in the prophetic tradition of Old and New Testaments. But the place where the rubber meets the road is in His use of the wineskins as a metaphor for the people of God. His audience knows that old skins have stretched as far as they can when the first batch of new wine was placed in them—when they themselves were new. If new wine is again put into the old skins they will burst under the pressure of fermentation. He calls upon His people to become new—to become born again—so that they will stretch with the fermentation of the Holy Spirit in them.

Imagine it! The Spirit of the living God, who is God as surely as are the Father and the Son, is presented as not having reached full potency in us. The Spirit is all that the Spirit can be, whether we have experienced the explosive in-filling recounted in Acts or not; "and yet…not yet." That Spirit is in the process of expanding to fill us more and more—and expecting us to expand with Him. But what makes for even more mind-blowing reality is that repentance is a process rather than a unitary event. It is the phenomenon in which we turn away from the life and personality we have made for ourselves and toward the life and personality that God is creating for us. In fact, it is a process that will consume a lifetime and be completed only when we stand before the throne to hear Him say, "Well done good and faithful servant" (see Matt. 25:21,25; Luke 19:17). How else would we place statements about wine and skins into the context of John the Baptist's (and Isaiah's) call to pave a highway in the desert for the King and Jesus' frequent use of agricultural metaphors for spiritual growth— not to mention His own claim that progressive association with Him enables freedom and truth to prevail in the disciples' lives (see John 8:32)?

In a First Corinthians 12 world, that process is as true for our communal life in Christ as for our individual lives in Him.

> *Now to each one the manifestation of the Spirit is given for the common good. To one there is given through the Spirit the message of wisdom, to another the message of knowledge by means of the same Spirit, to another faith by the same Spirit, to another gifts of healing by that one Spirit, to another miraculous powers, to another prophecy, to another distinguishing between spirits, to another speaking in different kinds of tongues, and to still another the interpretation of tongues. All these are the work of one and the same Spirit, and He gives them to each one, just as He determines* (1 Corinthians 12:7-11).

The operant phrase for us would have to be "as He determines."

Our experience of the Holy Spirit teaches us today, just as in the days of the Book of Acts, that the gifts are ordered and distributed on an as-needed basis. The Spirit determines the need. He also determines the ordering of the composite-sharing, by multiple members of the Body, as God's will unfolds in shared ministry—just as it did in the prayer for Qaumaniq, and surely as it did when so many prayed for the fires to cease in Southern California.

There was an evident progression in God's call to prayer when wildfire broke out again in Southern California in fall 2007. At least a half dozen prayer ministries, including PrayNorthState, called all of their networks to prayer and thousands responded. The prayer was that prevailing Santa Ana winds would die, that desperately needed rain would come, and that predicted winds from the west would help, as they did in 2003, and not hinder. The Santa Anas were history in three days, rain came on the fifth day, and the west winds blew fires back on themselves instead of spreading them. "The body is a unit," Paul writes in that seminal chapter, "though it is made up of many parts; and though all its parts are many, they form one body. So it is with Christ" (1 Cor. 12:12). In a profound way, because we share the Spirit of the Living God, the gifts of the Spirit have us.

The Kingdom Paul describes in First Corinthians 12 is one in which every component has integrity and is to be honored on that account. Yet, that Kingdom is also one in which every member is absolutely essential to the destiny of the whole and is also to be honored and sought on that account. First Corinthians 12 is just as surely a Kingdom description as is Matthew 11:2-6—in which the dead are raised, the blind and deaf restored, the sick healed, and none take offense at King Jesus as He is revealed in glory. But just as it does in our human bodies, it all comes down to a beginning at the cellular level. This means that if I want transformation to come to my community, I must passionately long for it to come to me. Repentance as a process does not proceed from one unfolding to another in the Body of Christ until it proceeds that way in thee and me. The transformation phenomenon that has been so ably documented by George Otis Jr. in hundreds of communities and nations always seems to begin with a small selection of leaders determined to repent until they become new wineskins.

Praying for Qaumaniq's healing the way we did was a stretch for me. We have taught in PrayNorthState for years that what God blesses He transforms, but did we dare to bless even this foul disease? Yet, we know only the enemy curses; our God is a God of blessing. We know God turns all things to good in those who love Him because He says so in Romans 8:28. We took Him at His Word, blessing what seemed unblessable.

The fruit was healing for Qaumaniq. But the larger fruit was in the stretching we all received as God asserted His authority to a new degree in our lives. His ways are not our ways, but He is willing to transform even the thoughts in our heads by the renewal of our minds, if we are willing to be stretched day after day to accommodate His vision.

I was stretched another way when we to prayed about the presence of Kryon. A hotel in our city had booked a New Age event. The purpose was to channel a spirit by the name of Kryon—an alleged 35,000-year-old ascended master who would supposedly enlighten the participants when he manifested himself at their call. A member of the management team for the hotel was very uncomfortable about hosting a demonic presence and called to ask if one of our teams might come and pray. Of course we would come.

We brought an interdenominational team to the hotel the afternoon before the conference. Our contact gave us the use of the conference room in which the summoning was to take place; and we decided to spend our time worshiping and praising God, rather than railing against the demonic spirit—as so many prayer warriors do. The Lord seemed to be saying that if we laid out a carpet of praise to our Lord, it would be His Spirit who came that evening, and a demonic entity would want no part of that space.

We know we have authority as Christians to cast out the agents of the enemy. But we also know—if we read Scripture—that Jesus only addresses these agents when He is directly confronted by them. This is true whether it is a man in a Capernaum synagogue who cries out, "What do you want with us, Jesus of Nazareth?" (Mark 1:24), or the man called Legion who hollers out the same challenge in the country of the Gerasenes (see Mark 5:8; Luke 8:28). Kryon was not present in that conference room, and we made a decision to honor only the Lord—giving Him all our attention—and giving no importance to the competition. By dedicating all of the available space to the Lord and His praise, we hoped to leave no place on which the interloper could stand. More than that, we hoped to invite the Lord to occupy and bless the gathering planned for that evening.

We worshipped until we sensed the Lord's contentment. I called our contact person a couple of weeks later, wondering how things had gone. At first she seemed confused; she had not noticed any dramatic indication that our prayers had been answered, and certainly the conference had gone forward as planned. "Did Kryon appear when he was summoned?" I asked. He had not. "Did this ever happen before at an event like this?" I continued. It had not; in fact, the organizers had been at a loss to explain the non-appearance. "How about the peace you sensed when we prayed in the afternoon?" She said that the peace of God had been palpable in the hotel since that afternoon—and she asked us to come again to bless the whole facility—which we were honored to do.

Our next visit sparked an escalation of God's presence on the premises. This time we included a celebration of the Lord's Supper as we worshipped in the conference room. The Spirit of prophecy broke out amongst us, and a composite word emerged to the effect that an economic renaissance would come to Redding and that the hotel district along Hilltop Drive, where we stood at that moment, would be the locus for it. We released a word that this very hotel would be especially blessed, but that the forerunning phenomenon would be that all of the management, and then the owner, would embrace Christ.

In keeping with His plan to build a prophetic community First Corinthians 12 style, many of us were given a piece of that composite revelation. We also were privileged to see, over the next two years, a progressive embrace of Jesus Christ by the management team of that hotel. Furthermore, we witnessed the designation of Redding as the fastest growing market in the country for investment housing—with many or most of the investors getting their first glimpse of Redding from a hotel balcony along Hilltop Drive. By 2005 Redding timber sales had returned to their pre-1993 levels after a decade-long decline that had shattered that primary local industry. Hotel room sales had broken the record set in 2004. The prophetic re-naming of Redding as Abundant Springs was gaining shape and depth into the bargain. God's fresh word squared with Scripture is always good, always worth waiting for, and always calls for a counter-intuitive stretching of how we think things ought to be done.

TOUGH LOVE FOR BELIEVERS

One of the biggest stretchings of my personal wineskin occurred on a mission trip to Fiji. Kaifafa is a local Fijian member of the construction team for Teach Us to Pray International—the ministry with which I serve in Fiji—and he was working one afternoon on a scaffolding that collapsed beneath him. Landing on his head, Kaifafa was immediately paralyzed from the shoulders down, although his organs continued to function. As the leader of the evangelism and prayer team, I got the call on the emergency and immediately hailed a cab and headed for the hospital in Suva to which he had been taken.

On arrival, I met Kaifafa's father, a local pastor and colleague, in the emergency room. We began to pray with authority as we laid our hands on the motionless young man; we commanded the process of injury to reverse in the name of Jesus and leave him in peace. Within ten minutes he was able to move normally and the x-rays showed no evidence that he had been injured at all. There was not so much as a bruise on his head. But that was not the faith stretcher for me in the encounter.

Reality is that I did not believe God was going to heal Kaifafa when I laid my hands on him and began to pray. I acted in obedience to a Lord who calls us to pray with the authority of His Name. In John 14:12 He goes so far as to say, "I tell you the truth, anyone who has faith in me will do what I have been doing. He will do even greater things than these, because I am going to the Father." Romans 10:9 reports from the heart of the Lord—for all Scripture is God-breathed—that faith is simply this: "If you confess with your mouth, 'Jesus is Lord,' and believe in your heart that God raised Him from the dead, you will be saved." Kaifafa's healing rested in God's hands—not mine—and God graciously offered me the chance to participate through obedient action. It was about what God was thinking, not what I was thinking.

It was a tremendous stretch for me to realize that God is exponentially and passionately more concerned about what I am willing to do in Him than in what I think or feel about it. He is so invested in what the Body is willing to do—each individual member coming together by choice and valuing one another more than themselves—that He claims in Psalm 133:3 that this chosen unity "is as if the dew of Hermon were falling on Mount Zion. For there the Lord bestows His blessing, even life for evermore." The Son says simply that "the Kingdom of Heaven is in the midst of you" (Luke 17:21).

But it is both easy and exciting to speak of miracles that come with this stretching and repenting. The most dynamic reconfiguring of our wineskins is usually much less dramatic and certainly less fun to talk about. I think of the many times each of us is called to repent our hardness of heart. The Lord seems to believe this call increases in importance to the degree we feel justified in the hardness.

In Matthew 18:21-35, it is clear that the unjust servant is collecting a legitimate debt from his fellow servant; Jesus' contention is that he ought to have mercy on his brother as God has had mercy on him. In Luke 12:13-15, a man asks Jesus to force his brother into a division of the estate that is coming to him; Jesus tells him to spend his energy on more important matters. Paul, in his first letter to the Corinthian church, urges the people to accept worldly injustice before going after each other in the secular law courts, where they can only hold the unfolding Kingdom in their midst up to ridicule (see 1 Cor. 6:1-11).

The Lord is far more concerned with the state of heart in the believer than with gratifying the desire for vindication. Jesus wants our eyes and attention on Him, and not on our prerogatives—real or imagined.

I am a case in point. I come from a dysfunctional family of origin that has stolen, or otherwise withheld, inheritance from me five times over the past 30 years. My task in the Lord each time a new legacy comes due and is snatched away has been to forgive and bless those who have wronged me— and to recognize Him as my cup and portion.

I come from a denomination that has embraced apostasy. This branch regularly elevates men and women to positions of leadership who publicly deny the Bible as the authoritative Word of God. In their own domestic arrangements, they defy the Bible's teachings on the structure of family—though Jesus, in Mark 10:6-9, calls "family" a reflection of the very order of creation. The leader of this national body has publicly declared that Jesus is not the exclusive author of salvation and given orders to bring lawsuits against those clergy and congregations who lead their flocks into more orthodox jurisdictions. Yet, the Lord has called me, and others, to an explicit ministry of blessing these leaders, even as we stand against them. We have been instructed to speak out against them only if we can weep over them as He does. We are ordered to walk a thin line between loving confrontation and hateful condemnation.

I don't find it easy. It isn't simply a matter of quoting Scripture and moving on. On the contrary, the struggle recurs and gores my heart on a regular basis. But the Lord says that in my weakness He perfects His strength (see 2 Cor. 12:9). He calls me to remove the log from my own eye before attempting delicate surgery on the eye of my brother (see Matt. 7:3-5; Luke 6:41-42). And each time I abandon my own sense of entitlement—even if I have to deal with the same issue the next day—I find myself stronger and more fit to deacon that Kingdom. When I am enabled to go beyond forgiveness to praying the blessings of God on those I might rather despise, I experience His pleasure and peace in a veritable flood.

In retrospect, it is not rocket science to see that the Lord is clearly permitting a level of injustice in my family of origin in order to prepare me for mission in my denomination. In the meantime, He has provided me with special appreciation for the unique gifts He deposits with Anglicans, alongside an excitement to share those gifts with other members of the family of God while embracing the gifts He has given to them. That sharing and mutual embrace is central to the ministry Diana and I have been given.

It should be just as clear for any of us who suffer setbacks and rollbacks that we serve a God whose will for good and abundant life for all cannot be ultimately thwarted. But often we have to simply choose to obey during what seems like darkness—comforted by the knowledge that God is not put into a funk by what we think or feel at any given moment. He is too busy being passionate about what we *do* in Him. And He always gives much more than He appears to take.

Reality is that the unfolding Kingdom is filled with setbacks and non-starters, even as it splashes signs and wonders of His glory all over the landscape. Frustrations are the material that toughens us for the long haul into which we are called.

Fiji is a nation in which the Holy Spirit has swept through hundreds of villages; unproductive land has been healed alongside the bodies of the sick, and ethnic reconciliation is on fast forward. It has also experienced governmental overthrows and political and social disruptions in the midst of dramatic renewal. Our own mission trips have seen hundreds healed and hundreds more receiving Jesus on each visit. Ministries such as Youth With a Mission are drawing many more into the Kingdom. People are learning business through instruction in micro enterprise; old enemies are repenting and forgiving one another; new congregations are springing up, and older ones are cooperating with one another for the sake of the Kingdom. Yet, the people we serve still live in grinding poverty; the bondage of pagan superstition still holds the majority of residents, and old cultural traditions like wife-beating die hard. Is transformation real or just a pipe dream? The answer must be, of course it is. And it remains an unfolding reality alongside the rest of the unfolding Kingdom that launched on that first Pentecost Sunday.

In our own city of Redding, we have seen thousands of healings from physical, emotional, and spiritual bondage of all kinds. Hundreds of people from every denomination turn out to pray for the city, daily for months at a time, and we have seen things like violent crime and death in traffic—or by suicide—decrease in measurable proportions during these times of prayer. With the permission of city officials, equally large and denominationally diverse groups converge on City Hall to read the entire Bible over the city; and the peace of God descends on the city at such times and with such clarity that even pre-believers comment. Large cross-sections of the Body have combined to bless the city with concerts featuring nationally known Christian bands, festivals of love in city parks, and going out to neighborhood homes to cut grass and do chores for people who cannot do these things easily for themselves. Yet, we still have an unemployment rate well above the state average; drug abuse and domestic violence are rampant, and some churches and pastors continue to think it too dangerous to expose their members to the thinking and practice of other kinds of Christians in the city. Is the cup half full or half empty?

This mixed blessing aspect of the process of unfolding the Kingdom is typical of nations and communities around the world who have experienced a measure of the transformation process. Uganda still has high incidence of the AIDS virus, despite a 50 percent reduction in new infections over the past few years. The drug cartels still wield incredible power in Columbia—as do Marxist insurgent forces—in the wake of a great awakening that swept drug infested cities such as Cali in the mid '90s. Eastern Canada has seen tremendous progress in displacing drug abuse and suicide with a burning hunger to worship the Lord Jesus Christ in Native Americans who travel hundreds of miles on snow mobiles for services that last for days. Yet, because pastors in Canada hold up biblical family values as authoritative, they can be fined or jailed for preaching what politically correct officials interpret as hateful. But nothing in the *not-yet* dimension of the Kingdom coming to these nations is derailing or negating the achievements that God has truly brought to pass. What He has done, He has done.

CHARISM TRUMPS COMPETENCE

Mark 8 contains a wonderful sequence that I think of as the story of Bible math. Jesus and the disciples are heading across the Sea of Galilee when the boys realize that they have forgotten to pack food and have only one loaf of bread between them. (We covered this material in *Living As Ambassadors of Relationships*, but it is worth a do-over here.) Naturally, they begin to blame one another for the lapse—until Jesus gets into the discussion with a warning to avoid the leaven of Herod and the Pharisees. (See Mark 8:14-15.)

The so-called leaven of Herod is simply a can-do spirit that says human invention can take care of human need. Herod was—by secular standards—one of the best Kings Judea ever had. He led a massive public works program and managed to fund it. He won concessions from the emperor of the mightiest empire the world had ever seen. Yet, this paranoid king killed any who opposed him and was so opposed to the purposes of God that when he learned of the birth of Messiah, he murdered every boy baby in the kingdom to eliminate a perceived threat to his own power (see Matt. 2:16). Like another effective king before him—Ahab—Herod is an enemy of God and so is the spirit that animates him.

The leaven of the Pharisees is just as poisonous, and just as reasonable by the standards of fleshly reckoning. They live in such fear of transgressing His holiness that they have become the party of do-not-look and do-not-touch. They search the Scriptures but cannot imagine a God bigger than their imagination of Him. They are legalists—knowing that the Law forbids work on the Sabbath, but un-knowing a God of compassion who encourages acts of Sabbath mercy, like pulling a farm animal from a well—written right into the Law (see Matt. 12:11-12). They cannot engage with Jesus at the table because they are busy watching Him to see if His table manners are a scandal—and so they miss the real interaction between the Lord and the prostitute who washes His feet with her hair (see Luke 7:36-39). Though they seek to serve, it is the Law they know and not the Father.

The Herodians are arrogant enough to believe they are doing what God *would be doing* if He were actually present in the world. The Pharisees are arrogant enough to believe they can protect a God who does not need their protection; it is their attitude of militant fear of wrongdoing that prevents them from doing right. Jesus actually calls us to a bold humility in which we understand our own helplessness to generate life, while at the same time embracing a serene confidence in the One who can. We are called to search the Scriptures, not as a protective measure but as a relational activity. But we are also called to risk everything on what we know of God's heart and discover the bridge that is there only when we have stepped on it, even if we don't know the scriptural address— like Indiana Jones stepping off of the precipice in the *Last Crusade* movie because only the Holy Grail across the chasm can save his father's life.

Jesus next asks the heart of the Bible math question. "When I broke the five loaves for the five thousand, how many basketfuls of pieces did you pick up?" They answer that there were 12. "And when I broke the seven loaves for the four thousand, how many basketfuls of pieces did you pick up?" They answer that there were seven; He wonders if they still do not understand. And the Bible math reveals itself. (See Matthew 16:9-12.)

If there were 12 baskets after breaking five loaves for 5,000 people then there should have been many more than seven left after feeding 4,000 on seven loaves. By earthly standards the math simply does not work, and that is the point. Bible math does not concern new theorems or alternative rules for multiplication and division. It is about choosing *whom* not what to believe. It is all about being bold enough to depend on Jesus and humble enough to know at all times how desperately we need to do just that. It is about bold humility.

It was an exercise in bold humility to pray with authority in the name of Jesus for Qaumaniq and Kaifafa the way we did. It was just as much about that for the pastors who envisioned Faithworks Coalition to seek a literal vision they could share—to believe that the pieces each of them saw would make a logically whole conception on which they could actually act. It is always such an exercise whenever we act as though the Kingdom is here because we have seen God's deposit on His own promise, and again when we accept with grace the fact that we haven't a clue about the date or the details.

There are things that we can do and watch for, which place our visible dependence on the charism—the gift—and not on the chimera of our own competence. There are simple, albeit counterintuitive, measures that pave the highway in the desert for God and the Kingdom He is unfolding in our midst.

One is to reflect that the apostles were honored to make common cause with any Christians who confessed the summary statements of the faith that we summarize in the ancient creeds of the Church.

God is One—Father, Son, and Holy Spirit. Abba, the Father, created all that is and He is Creator still. Jesus, the Son, is fully God and fully man; He came to summarize and complete the creation, and to redeem it as well. Through Him, and Him alone, we have forgiveness of sin, adoption as sons and daughters, and eternal citizenship in that Kingdom for which He died and rose. The Holy Spirit is a present and dynamic reality in the lives of all who believe in their hearts and confess with their lips that Jesus is Lord and the catalyst for the Body of Christ, the Church (see Rom. 10:9). The Spirit is the giver of both gifts and fruit that animate our abundant life. Baptism is the door, and the apostles never required a time of study and learning before that door could be opened; asking was enough.

In Acts 15 the Jerusalem Council asked only that Gentile converts—from outside of Judea no less—refrain from any participation in idol worship, from eating blood and the meat of strangled animals, and from sexual immorality. (They took for granted that converts would receive the Hebrew Scriptures as the reliable Word of God that they are.) Why on earth would we shrink from sharing communion, ministry, or any kind of service to God with another, simply because he or she is of another Christian denomination than the one we call home? The Bible has no answer for such a question.

In Northern California—and I can only speak for my own region with any authority—virtually every ministry that God has made into a region-impacting blessing has been an interdenominational effort. From Faithworks Coalition building transitional housing and cutting welfare rolls, to Anderson-Cottonwood Christian Assistance feeding the hungry and teaching them to cook at the same time, the Holy Spirit visits unusual favor, power, and authority on these combinational groups of Christians. From Teen Challenge setting free the captives of substance abuse, to Carenet and Lifelight Pregnancy Centers partnering with each other, with Salvation

Army, and with multiple churches to care for pregnant women and the men in their lives, it seems that the more partnering they do the more they prosper. From Outreach America collaborating with whole communities to put on youth and family fairs (bringing some really good music alongside the Gospel at regional county fairs) to Jesus Culture gathering 1500 young people at the Redding Convention Center to send them out serving the people they meet on the streets, it is clear that the gathered Body of Christ is entering public arenas where the popular wisdom of our time says they shall not go. And this is but a partial list of the ways and personalities through whom God is getting glory for Himself in one thinly populated region of a thickly populated state.

I am not speaking of a syrupy ecumenicalism in which people of different traditions stand on their best behavior and commit to mutual toleration. The oneness of the first-century Church is on the table here, in which there was one Body in cities made of many congregations, each with its own style and emphasis—the Church of many gifts serving one Lord. The people I describe are robustly proud of the special gifts and perspectives God has given to them, even as they share a love for Him and for each other. They have simply chosen to learn from one another, as the Great Commission commands.

A second point of reference is Jesus' command to the disciples to make no provision for themselves as they go out on mission. In Luke 9 He gives power to heal and cast out demons as they preach the Kingdom, a Kingdom they do not yet understand (see Luke 9:1-2). "Take nothing for the journey—no staff, no bag, no bread, no money, no extra tunic," He tells them (Luke 9:3). They get the same thing in the next chapter, except this time they are going where even the Christ has not yet gone, there are six times as many disciples on the road, and they are instructed to bless, hang out with the people, meet their needs in the Spirit's power and gifting, and share what God has done for them—in that order—if we understand Luke 10:1-9. They return rejoicing at the miracles they have seen, and Jesus tells them to joy instead that their names are written in His book (see Luke 10:17-20).

In spring 2006 it was my privilege to keep a vow I made to the Lord to visit the Little Bighorn battlefield as a pilgrim—hearing in my heart the importance to the Lord for this watershed in American race relations to be acknowledged in bold humility. Bold humility, incidentally, meant to me that I would only pray on the battlefield after offering proper protocol and respect to the Native Americans who were its earlier stewards. I would go there, however, without waiting to know how to do the protocol—inasmuch as I had no contacts with local Indian elders. I left Redding with my friend, Pete Bowers, who knows (as I do) reconciliation with any and all to be a prime component of his ministry.

On arrival we went to the socially central trading post, and I was invited into conversation with a man named Kale, a leader in the Crow Nation. Crows were first claimants of the land on which the battlefield rests—they were resisting Indian as much as White invasion and for that reason had thrown in their lot with Custer on the day. In a series of unplanned and seemingly uncaused encounters, I found myself first vectored by Kale to a gathering of Crow elders that was to conclude that very night, and then standing face to face with an elder named Art who listened to my request to pray for authentic peace between our peoples on his ancestral land. He gave his blessing with gladness, adding only that he wished everyone would "ask permission before asking forgiveness."

The next day we prayed and celebrated the Lord's Supper on the hill on which Captain Benteen and Major Reno withstood a day-long assault. The Lord had directed us to this place because it was a place of life and death—most of the combatants on both sides survived the battle—while Custer Hill was a place of death alone. As we prayed and ate and drank we saw a lone hawk circle an Indian grave marker at ground level just over the lip of the hill, something that does not happen in nature. We sensed the Lord telling us that the return of freely grazing buffalo on the battlefield would signal peace and not just the absence of conflict between our peoples. When we reported to Kale at the trading post, he told us the herd belonging to the tribe had been drifting toward the battlefield to graze for some years, and was now only about two miles distant.

"Taking no provision" means that vision trumps planning. It envisions a radical dependency on God to conceive, to conceptualize, and to create what is on His mind and place it on ours. It means using the mind God gave us, but only after seeking His face and mind as though it were our own—and that often calls us into what planners name the counterintuitive approach. "Taking no provision" was applied as a pragmatic principle when leaders envisioned each of the ministries cited above, from Faithworks to Jesus Culture.

It is not literally about whether we had money for gas and food when we left Redding for Montana. It is about trusting charism instead of competence for the performance of our mission. It is about gifting, not get-go.

Pastors and leaders in Siskiyou County are applying the same principle on a slowly expanding basis, as they witness the unfolding of God's promise to bring revival in the wake of word getting out about Gerry's healing. Since 2002 they have banded together in Mt. Shasta for an annual Fourth of July Christian festival called Day in the Son, for which the Lord always provides the hot dogs, the music, and the testimonies they need. They have gathered a hundred-strong in little Fort Jones (population 700) to pray at the gates of their valley and watch the Lord stop a lusty snowstorm at their prayed request—figuring how much more He will show His face to His people in that valley who earnestly seek Him.

Leaders from several Siskiyou County towns now gather for their own annual public reading of the Bible and for an annual youth gathering called Kaleo, which brings in young people from all of the area churches. Any of these things would have been unthinkable a few years ago, and the unfolding promise is only beginning to be fulfilled.

A third point to encourage us is that scattering is good for us. In the beginning of Acts 8 we read:

> *On that day a great persecution broke out against the church at Jerusalem, and all except the apostles were scattered throughout Judea and Samaria. Godly men buried Stephen and mourned deeply for him....Those who had been scattered....went down to a city in Samaria and proclaimed the Christ there. When the crowds heard Philip and saw the miraculous signs he did, they all paid close attention to what he said. With*

shrieks, evil spirits came out of many, and many para-lytics and cripples were healed. So there was great joy in that city (Acts 8:1-2;4-8).

Things are going very well in Jerusalem—as we might expect in the weeks following such a major outpouring of the Spirit and the power of God. Thousands are coming to know Jesus and to exercise powerful gifts to heal the sick and speak the word as it has never been spoken before. When the authorities question their right to heal beggars on temple property, the apostles give such clear and convincing answers that the priests have no apparent choice but to let them go (see Acts 4:1-21). Everything they touch is turning to Kingdom gold, except for the little detail that they have forgotten the command to preach the Gospel in Jerusalem, all of Judea, Samaria and the rest of the world (see Acts 1:8). Things are going too well.

God is equal to this new challenge—the challenge of success. He moves the leaders of the Body to establish a new layer of leadership under Stephen and Philip and the other deacons. He permits Stephen's death—following one of the best evangelistic sermons ever preached—and the scattering of the younger generation of leaders beyond the city in the persecution that follows. They are not especially frightened by the chaos—as far as we can tell by reading Acts 8. They just keep doing what they are called to do wherever they land—from cities in Samaria to desert roads to Syrian Antioch. (See Acts 6–8.)

For those of us who wonder if every time we experience this scattering in our lives and ministries it means we are forgetting what God commands, Jesus tells us that doesn't matter: "But this happened so that the work of God might be displayed in his life" (John 9:3). In Romans, He says through Paul, "And we know that in all things God works for the good of those who love Him, who have been called according to His purpose" (Rom. 8:28). Certainly the Holy Spirit convicts us of sin when we need it, but He always has a far greater, and more blessed, purpose for us at the end of the day.

The year 2006 was a banner year for PrayNorthState in many ways. We coordinated a three-month prayer project in our county that yielded documented fruit, like a 40 percent reduction in traffic death, a cut in the youth death rate of 50 percent, and nearly 60 percent fewer hospital admissions for cancer when compared to the same quarter a year earlier. A number of California cities began public reading of the Word of God on our model, and we continued a pattern of faith-based observances in public venues like the 9-11 Commemoration at the courthouse and the Culture of Life Rally back at City Hall. We completed three very successful overseas mission trips into the bargain. God did it all, and I risk being called a braggart, only to bring into perspective the last three months of the year when we were hit with unprecedented backlash. Our ministry was never far from bankruptcy—parachurches seldom are—but at this point, Diana and I were forced to consider shutting down the ministry if things did not improve in early 2007.

Into that train wreck strode a dynamic and loving God who spoke to me as clearly as He ever had. "I call upon you to sow into the future and pay no attention to what you see around you. Have eyes only for me and where I am calling you." When I replied that I was not certain I had a future, He said, "Your job is to seed the future; My job is to give you a future to seed."

He then began to tell me—with several friends and colleagues hearing the same word—that He wanted focus on the media and writing dimensions of our ministry for 2007. (We began a local radio talk show in 2001 and a regional television program in 2004.) Although radio and television had always been a small corner of our calling in my mind—and not well funded at that—I began looking for ways to expand the number of stations that carried us. I also submitted a proposal for *Living As Ambassadors of Relationships* to three publishers, to whom an author friend had written letters introducing me. By the time we were well into 2007, our radio hour was on four outlets with more stations preparing to accommodate us and a new program on young people in leadership under development. The book was accepted for publication, despite the fact that no new author expects to get away with only three submissions. God meant it when He said, "Your job is to seed the future; my job is to give you a future to seed."

A Kingdom of Neighborhoods

First Corinthians 12 refers to a communal understanding of *ekklesia*—the word we hear as "Church" is *the called out ones* in New Testament Greek. It is as much about the integral value of constituent congregations to the whole gathering of the Body of Christ as it is concerned with valuing persons. Paul knew, as well as we do, that the human body is organized as organs and limbs and bones and hormonal systems as well as along cellular lines. He also knew that there were multiple congregations in the cities he visited but only one church in the city. His letters were passed from gathering to gathering.

New Testament leaders knew and celebrated the fact that each of these congregations had its own way of worshiping the same God and its own way of serving the same Lord. That is why Paul says there are many gifts and one Spirit; it is why he exhorts the faithful, "If it is possible, as far as it depends on you, live at peace with everyone," in Romans 12—that other chapter that compares the Body of Christ to a human body (Rom. 12:18).

The stretching of wineskins is a corporate call to the faith community as much as to individual believers within those communities. The denominational units of the Body have received unique identities—some are really good at enlivening worship, and others are really superb at helping families to strength. Some are really gifted at drawing the gifts of the Spirit from their members, while others are the best they can be at producing ambassadors of reconciliation. Still, others are unusually impassioned about feeding the hungry and clothing the naked—and good at organizing such ministries of compassion. Since all of us are called to these ministries as pre-requisites of the Great Ministry of blessing, hanging out with, meeting needs of, and then witnessing our faith to the people we meet (see Luke 10), we need the rest of the Body to teach us what they know in greater facility than we do. And they need us to share, not hoard, our gifts.

God has not called us to be a soup pot and still be found in the same bowl with the rest of us, but instead, to be more like a big salad in which every element can be tasted in all of its freshness and fullness. He indeed calls those who have ignored the Word of God—as summarized in the creeds—to get back on track. But He must be flabbergasted when we refuse to worship or serve with our brothers and sisters, because we don't care for their style of prayer (hands up or hands down), or their standard of baptism (kids first or adults only), or their interpretation of this or that passage—providing they believe the passage itself is of the Lord. He makes it very clear in the parable of wheat and tares that it is not our place to do that kind of sorting (see Matt. 13:24-29).

Reality is that we stand on the shoulders of individuals and communities who have gone before us. In my city alone, there are dozens and perhaps hundreds of men and women who, for many decades, have prayed for and looked for the kinds of Kingdom activities we see today. Most have names that few would know outside of Shasta County—and in the Kingdom of God. Some are still among us, like Tim and Carole Moore and Clif and Roberta Peterson; while others are watching the fruit of their labor unfold in Christ while seated at His side—Ed Petersen, Earl Johnson, and John Morrill come to mind.

Reality is also that each time the Body makes a loving move to launch a new ministry that partakes of the oneness for which Jesus prays in John 17, we displace the culture of death made possible by our sin with a culture of life—and so the next movement of the unfolding Kingdom is facilitated by ground made ready for it (see John 17:20-26). Events like the March for Jesus, National Day of Prayer, Pray Until Something Happens, and the many festivals of loving faith that have blessed our city in the past decade have made room in the spiritual landscape for the ones that follow and expand on their vision. Ministries like Youth for Christ, Child Evangelism Fellowship, Power Surge, and Moms in Touch, have paved the way for a ministry like PrayNorthState's walking and blessing public school campuses with permission of administration, which paves the way for renewed outreach and effectiveness of these earlier inroads. And faithful institutions like the Good News Rescue Mission, Salvation Army, and Teen Challenge just keep on keeping on—banding together with the rest of us for the goal of the prize.

Christians who discern the Kingdom in the midst of this very gathering of all of the streams and all of the rivers are the mother and brothers and friends of the Christ to whom He refers in Mark 3 and Luke 8 (see Mark 3:31-35; Luke 8:19-21). But the best reality of all is the truth of what Jesus says in John 15, that He is the vine and we are the branches (see John 15:5). We will do these things as we join Him in seeking those who do not yet know Him.

My friend, Jack, tells of a class of student pastors who were instructed by their leaders to avoid an especially muddy stretch of parkland when they were out for a picnic in that park. One of the students paid no attention to the instructions—which were quite clear—and ended up in the mud. The more he shifted in his efforts to escape, the more deeply he sank into muddy bondage. By the time anyone noticed his predicament he was up to his hips and there was no escape. The instructor intended to go out to his rescue, but he called class members together and had them lay branches on the ground to enable the instructor to walk out without himself getting bogged down. He then went to the hapless student and, with the help of other branches, got him out and back to the solid ground. That's right—with the help of the other branches.

The Kingdom of God is an unfolding reality with each deposit on the promise that God has made, bringing the whole picture into clearer focus. He is the vine and we are the branches.

Chapter 3

∽

Prophetic Acts With Impact

Loren was near the end of his battle with cancer when his best friend came to the Tuesday Morning pastors' prayer meeting. Wendell asked that we pray for a man I had met but hardly knew—pray for him as though the Kingdom depended on it; he said that Loren had only days to live, unless the Lord came in major league power. While we prayed for him I was given a vision—a weird vision, but then my visions are usually pretty out there. I saw Loren in his hospital bed, and his abdomen—where the cancer was concentrated—had become a football field. The two-minute warning had sounded and God spoke to me, saying, "Tell him to throw the Hail Mary!"

Anybody who knows football knows that the Hail Mary is a desperation pass in which the quarterback tells everybody to go long and hopes somebody will catch it when he launches the rocket. Any pastor with an ounce of professionalism knows that stupid football patter is not what you bring to the bed of a dying man. (The same could be said for any lay person with an ounce of common sense.) I approached Wendell in fear and trembling and described my vision to him, with apologies. But Wendell laughed and said that Loren, a fanatical football fan, would love the image. "Well," I said, "you be sure and tell him about it when you see him." Wendell's response was that I had to tell him myself—in person—since I was the one to whom the Lord had spoken.

With heart in hand I went to Mercy Hospital and walked into Loren's room to see a semi-comatose man clearly close to death. I reminded him of who I was and related the vision that I had seen. Loren laughed softly, opened his eyes, and asked me to pray the vision. Two days later he walked out of the hospital a healthy man. What we all witnessed in Loren's case is the model for what I call a prophetic act with impact. The prophetic act and its impact are demonstrable and documentable—and so clearly identifiable as a miraculous intervention of God that there are simply no circumstantial ways to explain it away.

In today's prophetic community that God is constructing of His Church, He is doing more and more of these prophetic acts with impact. They are the paving stones of the straight highway we are called to lay in the desert for our coming King. They are the stuff of the Holy Spirit transformation that is breaking out in hundreds of communities all over the world. They are the very antithesis of the breezy statements that we so often associate with prophecy, to the effect that there has been some sort of shift in the heavenlies, leading to a restructuring of life in our world—albeit invisible and shapeless to our eyes—to be believed simply because the prophet says that it is so.

God cherishes every prayer we utter, and He is especially sensitive to prayers of intercession because on those occasions we are valuing others above ourselves. But intercessory prayer, as we prayed for Loren or for Gerry or Qaumaniq, becomes prophetic intercession when the focus becomes the Kingdom, rather than one or two for whom the Kingdom is established. Prophetic intercession is Kingdom or strategic intercession; its subject matter becomes issues that, when answered, facilitate the coming of the Kingdom to a community. When we pray for a person with cancer God is pleased to answer. When we pray that God will eliminate cancer from our community— and when we do this in company with a cross-section of the Body—God gets excited and galvanized into action that is strategic in scope.

Prophetic Intercession As Project

The Arrowhead Project was a ministry of Sierra Ministries International, a Nevada County, California, group with similar focus and style to our own PrayNorthState. In spring 2003 their leader, Pastor Dan Prout, organized 125 praying people from many denominations into three teams. Their commitment was to pray each day for the topics assigned to their respective teams. Team 1 asked God to reduce the numbers of crimes in their county. Team 2 petitioned the Throne about unemployment. Team 3 went on their faces over the issue of workman's compensation cases treated at the local hospital. Dan gathered baseline statistics from the relevant authorities and the teams prayed for 90 days; he then gathered updated stats so that they could compare numbers with the same three-month period a year earlier. The documented impact of God's response to their consistent and concerted prayer was remarkable—to say the least.

Crime was reduced anywhere from one quarter to two-thirds, depending on the specific category of the eight that are included in Part 1 Crime. Unemployment was down by about one percentage point—just as spectacular in its way as the crime result. There were no hospital admissions for workman's compensation related issues during the three-month period. But that was not all she wrote: owners of the most prominent gold mine in the county announced the discovery of a new and very rich vein. There had been no new gold sources opened in the county in more than a century. Although the teams did not intercede specifically about gold, a recent prophecy stated—and was fulfilled—that gold would again flow in Nevada County. When we show up God loves to show off.

Everyone who hears this story marvels at it and praises God for it. Only a few find a fire burning in their bellies to go and do likewise. That fire caught in me the first time I heard Dan share it. I began to ask God to authorize me to lead such a project in Shasta County, where I live. For more than a year He kept quiet when I prayed about it, and when He did give me the go-ahead He simply said, "Call it *Paah-ho-ammi*."

There was one little problem with the word the Lord gave to me. I had no clue what *Paah-ho-ammi* might mean—or even in what language it might be! We work with Native Hawaiians, American Indians, and Jewish people in the reconciliation side of our ministry, and the word sounded vaguely like it could have come from any of their language stocks. I asked the Lord repeatedly over the next several weeks to tell me about this word, and He was as silent as I had been to Him during the first 22 years of my life—when I lived without Him. But I had my marching orders, and I began approaching pastors and other leaders about coming on board with a Shasta County Paah-ho-ammi project, even as I continued to seek His face for more information about it. As anyone can imagine, the moment of high drama always came when I told them what we were planning to call it.

"Paah-ho-ammi. Interesting. What does it mean?"

"I don't really know."

"Foreign language—sounds like. Which one?"

"I don't know that either."

"Uh-huh. Where did you get it—the name?"

"The Lord told me to call it that."

"Oh—good—uh—Why don't you come back to see me after you've had some therapy?"

Even so, I was able to gather about 135 Christians from across many denominational lines to commit to service on the prayer teams. Simpson University—a Christian liberal arts school in Redding—gave me use of their facility at no charge for the launching service. Because I like to bookend things, we decided to begin Paah-ho-ammi, which I short-handed to PHA, on September 26, 2004—the feast of Yom Kippur. We would end it on New Year's Day—the traditional feast on which Jesus is formally named by His earthly parents. Team 1 would pray about Part 1 Crime, just as in Nevada County. Team 2 would pray reduction in unemployment and increase for indicators of economic prosperity in the county. Team 3 would assault the throne over traffic fatalities and cancer admissions to the hospital. (God had spoken to a number of us in NorCal regarding His intention to make the region a cancer free zone.) All of the team members agreed to pray for protection of young people in the county; we were averaging two deaths each month in kids aged 14 to 24 when we decided to attack this epidemic of sudden death. And so we began to pray.

When we updated our stats in early 2005, we were just as astounded as the folks in Nevada County. Overall crime in the areas patrolled by the county sheriff was down by 22 percent. Unemployment was down by about seven-tenths of a percent—very good on such an indicator—and Redding had just been named the number one investment housing market in the country. In addition, we became the fastest appreciating real estate market in the state, and timber orders, which had been devastated by environmental decisions in the early '90s, reached a level on par with their 1993 heyday. The indicators were good, but the most spectacular impact of this prophetic act was in the public health arena.

Traffic fatalities in the county overall were down by about 20 percent against the same period a year earlier, but there were no fatalities at all on the roads anywhere in Northern California during the most traveled weekends of the year: Thanksgiving, Christmas, and New Year's. We had only been praying for Shasta County, but God released the gold over us just as He had in Nevada County! On top of that, we found cancer admissions to Mercy Hospital were reduced by 21 percent, and there was an approximate 80 percent drop-off in deaths among young people during the period of prayer!

We found other unexpected fruit in terms of both danger and opportunity. The danger was that God did not continue to provide such bounty when the people stopped their praying on a regular basis. In Second Chronicles 7:14, God promises an answer when the people called by His name are actually praying, but not when they merely have a history of prayer. Jeremiah 29:11-13 promises that when we seek His face we cannot fail to find Him, but it does not promise that He will be always before us after we stop looking. And First Thessalonians 5:17 says to pray without ceasing, not to cease prayer when we have what we want. The youth deaths began to climb again after the end of the project, although (praise God) only about halfway to where they were before we began. Prosperity indicators remained healthy through 2005—although the econ team was the most faithful in lifting their concerns before the Lord throughout the year. And the sheriff's office announced an overall 11 percent reduction in county crime for 2005—not 22 percent, but a tremendous blessing.

The next time we ran Paah-ho-ammi was the spring of 2006, and God was already escalating the process of His glory. This time we prayed from February 2—not because it was Ground Hog Day, but because it was the day Baby Jesus is presented in the Temple at Jerusalem—through May 3, the National Day of Prayer. We gathered a little more than 200 people of prayer into the teams and we found a dozen churches willing to take one to two minutes in every Sunday morning service to pray all of the PHA topics as a Body. (None had been willing to do that in 2004.) We added suicide as a topic for the crime team this time out.

The harvest God brought in this time was mind blowing! Suicides were down by about 12 percent in our county— even though they doubled throughout the rest of the state—and county crime was again reduced by 22 percent. Unemployment was sent down a full percentage point this time and economic indicators climbed higher than before. But the public health sector again posted the greatest glory for the Lord. Youth deaths were cut in half, even after we added more categories for a more accurate accounting. Traffic fatalities were reduced by 40 percent and cancer admissions were down a whopping 58 percent!

We did not include abortions in Paah-ho-ammi until 2007 because of difficulty in objectivizing the statistics, but many of those who pray for women in crisis pregnancies were part of the public health team, and the local Carenet Pregnancy Center led it. They prayed in accordance with the same teaching that governs all of our prayer projects. Our best estimates are that abortions in the county fell off by about 20 percent from 2005 to 2006—and in 2007 we discovered a way to be a good deal more linear in our figuring so as to include this issue from that point on.

By the third time around, on what has become an annual event, we had come to understand that our primary objective in Paah-ho-ammi is to displace a culture of death with the culture of God's abundant life. This represents a serious escalation from an original intention to document God's response to some concerted and strategic intercession for our community and proclaim it from the rooftops! But it also stands as an equally serious escalation in God's call to permit Him to set our priorities, even as He perfects His strength in our weakness (see 2 Cor. 12:9).

SEEKING A CULTURE OF LIFE

When the two pro-life ministries in town—Carenet Pregnancy Center and Life Light—chose to hold their principal fundraisers on the same day in 2005, the County Board of Supervisors declared that week in October to be Culture of Life Week. They used it to honor life-affirming ministries, whether faith-based or not, and to recognize that the disproportionately high incidence of drug addiction, suicide, divorce, and domestic violence in the NorthState region were symptoms of a spiritual culture that makes death more natural and magnetic than life. In 2006 the same proclamation was issued, and Shasta County saw her first Culture of Life Celebration—a rally in the plaza of City Hall in which many who had, once upon a time, chosen lifestyles of bondage shared how knowing Jesus had set them free. Into this backdrop swam Paah-ho-ammi 2007— utterly dedicated to laying a carpet of prayer for a culture of life in Shasta County.

We launched on the National Day of Prayer—our numbers having grown from 135 to about 350 praying people of all denominations and streams. Their sole commitment was to pray daily, for as long or as short a time as they could handle and in whatever style was most natural for them. What had morphed from the crime team into the more broadly focused public safety team prayed this year for reductions in suicides and drunken driving arrests. (We reasoned—erroneously as it happened—that a reduction in arrests meant an increase in freedom from the bondage of addiction.) The economy team prayed again for less unemployment and more concrete indicators of prosperity; the public health team hung in with prayer that traffic fatalities and cancer admissions would be fewer. They added prayer that decisions for life—based on client statistics from Carenet—would increase. All teams prayed again for protection of youth against sudden or violent death. The project would conclude on the traditional festival of Jesus' transfiguration on the mountain as recorded in Matthew 17 and Luke 10—it was a tad more than the 90 days we seek as a parameter of prayer.

Results this time were ambiguous in terms of what we set out to achieve, but crystal clear in terms of God's agenda. Arrests for driving under the influence actually rose—by about 5 percent in county areas and by a hefty 65 percent in the city of Redding itself. As the project's leader, I was disappointed until I remembered that we always ask God to bless the efforts of law enforcement. His blessing was evident in that drunk driving collisions were actually down by 22 percent in the city despite our imperfect reasoning about what to pray for. God was actually and abundantly blessing our cry for a culture of life to begin budding. Suicides were reduced by an incredible 86 percent during the prayer period!

On the economy front, there was more ambiguity and even more glory for God. Unemployment showed a net increase as against the same period a year earlier, although it continued the downward trend that began in the spring of 2007. The slump in the housing market that had shaken the nation hit here as well—but for the first six months of 2007 it was 1 percent in our county, against 13 percent across the United States. Home building permits rose by 25 percent between May and June; foreclosures were rising at only a third of the statewide increase and sales later in the summer were falling at about a third of the statewide drop. Commercial property valuations in Redding were increasing at a pace to outstrip the record-setting year of 2005. There was a significant increase in total jobs in the county. Whether in protecting us from the bad news or making good news of His own, the Lord of life is declaring a new culture of life for His people who are called by His Name and seeking His Face.

In the public health arena, traffic fatalities fell by a modest 15 percent; while cancer admissions actually rose by 17 percent. (I am still scratching my head over that one—especially when I consider the many anecdotal examples of cancers being healed in this season—like the malignant melanoma in a man I know that went undiagnosed for eight months before God healed it through a combination of prayer and surgery; melanomas are simply not healed in nature after so long an access short of a major league miracle—the kind God loves to deliver.) But the most spectacular fruit of this project dedicated to a culture of life emerges from the decisions for life in crisis pregnancies in the county—they rose by an unbelievable 130 percent!

While suicides were reduced by 86 percent, decisions for life were increased by more than 100 percent. Youth deaths declined by more than 60 percent as well. We do not need to ask God to bless what we are doing; we need instead to do what He is blessing—even and especially when we pray. And when we sow the teaching that God has revealed, He escalates the harvest 30, 60, and even 100-fold!

What exactly is that teaching for Paah-ho-ammi?

First of all, we believe the Body is called to war. In this war, we practice the weaponry of spiritual warfare; for our war is indeed spiritual and that means our strategy is to love as Christ loves. In Romans 12:14 Paul reiterates what Jesus says in the

Sermon on the Mount—that we are to bless and curse not—and each time He sends the disciples ahead of Him (see Rom. 12:14; Matt. 5:43-48). He makes no exceptions, and so we bless without exception and without reference to what we think someone deserves. And we reflect that when God blesses He transforms more and more into His likeness.

We are also to forgive and condemn not. In John 20:19-23, Jesus sends the newly blessed apostles out, as He has been sent—to declare His peace. He tells them that the sins they forgive are truly forgiven and those they retain are retained—by them. It is the same message He has preached since He told them that if they could not forgive they could not be forgiven. It is not about what we deserve—His mercy is what happens when we do not get what we do deserve. There are no exceptions.

We are called to celebrate the Lord's Supper whenever we get the chance, doing this for the remembrance of Him is what the Scriptures say (see Luke 22:19; 1 Cor. 11:24-25). In Luke 24 the men on the road to Emmaus do not recognize the risen Lord when He falls in beside them and begins to chat. They do not recognize Him when He opens their minds and hearts to the Scriptures about Himself—although they say later that their hearts burned within them. It is only in the breaking of the bread that they see Him for who He is. And we are no different 2,000 years later. (See Luke 24:13-35.)

These three weapons: blessing, forgiveness, and the Supper are the only weapons we have been given by the Lord our God; when we engage in war by prayer and by honor they are the extent of our armament.

Now some will say at this point, "But what about repentance?" I can only respond that, in a world steeped in use of the weapons of destruction and domination since Cain killed Abel, the exclusive use of blessing, forgiveness, and the Supper in spiritual warfare is the very essence of repentance.

"OK, but in Revelation 12:11 it says that the devil is overcome by the blood of the Lamb and the word of their testimony." This is true, and we speak of the Supper in this tactical sense as addressing the bloodguilt with the blood. But more than that we understand warfare as preparing the ground—paving the highway—so that our testimony falls into ears and an atmosphere made ready for it. Saint Francis of Assisi was so oriented to this kind of prophetic action that he famously called on his disciples to preach the Gospel by all available means—even using words where necessary. In a profound sense, these weapons constitute our testimony that something greater than law and prophets is present, even as they pave the way for it.

"Yes, but in Hebrews 4:12 I read that the Word of God itself is living and active and sharper than any double-edged sword; it penetrates to the marrow of the bones and to the ends of our hearts. How about that?" That is absolutely on the mark! And the Word of God says what? We are to love one another, whether we feel like it or not, and whether the love is deserved or not. We are to forgive as we are forgiven. And we are to do what we do in the Supper—whenever the Lord shall provide for the setting of a table in the presence of His enemies—for the remembrance of Him. Because the enemy of life cannot comprehend these tactics, there are no more devastating or transforming methods with which to assault the gates of hell and usher in the Kingdom of Heaven.

All Paah-ho-ammi prayer is structured around the principle of blessing and forgiveness, and the Lord's Supper is celebrated at every team meeting and at the general services held at the beginning and close of the project each year. But two other teachings emerged from this particular event in the coming and preparation of God's Kingdom in our region. The first was that "doing" precedes "knowing" in the Kingdom of God, and the second was that every time we leave our comfort zone in the name of the Lord, we enter the Kingdom zone in terms of the fruit He will give.

The Lord's word to me was to proceed with Paah-ho-ammi before I knew what it meant or where it came from. I knew from the fruit of Arrowhead that God had birthed this prayer and this project—and I did need to know it was His before going ahead. But His Word makes very clear that doing always precedes knowing in the Kingdom. In John 8:31-32 Jesus does not say that when we know the truth we will be set free and enabled to follow him (see John 8:31-32). On the contrary, He says that if we follow Him—if we hold to His teaching—we will come to know the truth and be set free in it. In Isaiah 55 God says plainly that our thoughts are not His thoughts; we can hardly expect to understand Him (see Isa. 55:8). But He adds that His Word does not fail to accomplish that for which it has been sent (see Isa. 55:11). He promises peace and plenty to those who follow His Word prior to comprehending it. Jesus promises that what He utters in the darkness will be trumpeted from the rooftops—by those who are faithful.

Even the famous proclamation in Joel of the outpouring of the Spirit on all flesh follows the obedience of the people in calling a solemn assembly to seek God in repentance in the earlier parts of the chapter (see Joel 2:28). And the witness is eloquent and unequivocal that the children of Israel had no clue what was in store for them when they set out from Egypt because Moses had convinced them, with signs and wonders, that God was calling them. We preach a Gospel of power and not of mere words—power first and then come the words.

Just as central to the witness of Paah-ho-ammi is the fact that whenever we leave our comfort zone at His word we enter the Kingdom zone in terms of the peace and power of His love that we will experience. He says that we will do greater things than what we have seen Him do—if that is not beyond the bounds of the familiar, I don't know what is. Yet John 14:12-14 has been proving true for two millennia—it's just that it is more comfortable to marvel at what other people do in the name of Jesus than to undertake those things oneself.

No prophet was ever comfortable obeying the Word of the Lord—unless we think John the Baptist enjoyed camel's hair against his skin and the taste of wild locusts. (Did Ezekiel really like lying on his side for over a year and eating bread baked over dung?) Yet, we check in with Peter through the pages of Matthew's account and see that he walked on water when his master called (see Matt. 14:29). He was the first to confess Jesus as the Son of the living God and to hear Jesus say that only when we are willing to give up our own life are we set to find real life (see Matt. 16:13,24-25). Yet, his confession in faithfulness that Jesus was the Son led directly into the trip up the mountain of transfiguration where Jesus is revealed in all of His glory for the very first time (see Luke 9:28-36). All God asked me to do was risk a little embarrassment when I went to tell those pastors that I didn't know where a name came from but that I wished they would help me anyway. The fruit of that bit of faithfulness has been beyond my wildest imaginings.

FAITHFULNESS TRUMPS

There is actually a third teaching that emerges from the Paah-ho-ammi experience of prophetic acts with impact. It is that faithfulness trumps giftedness every time.

Mark 9:14-29 recounts the story of a demon-possessed boy whose father brings him to the disciples for healing and deliverance. When the disciples are unable to deal with the situation, the father goes straight to Jesus, asking Him to cast out the spirit if He can. In one of the most charged verses in all of Scripture, Jesus blasts him with, "'If you can?'...Everything is possible for him who believes" (Mark 9:23). The father's words are immortal—"Lord, I believe; help my unbelief" (Mark 9:24 NKJV). Jesus heals and delivers the boy at once, and sets up the reason this passage is important for prophetic acts with impact. When the disciples want to know why they could not cast it out, Jesus replies, "This kind can come out only by prayer" (Mark 9:29).

The disciples had prayed for the boy—and nothing happened. Yet, Jesus cites prayer as the solution to the dilemma. He can only be meaning that they have not yet prayed enough, that sustained prayer is the ticket—the kind called for in Isaiah 62 when the Lord calls His people to give themselves and Himself no rest as they keep watch on the walls of Jerusalem.

How often do we say—or hear others say—after a moving testimony of God's goodness in our land, that we would like to do those things too, but we lack the gift? Yet, Jesus says not that the gifted will be saved, but those who endure to the end. (See Matthew 10:22; 24:13; Mark 13:13.) When do we find Him recruiting gifted people for the work of His hand—in Old or New Testament? The people He binds to Himself become gifted only after they enter and remain in His service. He sent Moses, a man with a speech impediment, to proclaim His Name to the Jews and the Egyptians. He sent Paul, a man with an eye disease, to cast the vision for His Church of the called-out ones. The 12 disciples who become apostles are among the least gifted people the world has ever known. (Only Judas is reputed to have the education and the connections for success.) When we recruited for Paah-ho-ammi we did not call for prophets or apostles or people with proven gifts of intercession; we asked for anyone who would pray everyday—whether they were able to pray for hours on end, like my wife, or for the moments an attention deficit disordered person, like myself, could muster. And when we showed up, God showed off.

The bottom line of these teachings, which keep informing us of the escalating outbursts of God in our region today, is that we only come to understand the word God is speaking to us from inside obedience to Him. If we wait for comprehension before we act on what He says, we will never act, and understanding will never come. If—having verified that it is God who speaks—we act in faithfulness, we will find that we come to understand all things and that all things that we need will be given us as well. All gifts are available to the one who is faithful in what he or she has already been given.

There are several bottom lines on the prophetic acts that demonstrate the coming of the Kingdom in ways that can be documented for all to see with eyes to see.

Prophetic acts walk out the Word of God, whether spoken on the spot or applied from the Scriptures. In Amos 3:7, God declares that He does nothing without first informing His servants the prophets. In Joel 2:28 and again in Acts 2:17-21, He promises to inform all of His servants in the latter days. The emphasis is obviously on what God is doing, not merely on what He says; and He says in First Corinthians 2:4 and again in First Corinthians 4:20 that the message comes with a demonstration of the Spirit's power. Indeed, in Romans 1 He says that what He has done in creation is available for all to see so that we are without excuse if we plead ignorance. We have an obligation, as well as an opportunity, to seek occasions for the manifesting of His glory that can be documented as they are demonstrated.

Paah-ho-ammi is nothing more or less than walking out His word in Second Chronicles 7:14—that when the people of God pray, He cannot resist answering; but the prayer is to be sustained and concerted, and with focus on the things He desires if we would become a force for the Kingdom in our midst.

In PrayNorthState we use words like *prophetic, strategic,* and *kingdom* interchangeably when referring to intercession. That is because prophetic, strategic, and kingdom always refer to God's purposes and our destiny as a called-out people—as opposed to praying for what we want, however praiseworthy that may be. Intercession becomes prophetic— or strategic or kingdom-oriented—when it moves from the desire of our hearts to the desire of His heart. As much as He loves to grant the desire of our hearts, He gets really excited when we begin to care about the desires of His.

Prophetic acts must have a pragmatic dimension if they are to be truly prophetic. God speaks in Isaiah 58 of authentic fasting compared to the bogus—in the genuine, justice is turned loose and the hungry are fed. In Luke 7, Jesus compares the sinful woman of the streets to Simon, the pious Pharisee (see Luke 7:36-50). The latter makes a great show of his tolerance in bringing the Galilean rabbi to his home for dinner, but fails to offer the most elementary courtesy of having the feet of his guest washed and greeting him with a kiss of friendship. "You did not give me any water for my feet but she wet my feet with her tears. You did not give me a kiss, but this woman, from the time I entered, has not stopped kissing my feet. You did not put oil on my head, but she has poured perfume on my feet" (Luke 7:44-46). In Matthew 25, Jesus prophesies separation of sheep and goats; the sheep will not be the ones who spoke great messages, but who cared for the hungry, sick, and imprisoned ones (see Matt. 25:31-36).

In Redding, a couple of years ago, a local church bought 38 prime rib roasts for the annual holiday feast they offer to the poor. They were surprised when half as many as they were expecting showed up for dinner. They prayed and began feeding everyone—including the volunteers—as though they had plenty. When they counted the bones after dinner they found the Lord had supplied half as much more than they had paid for—because they needed it and because they depended on Him.

Perhaps my favorite is the couple in the rural Northern California town of Manton who built a home for themselves so that they could begin to impact their town for the Kingdom. They planned to have community Bible studies, worship times, and retreats in their home—if it ever got finished. One night, when both roof and flooring were incomplete and most vulnerable to warping from rain, the weather forecast called for heavy rain. We had taken a prayer vanguard team to the home that day to bless it, and we were directed by the Lord to speak the passages from Exodus over the home that describe the parting of the Red Sea under a strong east wind that the Lord sent (see Exod. 14). At the same time, one of us prophesied over an area behind the house—that it was to be a horse pen, housing Shetland ponies that would be used to give rides to neighborhood children. The couple looked on wide-eyed as this prophecy was spoken, because it confirmed exactly what they believed the Lord had been moving on their hearts for that piece of land. That night the rains were torrential, but the east wind was both strong and constant. When they went outside the next morning, they found much of their land under water but the house, including roof and flooring, was bone dry and undamaged from the storm. They gave thanks to the Lord and top priority to building the pony pen—and it is very much in use today as an invitation to children to bring their families near to the Lord's land.

Prophetic acts cannot be separated from sacramental outbursts—which are nothing but visible deposits on God's larger promises. (They are fully presented in the next chapter.) Jesus' prophetic instruction in Luke 9:13 is "You give them something to eat," when the disciples are faced with a hungry multitude and nothing in the cupboard but a few loaves and a couple of fish. God has promised in Isaiah 55 that all of the hungry will be filled. The implicit message in the miracle of

5,000 fed is to spend lavishly whatever we have and let God worry about the outcome. This incident leads directly into Peter's confession of Christ on the road outside Caesarea Philippi—a major escalation of the miracle of the loaves, because this time the Spirit of God identifies the Son and source of the loaves and moves on the man to confess Him (see Matt. 16:13; Mark 8:27). Peter's role is still to spend what he has—in this case all he has is confession at the risk of death by stoning for naming a man to be God. The process comes into further escalation eight days later when weary disciples accompany Jesus up the mountain and—brought about by the revelation released on them all in Peter's confession—Jesus is revealed in His glory (see Matt. 17:1-13). If being in the eternal company of the Son is the point of all Kingdom activity, then we reach a summit here in more ways than one.

The same process is walked out in the miraculous catch of fish recounted in Luke 5 and escalated in John 21 (see Luke 5:1-11; John 21:1-14). In the pre-resurrection event, Jesus tells the disciples that, having obeyed Him for the sake of obedience in casting their nets, they will later be catching men with the same technique—obedience for its own sake (see Matt. 4:19; Mark 1:17). In the post-resurrection morning, that is almost a repeat of the earlier event. He uses the unexpected breakfast of miracle fish to send them off on the rest of their lives as fishers of men and women.

The 2005 decision of Redding's Carenet Pregnancy Centers and LifeLight to hold their fundraisers on the same day required both courage and a high respect for prophecy. They draw support from many of the same churches and individuals. The convergent scheduling was inadvertent—and normally a bad prospect for both of them, as they would be diluting the support they could expect. When a prophetic statement was made that God had planned it this way, their leaders had to choose to obey a word they recognized as coming from God or take the safe course and reschedule their events as far apart as possible. They chose to leave the events where they were. They then took the even more courageous step of encouraging their supporters and volunteers to bless the other agency in every way possible—each ministry even made a financial donation to the other one. The fruit was that both ministries broke their own fundraising records, and they continue to escalate in favor and scope within the counties they serve.

You don't get much more pragmatic impact from your prophecy than that.

A Culture of Pragmatic Prophecy

God is moving on human hearts to perform any number of prophetic acts with impact on the communities in which we live. They are the currency of the prophetic community He is creating from the Church, which is His Body in these latter days. I describe some of the prophetic acts with the understanding that these are but a few examples from the infinite variety of outbursts of glory that He plans for us whenever we are willing to step out in His Name. Each of them—in the manifestation of their fruit—is a deposit on God's promise to transform our communities into provinces of His Kingdom when we seek His face consistently in the garment of bold humility.

Prayer Vanguard is a prophetic act because it walks out Luke 10:1-9 and Jesus' instruction to go into the towns and villages where He has not yet come and bless the people, hang out with them, meet their needs in the power of the Spirit, and share the faith that is in us—in that order. It is a ministry of spiritual reconnaissance. We take vanguard teams into churches, businesses, and schools. We only go where we have been invited. We pray for the blessings identified by the pastor, business owner, or school principal under whose authority we have come; we are equally respectful of God having placed a chosen person in charge of the installation, whether that person is a believer or pre-believer in the One who put him or her there.

Results are rarely as dramatic as what we saw when we blessed the church that drew all of the contractors to bless them once the contractors found peace in their bodies, but there are enough awesome exceptions to tip us off as to what we are looking for over time; for the Lord is usually doing a slow process of basting in His oil of gladness. There was the middle school in our county in which the principal asked us to pray for a cessation of drug use and violence on campus, the success of a reading program they were just kicking off that fall, and an improvement in the morale of the faculty, which had reached an all-time low. We also found out, as we began our walk, that a woman had been raped on the school's football field a few weeks earlier. Clearly, we were out of our depth and working above our pay grade—there was no way we could resolve these issues, but we knew someone who could.

We prayed through every classroom and restroom: the cafeteria, auditorium, and drama building; we spent special time on the football field and in the administrative offices. We went home and had no further contact with that principal until it was time to return the following fall. When we asked him how we ought to pray for the new school year, he said, "Wait a minute. Let me tell you what happened here after the last time you prayed." Drug use and violence had fallen like a runaway elevator. The reading program had taken off like a shot. And his faculty had returned from summer vacation pumped for the new year like he had never seen them before. He was—for the first time since coming to that school as its principal—ready to begin some serious vision-casting with his faculty leadership.

I love it when businesses and schools we have visited tell stories of God's wonders released over them—but especially the public schools. There is the grade school, in which we prayed that God would put a stop to the everyday fights that infested their lunch area, and the middle school that was so plagued by drugs and violence that vision casting by faculty was thought a too-expensive luxury item. We prayed for healing and peace in both schools, with special emphasis on a new reading program and faculty morale in the middle school. The fights at the grade school disappeared and did not come back for the rest of the year; when we returned the next year the principal asked us to pray now for his vision of the school becoming a community center. The drugs and violence were seriously reduced at the middle school and the reading program took off like a shot; most moving to the principal was the faculty morale at the end of summer. Yet the Lord saved His best for the escalating grace He gave much more slowly. Today the grade school is a community center and the middle school is a California Distinguished School—as are several other schools in which we pray.

God's biggest miracles take time—the time to slowly baste in the grace that has been released through sustained prayer and often remains invisible until the time is right. The principal of the elementary school was much more interested in it becoming a community center; the violence was blocking that goal, but he was quite clear as to which would be the bigger miracle and perfectly comfortable with the reality that it still took some years and regular prayer visits to achieve. The principal of the middle school was much more thrilled when his campus became a theatre arts magnet school a couple of years before it was named as a California Distinguished School—the miracle of that first visit was just setting things up for the larger and less visible work of God.

Celebrating the Lord's Supper on polluted land is a vanguard activity so special we put it in a class by itself. We go to places—by invitation only—where the social and economic distress is clearly the result of unredeemed sin on the land. (Frequently, the pollution is chemical as well as spiritual.) We walk the land, repenting of sin that is revealed to us by either prophetic or very earthly means, like interviewing residents or reading old newspapers. We speak as a cross-section of the Body, which we are, pronouncing forgiveness of sins as Jesus commands the apostles to do in John 20 and Matthew 18. We celebrate the Lord's Supper and make sure that we pour some of the bread and wine or juice out on the land—not because we think there is something magical about doing that, but because we know the Lord is very direct and we address the bloodguilt on the land with the shed blood of the Savior.

One day we were asked to pray over a little bedroom community a few miles outside of Chico, California. Satanists had been performing their foul rituals on the land for some months and—in addition to a spiritual atmosphere that would put anyone into a depression from exposure to it—traffic accidents on the highway passing the community had gone up exponentially. We simply did what we do in such cases, and we did it until the residents who were hosting us declared they felt the pall lifted from over their homes. The next day we learned the traffic accidents stopped as abruptly as they had begun. The Satanists—who were trespassing on the land they were fouling about once a week—have not returned in more than three years.

Of course we did not invent this kind of ministry. This type of prophetic act with impact has become a major component of the transformation movement worldwide.

There is a beach in Fiji that was visited by one of the land healing teams of intercessors for that nation. No one knew what might account for the condition of the place, but clearly there was ancient sin there because the off-shore coral reef was ecologically and in all other ways dead. The team blessed the land and whoever had lived and sinned there. They repented of the sin in identification with the people they had just blessed—as Daniel, Nehemiah, and Isaiah do over their people. They celebrated the Supper. Within a few weeks the reef had come back to life and was teeming with fish and other marine life—the life that belongs there and was welcomed back when God was welcomed back to His own land.

Hawaii's Spiritual Warfare Project saw God ministering in similar ways. Thousands of Christians representing every stream and tradition in the Body were called over a period of years to pray that all of Hawaii would come to know Jesus as the King of the Kingdom in their midst. They prayed daily for that strategic and prophetic goal, and on March 14, 1998, they went out to pray on the site of every pagan place of worship in the islands. They asked permission of each of the landowners on whose land they wished to walk, and in no case were they refused access. (Of course they had been praying daily, over a period of two years, for God to bless this day.) When they reached the hundreds of sacred temples— sites on which human beings had been disemboweled and sacrificed to pagan gods—they blessed, forgave, and celebrated the supper of the Lord. There were many miracles of weather and sea conditions to accompany their ministry. Within two days a two-year drought was broken. Over the next few months, thousands came to accept Jesus as Lord in the resurrected atmosphere of the islands. As it was in Fiji and Forest Ranch, even the land was healed.

Moo' Kini is a great promontory on the big island of Hawaii. When Leon Siu, one of the principal architects of the prayer project and a friend of mine, visited the cliffs two weeks after completion of the project, he was stunned at what he saw. The waters beneath the cliffs—which had been ecologically dead for a long time—were again alive with coral and fish and all of the other plants and animals associated with a vibrant reef community. God's teaching in all of this: what I would do for the land beneath your feet and beneath my waters, I would much more gladly do for you, if you would but turn for me to heal you.

Life—abundant life—is the currency and the economy of Heaven. Prophetic acts with impact are simply God's declaration in the here and the now, a proleptic piece of the Incarnate Kingdom and its story.

The Bible: Up Close and Personal is what we call the annual reading of the whole Word of God over the city of Redding. This Bible reading marathon involves about 300 people from more than 40 churches throughout the county. (It can be done with far fewer numbers, and in smaller towns they find that 50 to 70 are enough. What counts is that it's done by a cross-denominational group.) We obtain a permit from the city authorities so that we can read from the steps of our city hall. We read the Word in 15-minute increments over a period of about three days—until we have spoken all of it in blessing over our city and county. We operate on the principle that His words—living and active and sharper than a two-edged sword—shall never pass away. (See Hebrews 4:12; Matthew 24:35.) We take seriously what the Word Himself says in John 1—that in Him was life and that life is the light of humanity (see John 1:4). The impact is perhaps more immediately palpable than for any of the other prophetic acts we do.

During the first year we read the Word, the news media came down to check us out. (They have been very generous in their coverage in the succeeding years.) They interviewed people in City Hall, asking them how they felt about having the Bible read aloud right outside their windows. Without exception, they spoke of the peace that descended on the place when we began and that returns each year during the marathon. Camera crews also speak of the peace they can feel around the building—believers and pre-believers alike.

We will be doing our sixth year in 2008, and the activity is catching on in various parts of California—marathons were conducted during 2006 and 2007 in Roseville, Sacramento, and the little town of Etna—as examples. Readings are planned for other communities. The very presence of the readers is continuing the softening of the local atmosphere for other kinds of Holy Spirit activities, such as the appearance of prayer tents in multiple locations around the city last year—staffed by Christians of charismatic, evangelical, and mainline church backgrounds. They recorded many healings and testimonies of people accepting prayer for the first time in their lives.

The Lord is weaving an escalating tapestry of grace from the interplay of these and other prophetic acts with impact. Some of them are visible in their beginning and middle and end; while the fruit of others is coming into the bin over time, and over times that seemingly have a non-linear life to them. They are more and more on heavenly time, and we get to reap them in relays. But God is clearly pouring out His Spirit on the prophetic community of His Body, and the people of the towns, villages, and large cities are being blessed in ways they can only attribute to the Lord our God.

He is proving Himself to be more and more a God of escalation, of duration, and of warfare by honor. The next three chapters will be devoted to exploring each of these aspects of His character as they are played out in the unfolding manifestation of the Kingdom, wherein He has prophesied the coming of His Son and now brings to pass in the power of the Spirit and the prophetic acts with impact to those He calls His whole people. Our God is an awesome God. He is a God who has called His people to war, by giving the life of His Son, right into His Kingdom. But it is a war in which both goal and tactic are to love and honor those He loves and honors. We are privileged to pave the highway and prepare the ground so that every knee is able to bow and every tongue enabled to confess, as our testimony is both spoken and manifested in Him.

Oh yeah—and He did finally let me in on the secret of Paah-ho-ammi. About eight weeks after first giving me the word to go forward back in 2004, when I would pray and ask Him what the word meant, He began to speak to me about "looking it up." Not having a dictionary of tongues, I was pretty perplexed, but He kept repeating, "I told you to look it up." I opened my Bible concordance, which includes a very incomplete Hebrew dictionary in the back. There in plain sight were the three words He put together to name this project. The compound means, "Cry alas, My people," in perfectly good Biblical Hebrew. I cannot imagine a more appropriate title for a project of intercessory prayer—nor a more awesome God who supplies all things that we need, when we seek first His Kingdom and His glory.

If it isn't pragmatic, it cannot be prophetic—that is my conviction. On the other hand, what could be more practical than the Word of God unfolding in a world that desperately needs it—and desperately needs it in such overwhelming clarity that when we say the heavens declare the glory of God, we can see it with our eyes and touch it with our hands. We can document the impact because it is impacting the world in which we live in the tremendous love of the Son of God, who has chosen to live in it with us.

Chapter 4

SACRAMENTAL OUTBURSTS

The three churches were under major league attack from their own denominational hierarchy because of their stand for the Word of God in a denomination grown increasingly hostile to the authority of that Word. They were even being dragged into court to confiscate their land and buildings. We promised to bring an interdenominational team—a prayer vanguard team—to bless them on behalf of the whole Body of Christ. Prayer Vanguard is walking out, through prayer, the sending of the 12 to the towns and villages where Jesus had not yet come. It seeks a softening of spiritual ground and atmosphere through blessing, forgiving, and the strategic celebration of the Lord's Supper in places and among people who want to assume their place in the Body and under her protection. It is a key component of paving a straight high-way in the desert for the coming of the King—as John the Baptist instructed the faithful to do.

We came, as we always do, to represent the Body and the awesome Holy Spirit power that Jesus conveys when He says, "As the Father sent me so I send you," and in His com-mand to bless, hang out, meet needs, and share the faith that is in us (see John 20:21; Luke 10:1-9). (Believing, as we do, that God transforms whatever He blesses, we blessed the denomination and its leaders, as well as the congregations.) Because the Bible commends it, we planned to anoint the churches with oil that has been blessed by some 700 pastors and leaders from all over the world. (It is not magical for having been so handled, but it sure reminds us all of who we really are in Him.) The only problem was that the oil had spilled in Diana's purse; there was one little drip-drop left in the bottle.

It was a time of choosing. Would we, as a team, proclaim that we had come to anoint in blessing and leave it to the God who had sent us to provide the oil, or would we say that we wanted to anoint but would not be doing that today be-cause we had no oil? We chose to make our boast in the Lord, and we began to pray and praise the Lord, anointing as we went with the oil we had. (We anointed lavishly, choosing to believe that our God is not a God who rations.) At the end of a day, compounded by Los Angeles traffic snarls between three spread out locations, we found a quarter inch of oil left in the bottle. Diana said that each time I asked for the oil there was a little bit more—not a little bit less—than the last time I asked for it. We could only praise the Lord for His marvelous provision—His abundance in the face of what only looks like poverty. We had witnessed what I call a sacramental outburst.

A *sacramental outburst* is a miracle—of course—but with dimensions that we don't normally attribute to miraculous events. There is the miracle itself, but a second dimension of the miracle carries intrinsic teaching that can be sown back into later ministry. A third dimension is the element of escalation; when the teaching is sown back into Kingdom activity, the original miraculous intervention morphs into bigger and more elaborate manifestations of itself. What begins as an intervention of small enough scope that we can see and grasp it becomes an event of such scope we can no longer comprehend its boundaries. C.S. Lewis' definition of a *miracle* is paraphrased as God writing small what He normally writes large.[1] We can only remember the shape of it from when it was small enough to be seen with human vision. But we can praise the Lord, regardless of whether we are seeing or remembering.

This sacramental outburst in Los Angeles was characterized by the miracle of the multiplication of oil in the bottle. This satisfied the first criterion. The teaching was just as obvious when we look at the fact that there was more oil in the bottle each time it was used. When we spend lavishly what we have on the Kingdom of God we always end up with more, rather than less. Jesus said it much better in Matthew 6:33—seek first My Kingdom. The second criterion was met with the recognition of this teaching. The escalation would come later—but just as consistently in the biblical pattern— as the teaching was sown into the congregations over the upcoming season in their lives. Oil in Scripture is used to heal, anoint leaders, and set apart for service. How would these churches become launching pads for their own escalating ministry and models for others who would follow their lead? The activation of this third criterion is where the adventure really begins.

As we prayed through and anointed one of the churches that day, a team member prophesied that there was a cloud of long ago sexual sin over the place. She said that she could not escape the impression of someone being violated in the sanctuary. She added that even though the sin had happened a long time ago, it was inhibiting the vitality of the congregation; she believed it had been eliminated but not repented. Several team members—visibly uncomfortable—agreed that they sensed the same thing. The pastor was praying with us and confirmed that a previous pastor had been involved in sexual misconduct some 30 years earlier. He admitted that the pastor had been dismissed by the leadership in place at that time, but the facts had never been disclosed to the congregation and no effort made to deal with the state of denial that had made the sin possible over time. We agreed with the current pastor to stand in the gap for the congregational leaders of that time—most of whom were long dead. We confessed the sin on their behalf, and the pastor pronounced God's forgiveness on behalf of the Body of Christ.

God did an incredible work in all three churches during the months that followed. All prevailed in their court case—they were the first in their denomination to retain their property in that kind of a lawsuit. But the real news was that the pastors of all three congregations declared that in the wake of our visit the people were ministering in a freedom and an authority they had never demonstrated before. Although most of the congregation did not know of our visit, the spiritual atmosphere over them had been transformed from one of depression and a fortress mentality to one of Kingdom joy and limitless energy to bless their communities. The biggest change was in the church with the history. Their youth group had been on its last legs, but they have become a vital and growing body, reaching into their neighborhood schools, and a catalyst for new ministry in the rest of the congregation.

Sacramental outbursts are the practical and pragmatic ways in which the Lord gives substance to His own prophetic declarations. These declarations can occur before, during, and after the fact. The anointing of these churches is part of a tapestry of reconciliation and re-connection of the regions of California that God began to announce some months before our visit. It came as a shared prophetic statement delivered to a gathering of pastors and intercessors in Hollywood when a Northern California leader—asked to give his testimony about the fires and the retreat of 2003—first offered his blessing to the South, as a representative of the Northern region of the state. The host pastor was so moved by this blessing in the face of long-standing rivalry and hostility between the regions that he went to the microphone and—weeping prophetic tears— called upon the people of his own region to come into repentance for their treatment of their brothers to the north. It was the beginning of a process of reconciliation and sharing of leaders and teaching between the regions that is still underway. The whole process was described in a prophetic vision given to that same Northern California leader more than two years later: God showed a wave-making toy—the kind of liquid-filled box mounted on gimbals in which waves are made by shifting the container back and forth repeatedly. He said that there was enough living water to irrigate all of California with revival—if the same water was shared by rolling it from one region to another as it was with the toy. The prophetic statements escalated along with the prophetic events.

Practical escalations occur in many dimensions. The much larger and potentially more destructive fires of 2007—described in the first chapter along with the response that numbered thousands rather than hundreds of prayer warriors—expresses God's determination to permit whatever may become necessary to bring the regions together in prayer. Unity of the regions is not for one emergency or another occasion, but for the outpouring of His purposes of blessing and transformation of the state in an active partnership with His people in the state. Those who lead prayer receive and proclaim that message.

OCCASIONS THAT PARTICIPATE

Sacraments—or sacramental moments—are occasions that participate in the realities they represent without being, in themselves, the fullness of those realities. They are deposits on promises that God has made, like the non-refundable down payment we make on the house we want to buy as a demonstration that we are serious and capable of providing the full purchase price. When we baptize new Christians, we are obeying the Great Commission. But we also declare the blood of Jesus over those persons for the full forgiveness of all of their sins and the reception of the Holy Spirit to enable them to live as the children of God that they have just become. Whether we dunk or pour or simply sprinkle the water, we don't think the persons will never have to bathe again. We don't imagine they will never have to surrender again or drown in God's love again. We get it that God's will is not satisfied with the ritual bath; He wants His new person to swim in His river forever, beginning on that day. The Holy Spirit is really into it when we baptize—but what has happened on the spot is a deposit on all of the promise that the Spirit delivers.

It's the same thing when we celebrate the Lord's Supper or pray for healing in a person's body—or declare any other thing that the Lord has promised to perform. We don't expect hunger to be satisfied with a piece of bread and a swallow of wine or juice. It is an appetizer, and the Lord wants it that way. He wants to fill us with a ravenous hunger for His heavenly banquet table. He wants to remind us, every time He heals one of His people, that there is healing in His wings for everyone and that His Kingdom is a place in which all of the lepers are healed and the dead raised. He wants to whet the appetite for the whole of His Kingdom every time we eat and every time we pray in His name.

The clearest description of a sacramental outburst that I know comes in Luke 5:1-11. The boys have been fishing all night, and they have come up dry as the bones of Ezekiel 37. Jesus has borrowed Simon Peter's boat and delivered a teaching on the Kingdom from just off shore. Then he calls on the captain to put out into deep water and let down the nets one more time. There is no argument—Simon does remind the Master that everything possible has already been tried—but he obeys just for the sake of obedience. The catch is as overwhelming as it is miraculous; they almost sink two boats trying to haul in the fish.

The miracle is clear, but so also is the teaching. Simon and his friends have come up empty from their own resources. It is not that they are incompetent—they must be very good at what they do to own a small fleet of boats and have partners in the work—but they have come to the end of their competence, and it has not been enough. When they do what Jesus tells them to do, everything changes. The clear teaching that can now be sown back into the Kingdom on a regular basis is this: when (and only when) we do what God says, when He says to do it, and in the way He says to do it, simply because He said to do it, everything can be expected to change. But there is also the escalation.

Diana and I had such an encounter in Hawaii in 1998. While shopping for souvenirs to take to our children, we heard the unmistakable sounds of praise music out in the mall. God called for us to do what seemed silly at the time—just go out at once and meet those who were playing the music. We left what we were doing and went out to watch and pray for the people brave enough to set up so publicly and praise the Lord. On a break we stepped up and introduced ourselves. On what could only be a Holy Spirit impulse, we exchanged contact information and invited Jill and Tia Tahauri to stay with us, if they ever got to our region. Eight weeks later they called to take us up on our invitation, and the resulting relationship has escalated into friendships with Hawaiian leaders who are today poised to lead revival in that land. More than that, we have found ourselves blessed with multiple opportunities to minister among and to indigenous leaders from all over the world. And, although it is true to say that Diana and I have always had a heart to be reconcilers in all of the communities in which we travel, it is just as true to say that this complex of relationships with many people of multiple tribal backgrounds provided both perspective and launching pad for the reconciliation dimension of our ministry today. In my own case, a pattern of events was set in motion that prompted me to repent of my own unwitting participation in the suffering of tribal peoples. But it has also awakened in me a profound sense of identification with my own tribal background, as a descendant of Scottish Highlanders—and a deep sense of longing for all of us to see and appreciate one another as joint heirs of the sin that divides and the Sacrifice that unites. It all begins with a simple act of obedience when the call makes no sense from a fleshly point of view.

As it is with us, when Simon sees what the Lord has done, he is undone. He sees the tremendous gap between who he is and who Jesus is. He falls at Jesus' feet and confesses his own unworthiness (see Luke 5:1-8). Jesus picks him up and says, "'Don't be afraid; from now on you will catch men.' So they pulled their boats up on shore and followed Him" (Luke 5:10-11). The principle is identical for the rest of their lives, but the fruit is so much greater than a few hundred fish in a net as to be incomprehensible. There is a world to be caught and transformed, and the Lord is leaving the catching in their hands—under His instruction.

This expression of sacramental outburst is not unique. In Luke 9 there is an extended outburst that escalates before our eyes. Jesus sends the 12 to many places where He has not yet gone. He gives them "power and authority to drive out all demons and to cure diseases, and He sent them out to preach the kingdom of God and to heal the sick" (Luke 9:1-2). He orders them to take nothing but what He provides (see Luke 9:3); they do as He instructs, and the results are as dramatic as they are good. Even Herod hears of it and wants to see the man who is making all the commotion in the countryside (see Luke 9:7-9).

Escalation comes before we can even properly process the teaching. A short time later, as they are teaching and healing, the disciples report that it is late, the people are hungry, and they have no food to give them. They advise Jesus to send the crowd away so they can fend for themselves, but Jesus says, "You give them something to eat." He then blesses the five loaves and two fish that the disciples do have (Do we really believe that everything we have is a gift from God?), and they find that there is enough for a feast. In fact, there are 12 baskets of leftovers. (See Luke 9:10-17.)

The teaching is as simple as it was in Luke 5. "Take only what I have given you and spend it lavishly. The provision is my challenge; the obedience is yours." It is the very same teaching the Lord planted in our adventure with the oil, and it works just as well—and just as well after. The next escalation, of this same outburst, comes when the group is away from the crowds—but it is a bigger miracle.

Jesus and the guys are praying before a wall near Caesarea Philippi when He asks them who people believe Him to be. After they give the usual politically correct answers that could be obtained from a Gallup poll (see Luke 9:18-19), He skewers them: "Who do you say I am?"(Luke 9:20). Peter answers with what only the Holy Spirit could have told him, "You are the Christ of God" (see Luke 9:20). Jesus says as much about the Spirit in the Matthew 16 account.

It is a few days and a walk up a mountain before the disciples see Jesus transfigured before them into the full reality of who He is. This is a miracle so big that it doesn't even look like the miracle it is. Many people would say, "Well, that's fine and it is certainly unprecedented, but I think it is a bigger miracle to feed 5,000 people so that they can see who Jesus is than to have a vision on a mountain." But they forget that the 5,000 people were too busy eating to notice who Jesus was; all four of the Gospels make this clear. They also forget that the miracles point to Jesus; not the other way around. Peter and James and John have not seen a vision on the mountain. For the first time, they have seen reality, and the escalating process of revelation has been fueled by sowing the simple teaching that the provision is His challenge and the obedience is ours. That progressive revelation is the purpose of every act of God—from expecting us to bear His authority in order to feed the 5,000, to confessing Him as Lord, to blasting our paradigms with a fuller picture of reality than we can imagine.

He loves to say things like what He said to me, "Your job is to seed the future; my job is to give you a future to seed."

We understood that same teaching on that day in Southern California in slightly different terms. We heard, "Spend what you have lavishly in my Name and you will always end up with more, not less." We learned, as the disciples did, that the biggest miracles often don't look like miracles at all. (Is it any wonder that John the Baptist is known to Jesus as the greatest of the prophets, although he never performed what we think of as a miracle? All he ever did was to announce the First Coming—the greatest miracle of them all.) The churches we see coming to new freedom and authority in ministry experience a process hidden in time and manifesting slowly in each of the members. But it is a far greater work than the mere multiplication of oil, and both events were triggered by the keeping of a vow when the resources did not seem to be present.

Once again we find that when we show up He shows off.

From the prophetic standpoint, sacramental outbursts—with all of their features—are exactly what Jesus promises in John 14:12 when He says that the disciples will do all that they have seen their master do and greater things than these besides. We know that no learner is greater than his teacher, and Jesus says that as well (see John 13:16; 15:20). So this promised escalation, in even the things that Jesus has done on earth, can only reinforce, as it proclaims the reality, that what Jesus did in the Holy Spirit before His resurrection was a mere deposit on the promise of what He would do by the same Spirit after Pentecost. He spoke true when comparing Himself to a wheaten seed in John 12—one that must fall to the ground and die so that a field of wheat will spring up from the multiple seeds that are planted (see John 12:23-26).

Even Pentecost is a sacramental outburst. As we saw, the Acts chapter 2 image of the unfolding Kingdom, the quintessential expression of the outpouring of the Spirit of the living God—foretold by Joel and so many of the other prophets—is not in and of itself a pouring out on all flesh at all. When Peter went to the balcony and proclaimed the Gospel and the promise he quoted from Joel 2, the Spirit fell on about 3,000 who received Jesus as their Lord on that day (see Acts 2:14-21; Joel 2:28-32). Today, the Christian faith is twice the size of its nearest rival—Islam—and the creed of one third of the population of the planet, a little more than two billion people. That is what I call major league escalation—grounded in the teaching that we are to go into all the earth and teach one another to observe all that He has commanded, with each of us sharing the piece of the whole revelation that has been entrusted to us. That teaching is activated in the simple fact that Holy Spirit fell on each of the worshipers gathered in that upper room. It will be fulfilled when every knee shall bow and every tongue confess (see Rom. 14:11). In the meantime, His Kingdom has come in power before the end of the earthly lives of those who heard Him proclaim it—as He said it would in Mark 9:1—and we praise Him for the encouragement He gives in the escalating deposits on the promise that He makes.

I have made several mission trips to Fiji with Teach Us to Pray's Ken Greenlee and his teams. We have seen hundreds of miraculous healings over the course of six-day outreaches. More than 60 people received supernatural chiropractic adjustments on one trip, as prophetic prayer warriors ordered—in the name of Jesus—their vertebrae to come into alignment, the muscles of neck and back to cooperate, and pain receptors to stop sending messages of pain that were no longer of any use. We watched a man's leg grow six inches until both feet touched the ground; a woman's foot that twisted backward was made straight; a girl with a serious bone abscess that would not respond to treatment was healed; and a number of people whose severe arthritis had made them lame evidenced their healing by walking again. Migraine headaches disappeared, heart disease cleared up, and one young man was even healed of painful internal warts inside his nose. It was a heady time for the villagers in the ghetto of Vatuwaqa (pronounced Vata-wonga) in the capitol city of Suva. It was a mind-blowing time for us—coming as we did from all sorts of Christian backgrounds and degrees of familiarity with a Gospel of power and not of mere words.

Frankly, it should always be mind-blowing to see a Scripture verse like First Corinthians 4:20—or any other—become living and active in our presence.

On one such trip—in addition to the healings—the Holy Spirit enabled us to command rain to stop during working hours so that the construction team could complete building on three houses and a school. The earth was literally commanded to open to receive the pilings for the houses when the mire resisted all efforts to pound them in. On the strength of the signs and wonders that the people had seen, more than 700 people have left their gods behind and received Jesus as their personal Lord and Savior. Many chose Jesus each day in the clinic and in the prayer line, because they saw Jesus touching them through the hands of the workers who served and prayed for them there. Others made their decision when the preacher said, simply, "Your god, Krishna, gives good advice for the living of a holy life. But who, besides Jesus, has ever offered practical help for the living of that life? How many of you have been touched in your body this night in the name of Jesus? Now how many of you would like to receive Him as your Lord and Savior?"

The teaching inherent in these miracles—and so central to the concept of sacramental outburst—was a simple word from the Lord, "I will teach you in that very hour what you are to do and what you are to say." None of us knew from one moment to the next what to do or how to pray for it. Conditions seemed to constantly militate against what we thought of, and prepared for, as the mission. Even the team of intercessors praying around the clock from California—and on whose shoulders we stood as we did seemingly absurd things like commanding rain to stop—were given daily direction for prayer by Diana, who led the team and spoke with me daily by phone. The Lord has kept us off balance on each of these trips and in the shadow of His wings.

But the escalation of the fruit was the best part.

FRUIT THAT ENDURES

Of far greater significance for the Kingdom than any individual miracle was the fact that the Fijian teenagers and young adults who had gone with some of the Americans through the village for days and prayed for the people continued to return to the village after the Americans went home, fully confident that the Lord had called and empowered them to minister to their own people—and the people themselves recognized that the Spirit of the Lord was on these young people. Business interests in the city saw this Spirit as well; they are working with the people of the ghetto as never before and planned to partner with our team when we return to Fiji—not because of what they expect us to do for them, but because of what they expect us to coach and mentor and facilitate of the work of God in their own people for leadership. Local church leaders of different ethnic backgrounds, who used to shun one another, are now walking arm in arm through the settlement and ministering together. The teens have been invited to come to the village twice a week to pray; they have also set up a Sunday School at the request of the villagers, and they work alongside the churches already there. This is a major change between the trips—an escalation of God's grace and glory.

Of far greater significance for the ministry teams who come from the States and return to our ministries at home is the fact that more than 40 people of prayer stood watch round the clock while we served in Fiji. When it became clear that the Lord was forbidding Diana to come to Fiji because He wanted her to coordinate the intercession work back in California, it was a big disappointment to me, because I wanted my wife to be with me, and also a disappointment to Ken Greenlee who wanted my wife to lead the women's programs for the outreach. But it became abundantly clear, as miracle built upon miracle and disaster after disaster was turned into victory on one trip after another, that all of us walked on the carpet of intercession laid down by Diana and her people in faithful, albeit unglamorous, service. As we compared notes between what God would show them, as He called them to pray for various things, and what we were actually seeing and experiencing on the ground, it became crystal clear that even life-threatening situations were dissolving in the prayers that rose. I know that my life was saved when we experienced multiple near misses on rain-slicked streets in traffic, and I am just as sure that a teen-aged worker on our team was spared a broken back and possible paralysis when a ridgepole weighing hundreds of pounds fell on him one afternoon. God sent a vision of the traffic hazard to the folks in California, and the boy—although weeping in such pain he feared to move when we loaded him into the cab for the ride to the hospital—was able to move by the time we got him there and showed no x-ray evidence of broken bones; he walked out of the hospital on his own steam.

None of us will ever again take for granted those who war in the prayer closet—and how desperately we need their service before the throne.

A recent trip saw more spectacular healings. For instance, a paralyzed man was healed, while others had sight and hearing restored. But the escalating glory to God is in the less dramatic appearing fruit from earlier outbursts. The man whose leg grew out received Jesus as His Savior, along with his wife; and they can't stop talking about what God has done for them. As a result, the Hindu priests of the village are sending their sick to the Christian pastors who work there for healing prayer—and God is answering to such an impressive degree that the wife of one of the priests has become a Christian. Two of the congregations serving this predominantly Hindu community have grown exponentially, and there are three new ones worshiping and ministering in Vatawaqa. The people who now know Christ are praying for each other, having learned that it is the Holy Spirit—not the pastors—who has the power to heal and enliven them.

Vatuwaqa has witnessed sacramental outburst upon sacramental outburst as more and more people are becoming ambassadors of God's reconciliation. The glory is escalating—even impacting the mission team in unexpected ways. One of our medical team members, David, was healed of his cancer while ministering to others in the ghetto; the healing was medically confirmed after his return home to Arizona. Another, having forgotten most of the textbook Hindi she had learned in school, found herself instantly fluent in the street dialogue of that language, which she had never spoken before. God chose us to participate—along with the Fijians—just for the sake of His great love and His great joy—in doing the unexpected. This is what His Kingdom is all about.

I love to tell of the wonders God does in third world countries—but it is a myth to say that He only or primarily does miracles in those places. Most of the signs I describe in these chapters took place in California—one of the most technologically advanced and self-satisfied places on earth. We are just more inclined to take the event for granted and the glory for ourselves. We do not combine our testimony with His shed blood as we should—and so we do not see our communities transformed into provinces of His Kingdom as He so desperately craves.

I have personally witnessed the Lord make a banquet for 1,100 people out of six fish and some fruit punch—on the Hoopa Indian Reservation near Eureka, California. When the people came and the Indians were caught short of food, they went to prayer and worship. They showed up and the Lord showed off.

I can also bear personal witness to the escalation of that miracle when the local churches made a habit of worshiping with the coastal Native peoples over several years, joining with them to raise funds for the purchase of four acres of land on an island in Humboldt Bay so that a monument could be raised to their ancestors who had been slain in an 1860s massacre. In the summer of 2004 the Eureka City Council voted unanimously to cede, not four, but forty acres of Indian Island to the Wiyot Tribe; all of the funds raised could now be devoted to the purchase of the headstone; and a city council had done something unthinkable—voted unanimously on such a hot-button political issue as native reparations.

It was an escalation of the sacramental outburst that first manifested as a feast of fish—the Lord had gone fishing for men and women. But He is far from satisfied.

> *When John heard in prison what Christ was doing, he sent his disciples to ask him, "Are you the one who was to come, or should we expect someone else?" Jesus replied, "Go back and report to John what you hear and see: The blind receive sight, the lame walk, those who have leprosy are cured, the deaf hear, the dead are raised, and the good news is preached to the poor. Blessed is the man who does not fall away on account of me" (Matthew 11:2-6).*

About this powerful snapshot of the Kingdom of God, Jesus, the Son of God, says this: accept no substitutes! All of the law and the prophets of the Old Covenant pointed toward the coming of God's Son and Messiah. The law is fulfilled; all of the prophets and the prophetic community of the New Covenant point toward the coming of the Kingdom that the Son has won. Accept no substitutes!

If we are called into becoming a prophetic community, then we are called to a community that celebrates the mighty acts of God in establishing His Kingdom even as we become the people who perform those mighty acts in the name of the Lord Jesus. He says that we will do greater things than even these things that we have seen Him do prior to His exaltation to the right hand of the Father. So we are and so we do.

Jesus fed a few thousand people on the two occasions recorded in Scripture—5,000 and 4,000 men, respectively, and the thousands of women and children who would have accompanied them. Yet, Christians have fed hundreds of millions since then—in the provision of food to hungry nations (inspired by the same Holy Spirit who moved Paul to take a collection for the famine-plagued Judeans), in the Holy Spirit birthed improvements in agriculture and distribution, and in the obviously miraculous events like the feast in Hoopa.

Jesus healed a few thousand as well—as many as one man could get his hands upon in a three-year span. Yet, Christians have healed uncounted millions through the medical advances that God gave when He entrusted the scientific method and His own zeal for redeeming the human body that He created to His Body, the Church, and through the love that sends medical missionaries all over the world at their own expense. And this count does not include the multitudes who have witnessed God's direct intervention into their bodies, like the woman who was healed of diabetes when I was privileged to pray for her after I preached at her church. This is all done through the activity of Christians who dare to believe that God's promise to use them as His hands and feet was authoritative.

COMMISSIONED UNTIL HE COMES

Jesus led about 120 disciples into larger life—if we read the account of the assembly of post-resurrection worshipers in the upper room out of Acts 1. God partnered with the apostles and exploded that number to 3,000 on the day of Pentecost; the Church has been growing ever since. When He said "greater things than these," He wasn't blowing smoke (see John 14:12). Yet, He also calls us to be manifestly dissatisfied with what we have witnessed.

"I have posted watchmen on your walls, O Jerusalem," He says in Isaiah 62:6-7. "They will never be silent day or night. You who call on the Lord, give yourselves no rest, and give Him no rest till He establishes Jerusalem and makes her the praise of the earth." The watchers on the walls are, of course, the prophets of Israel; in the Old Testament they were the prophetic figures who resided in Israel, and in the New Testament they are the whole prophetic community operating under the guidance of those who hold the prophetic office and the other offices of the five-fold ministry. Jesus calls on the community—in the Great Commission of Matthew 28—not just to preach the Gospel all over the world and let the chips fall where they may, but to make disciples of the nations of the world. In the end, there will be those who still reject Him and the life He lives to give, but we have no authority to rest until He says, "It is finished." In the meantime, our job is to praise Him to the skies for what He has done and to hold His feet and our own to the fire until all has been accomplished.

The primary way in which we fulfill the commission in our communities is to participate in and oversee the escalation of the sacramental outbursts He launches in our midst. This is the work and the joy of the prophetic community.

The prophetic word over Gerry Sprunger was that, when word of His healing got out, revival would come to Siskiyou County. Since that time more than 100 people have gathered in a small church in the county's Scott Valley to walk and pray their land. It was snowing hard when they began to worship, and the preacher led them in prayer, asking the Lord to stop the snow when they left the building—which He did while also supplying a double rainbow, for which they had not even asked. But the larger miracle was a gathering that size in a valley so sparsely populated in the first place. Youth groups, Bible studies, and prayer vigils have begun in places where they never existed before, and young people are taking leadership alongside their elders who are willing to think and move outside of the box. A group—led by lay people—gathered at their tiny city hall to speak the entire Bible over the town of Etna, and the Christians of Yreka did the same thing in a public park a few months later—they intend to make these readings an annual event. Speakers and teachers of the stature of Josh McDowell are coming into cities of the region with less than 10,000 in population because the leaders are begging God to send workers into the harvest field. Teams of Christians plan to pray their own Paah-ho-ammi project every day over issues of Kingdom significance in their communities, such as crime and the economy and medical scourges like cancer. God has said that He would eliminate cancer from Northern California, and these folks are giving themselves no rest, as they give Him no rest.

In doing these things and in seeking God's intervention day and night, they echo the cries of the little ones who triggered the Azusa Street phenomenon in 1906 and the Jesus People movement of the 1970s. They are no more a majority in their cities and denominations than were Dennis Bennett or, John Wimber, and their bands of brethren in the 1960s and the 1980s—or a Vineyard congregation in Toronto or a group of impoverished Native Americans of Eastern Canada in the 1990s. They simply came before the Lord and let Him decide that they formed a critical mass of intercession as a cross-section of the Body of Christ.

They are setting the conditions that God calls fertile for transformation. Each of these gatherings and co-laborings helps to refresh the atmosphere and re-direct the spiritual polarities that have been polluted by sin. Native American Christians are participating in this action of the whole Body, and the ground is being prepped for addressing the crimes committed against them in the county. Sustained prayer, acts of personal sacrifice, and the gathering of the Body are the prerequisites for the promised revival. It has been so in more than 500 communities and some 20 nations across the world in the past decade. Can the transformational revival be far behind?

Yet, it must be remembered that even in nations like Fiji, what has been documented is a sacramental outburst. The sweeping in of the Spirit of the living God has been documented in some 200 villages, and healing even includes dead coral reefs that now teem with marine life. Drug addiction, domestic violence, and babies having babies, is still rampant in the nation. Fiji has been wracked by her third coup in many decades, and corruption is as resistant to treatment as any other infection. But the people have seen a vision of what a transformed nation can be; the signs and wonders cannot be denied. Business people, the churches, and government officials are all praying and working together. They are honoring one another and praising the Lord more and more.

Divine appointments are also rampant. One such incidence was the Lord diverting me to visit Mr. Chun, on the way to bless a construction site, and the resultant healing of his shortened leg, which has brought so much fruit in the changed lives of people who now embrace Jesus. There was the case of a police officer who came by intending to investigate our mission. After his initial suspicions were dealt with, some of the workers gave him a pair of the eyeglasses we distribute. They also prayed for healing of the pain in his leg, and it was instantly released. When I arrived on the scene, he was posing for pictures with the people he had come to interrogate. The transformational activity we have seen is a deposit on the promise of a thoroughgoing transformation that we have not yet seen.

We are called in the prophetic community to be ambassadors of reconciliation across the board. That is the whole point of the Great Commission, according to Paul's message in Second Corinthians 5. In California, the miracle of the fires in 2003 has been escalating since the testimony and vision of regional reconciliation was released in the service at Hollywood Presbyterian Church. Many leaders from north and south now make a concerted effort to import each other to their respective regions so that insights and strategies that are blessing their region can be shared with each other. There have been statewide gatherings for just this purpose. Several ministries make it part of their regular routine to gather at the state capitol for times of prayer and worship; relationships have formed with legislators and officials, and some ministries are even given the use of rooms in the capitol—by legislators—from which to launch strategic prayer for the state.

Spiritual warfare is the primary prophetic activity by which land and people are prepared for transformational revival, and the Lord has given very specific weapons for this purpose. The scriptural basis for their designation was described in Chapter 3, but the bottom line is that all of them revolve around prophetic prayer—which is simply prayer with the Kingdom as its focus—and the ministry that gushes forth when prayer opens the floodgates. The weapons to which Paul refers in Second Corinthians 10 are blessing, forgiveness, and the celebration of the Supper of the Lord.

Blessing is not just a tactic or a tool that we can choose when the task at hand seems to call for it. The Word of God is adamant about blessing and cursing not. That is not always the easy choice—especially inasmuch as most of us are pretty assured that we are somehow morally better than many of the folks we pray for. One day we were vanguarding a public high school when one of the intercessors called me into the counseling office in which he was praying. He pointed to a little statuette of Buddha on the windowsill and said, "Surely you don't expect me to bless that." I told him that was a hard one, but I suggested he consider that the counselor knew we were praying in his office. "Suppose the Lord answers your prayer to blast that pagan idol into dust.

When the counselor comes in on Monday, how excited will he be about the Gospel when he sees his prize knicknack on the floor in chips?"

When we prayed in the space to which Kryon would be summoned, we did not curse; we only blessed, and he could not be found. It was the same when we prayed at the museum of art in Los Angeles while Buddhist monks attempted to release thousands of demonic spirits into the ocean off of Southern California. We blessed and the monks were completely frustrated in their efforts. In prayer over Qaumaniq's cancer, we blessed and gave thanks for the disease having brought all of us to such fervent prayer before we dismissed the cancer and called on the Lord to replace it with His peace and His health. We are certainly entitled to send evil things packing in the Word of God—but we need to know that this is a defensive action when we are cornered and confronted. (Jesus sent the disciples out to heal the sick and cast out demons, but how many times do we see Him casting out demons that are not confronting Him?) If we would take the offensive in spiritual warfare, we must choose to use only the weapons of the Lord who fought evil while hanging on a Cross. He blessed and forgave and presented Communion to the men who would desert him in the grove at His arrest.

Some will say at this juncture, "Well, what about the time Jesus cursed the fig tree? How about that?" In Mark 11:12-26, Jesus does indeed curse a fig tree that bears no fruit on the day He enters Jerusalem—for His time has finally come—but this incident is the exception that proves the rule about blessing.

What we can easily forget is that—to Jews—the fig tree symbolizes Judaism like Uncle Sam symbolizes the United

States to Americans. Mark takes care of that with his habit of bracketing episodes he thinks really important and best used to illustrate a central core. Jesus encounters the fig tree bearing no fruit—only pretty blossoms that have no practical value. (It is not the season for figs, but the presence of the Author of creation ought to be enough to stimulate fruitfulness—to make it the season.) Jesus says, "May no one ever eat fruit from you again" (Mark 11:14), before leading the apostolic band to the temple, driving out the moneychangers, and beginning to teach about His Father's house being a house of prayer for all nations. When He passes the fig tree later, the disciples are astounded to see the cursed tree completely withered (see Mark 11:20).

What we have here is a symbol—couched in a real incident—of the failure of Judaism to bear fruit, even in the living Presence of her fulfillment. (We need to distinguish here between the Jewish people and Judaism—between the people Yahweh loves and a belief system they have perverted into a collection of rules and regulations that substitute for a relationship with Him.) Jesus enters the temple—this being the point—and finds no fruit there but lots of pretty blossoms in a sacrificial system that is polluted by the moneychangers. He gives the boot to the polluters, just as soundly as He curses the fruitless tree, but only to make way for His own presence and to clear a space in which to teach. With respect to blessing as a weapon for offensive action, reality is that most demons flee in the presence of His praise—just as they did in that Redding hotel conference room—because a carpet of blessing is like burning coals to their feet while it is like Heaven itself to ours and an irresistible invitation to God.

Any further questions about Jesus' attitude toward cursing ought to be referred to John 3:17-18. "For God did not send His Son into the world to condemn the world, but to save the world through Him. Whoever believes in Him is not condemned, but whoever does not believe stands condemned already because he has not believed in the Name of God's one and only Son." Jesus has simply voiced the reality of the fig tree as it already is—like the headless chicken that has not yet dropped to the ground. But He does this because He continues to love the people of the tree.

But what about forgiveness—doesn't the one desiring it have to ask for it? Of course Jesus expects people to repent; there is no way around it. But He often extends forgiveness prior to repentance: the case of the woman who washes His feet and Zacchaeas are just two cases in point. Prophets from Isaiah to Daniel to Nehemiah engage in what we know as identificational repentance—in which they plead for forgiveness for their people in identification with them. The greatest act of identificational repentance is Jesus' own death on that same Cross from which He blesses and forgives His enemies. And that same Jesus, in Matthew 16:19, promises us unlimited authority to set at liberty what is bound in. In Matthew 18 and John 21, He warns that sins we retained will bind onto us.

Reality is that sin and its agents can only counterfeit life where it is unforgiven. When the healing team prayed at the beach in Fiji, and at the promontory on the big island of Hawaii, they forgave the sins of human sacrifice committed there by their ancestors—forgave in the name of the One who had forgiven them. When we went to Forest Ranch, we both begged and pronounced forgiveness of the people who had literally worshiped the devil there. After we made a second visit to the other end of the community—using the same weapons of warfare as before—our hostess reported that the same men who used to congregate around the convenience store at the heart of the little community to get drunk each day were now discussing ways to benefit their town, and they were sober.

And then there is the supper of the Lamb. I had never before scattered consecrated communion elements before we did it that day at the satanic altar in Forest Ranch. I simply did as the Boss told me to do as we were entering the site. We referred to it as "addressing the bloodguilt with the blood." I do know that the results were spectacular—traffic accidents ceased the next day on the road going past. I know that we celebrated the Supper on the bank of a polluted stream—anointing the water with it—and then found the water drinkable. We have visited two different suicide points since then, cliffs from which self-destructive people drive their cars into eternity. In one case, the deaths decreased significantly, while in the other, there were no attempts for a month. I would like to say they stopped altogether, but I'll have to say we need more celebrations of the Supper on these fields of spiritual battle. Jesus did not do this thing—and command us to do it for His remembrance as often as we could—in order to prepare us for the battles to come. Eating and drinking in the presence of the enemy is a time-honored act of warlike defiance; it also has the virtue of throwing up the shield of faith from the inside out and cranking up the sword of the Spirit, which is His incarnate Word.

Jesus' statement in Matthew 11:12 is as enigmatic as His metaphor of the wine and the wineskins for progressive repentance in Matthew 9:17—but full of insight for the connection of these seemingly passive weapons in pursuit of sacramental outburst. He says, "From the days of John the Baptist until now, the Kingdom of heaven has been forcefully advancing, and forceful men lay hold of it" (Matt. 11:12). (More traditional translations, like the New King James, speak of taking the Kingdom by violence.) It is, of course, logically absurd to imagine that we can possess God's Kingdom by violently wresting it from His hand—until we remember that the one force in the universe that even the Lord of the universe cannot resist is the helplessness of His people. From the cries of the captives pouring out of Egypt 4,000 years ago, to the cry of a widow in Zarephath whose son has died in the days of Elijah, to the woman with an issue of blood who took hold of the Lord's garment as He walked through the crowd, there is no resistance in the Lord our God to the ceaseless yearning of His people for release from bondage. He tells the disciples in Mark 9—when they fail to cast out the demon in the boy—that this kind comes out only in an atmosphere of sustained prayer. He tells Paul in Second Corinthians that His strength is perfected in our weakness (see 2 Cor. 12:9). And so we do take the Kingdom by force, when we make ongoing admission of our inability to force anything.

But perfection of strength is itself an escalating process—as anyone knows who has ever conditioned a body. If we want to do 50 reps with a given weight, we begin with five and add on over a period of weeks until we are doing 50. Once we are doing 50, we find that we can lift a whole lot more weight than we could have even imagined when we began. Jesus' favorite metaphors of the Kingdom are all about escalating growth: from the parable of the sower, to the mustard seed developing into a massive flowering tree, to the disciples themselves being the leaven in the loaf. Each depicts escalation following application of His teaching—and His teaching always comes associated with a powerful deposit on His promise of abundant life—whether healing the sick or feeding the hungry or calming a storm at sea.

Diana and I experienced a sacramental outburst in our personal life and ministry on a trip to Maui in 1998 that God continues to escalate today—and into tomorrow. While waiting for our transfer flight from Oahu, we saw a man saying good-bye to friends. The Spirit of God was clearly all over him, and we were rising from our seats to bless him when God spoke clearly to me that we would meet this man at a time and place of God's choosing—but not now. We were to pray for him in the meantime. The teaching was just as clear—that when we obey God everything will change and until we obey God nothing will ever change.

Three years would pass before we would actually meet Suuqinna and his wife, Qaumaniq, in another airport. In the meantime—beginning with that 1998 trip—we were led into a process in which we met and ministered with and came to love mutual friends of theirs from all over the world. As the process escalated, the teaching never changed. It has escalated over the years into an international dimension of PrayNorthState (the ministry itself had not even been conceived in 1998). Furthermore, it has taken us to places as different as Scandinavia and the Philippines and called us to testify of God's calling for Holy Spirit transformation that begins—from our human end—with a repeated decision to become new wineskins so that the wine He pours out can come to full potency in us.

Paah-ho-ammi carried for me the same teaching as the encounter with Suuqinna in the airport. When the Lord told me to, "Just call it Paah-ho-ammi," without giving me a clue of what that word meant, He did not need to remind me that things change whenever we obey His thoughts and ways—which are not our thoughts and ways—and that nothing changes until we do.

The fruit of Paah-ho-ammi has been escalating over the past years as it has become an annual event—the progression from a 12 percent reduction in suicides to an 86 percent drop-off is just one example. But the larger escalation is in the linkage between the Paah-ho-ammi prayer project itself and the many prophecies spoken over our region, such as the one that names Northern California a cancer-free zone. Others call for the region to be a habitat for a culture of life, because decisions for life abound, where once the decisions were often for death in various forms. Such prophecies are grandiose in the extreme and yet pragmatic to the core. (They would not be truly prophetic otherwise.) Their fulfillment depends on sacramental outbursts—deposits on God's promises—and Paah-ho-ammi is only one such. God depends on our choice to obey so that the teaching may be sown and the escalation poured out in the receptive atmosphere of human repentance.

The Church on earth lives to proclaim the Gospel that the Son has come and abundant life is available to all who will confess Him with their lips and believe Him in their hearts. The primary activity of the prophetic community, which is the Church, is to prepare the ground for the coming of the King in the proclamation of His Name. This activity is what we call spiritual warfare, and it is fought in terms of the blessings that God pours out on His people and on His creation through the gathered ministries of the people of His Name. As we are faithful to obey through blessing, forgiveness, and the celebration of His presence in the presence of His enemies, we are seeing outbursts of His goodness—the deposits on His promise to manifest the wholeness of the Kingdom in our midst. As we bank on the promise itself, we are seeing escalation upon escalation of the mustard seeds He has already released among us. The whole process is the heart of both the making and the fulfilling of prophecy today and tomorrow—on the third day He comes.

Endnote

1. C.S. Lewis, *Miracles* (New York: MacMillan, 1947), 134-5.

Chapter 5

WAITING ON THE LORD: THE MOST DYNAMIC ACTIVITY

When Diana was still a teenager, the Lord spoke to her one day about the man she was to marry. He said that He wanted her to begin praying for that man—that he would be having a blessed day, that he was drawing close to the Lord if he knew Him, and that He would seek the Lord if he did not—and other generic stuff that a believer would pray for someone she loved. "But," Diana reminded the Lord, "I don't know who he is." The Lord returned, "That's alright; I do. You just pray for him and let me worry about who he is." Diana prayed for me every day for the next four years—and then for as long as we both shall live.

It would be two years from the date of her conversation before I even met Jesus in a high school classroom while my students took a test. It would be another two years after that before Diana and I met. Still another two years would pass before we were both convinced that we had found the one for whom God had been preparing us since He placed us in our mothers' wombs. Our God is a God of duration who perfects His gifts and His plans over time—like we prepare fine wine or mentor our children for the leadership that will one day be theirs. We are called to wait on and in Him, just as He called Diana to wait in 1968.

We tend to think of waiting as a passive pursuit. It is the most dynamic activity we can engage.

Jesus employs the apprentice method for training and releasing His disciples. It could just as well be called the method of dynamic waiting. An apprentice attaches himself to the master—usually at the master's invitation. In training the master performs a task while the apprentice or disciple observes. Next time the master permits the apprentice to assist in the procedure. Later the master calls the apprentice to complete the task with the master's assistance. Finally the apprentice is sent to perform the task as though he were the master.

In Mark's Gospel this progression is especially clear as Jesus mentors the disciples for healing the sick and delivering the oppressed. In the first chapter—right after calling the disciples—Jesus casts out a demon on a Sabbath Day visit to the Capernaum synagogue, heals Peter's mother-in-law of a fever, and cures a man with leprosy—while the disciples watch (Mark 1:21-29;40-42). By the beginning of chapter 2, He is already working with the assistance of those who lower the paralyzed man into the room where He is ministering (see Mark 2:1-12), and in chapter 3 He is appointing His disciples as apostles (see

Mark 3:13-14), "that they might be with Him and that He might send them out to preach and to have authority to drive out demons," although they remain with Him for the time being. By chapter 6, Jesus is sending the boys out two-by-two, with no resources other than the Spirit with whom He has filled their hearts (see Mark 6:7). They will return and depart multiple times—amping up the process repeatedly—before the Jerusalem climax of death, resurrection, and Pentecost, but the principle is that they are waiting upon the Lord and His coach-and-release brand of mentoring throughout.

Waiting upon the Lord is so important—and so contrary to the way most of us think we ought to be—that God says, "Those who wait on the Lord shall renew their strength…[and] mount up with wings like eagles" (Isa. 40:31 NKJV). In the more modern NIV, it morphs into "Those who hope in the Lord will renew their strength. They will soar on wings like eagles; they will run and not grow weary, they will walk and not be faint" (Isa. 40:31).

In the Old Testament, waiting and hoping are inextricably linked in the Hebrew language; they are inseparable from faith in the Greek of the New. In Hebrews 11, God says, "Now faith is being sure of what we hope for and certain of what we do not see" (Heb. 11:1) and then completes the chapter with successive accounts of Abel making a sacrifice (see Heb. 11:4), Noah building an ark (see Heb. 11:7), and Abraham going on a journey of years until he arrives at where God has told him to go—and later letting go of the son for whom he waited all of his life when God tells him to sacrifice Isaac on the mountain (see Heb. 11:8-12;17-19). Moses spends more than a century waiting upon the Lord—from Pharoah's court to Sinai to Goshen and to Sinai again.

During that time the ten plagues are unleashed, the sea parted, the commandments given, and many battles fought as a desert is crossed and the people are taught to do very well on a single day's supply of food at a time.

That is how waiting upon the Lord is. Jesus is so willing to encourage waiting upon the Father, the Son, and the Spirit that He permits His mother to drag Him into a major expression of His anointing at a wedding in Cana (see John 2:1-10) after He has already told her to back off because it is not yet His time. And the reward for the wedding guests who have waited—who have avoided getting drunk on the wine already served—is to sample the best wine—the stuff of which the banquet master says, "Everyone brings out the choice wine first and then the cheaper wine after the guests have had too much to drink; but you have saved the best till now" (John 2:10).

Diana waited upon the Lord for four years; the life and ministry we share—and the children we raised—are the fruit of her waiting. But whether we are speaking of individuals ministering the Kingdom or whole communities entering it, the waiting gets really good whenever that Kingdom is advanced through dynamic waiting.

Most of the time when we speak of waiting on the Lord we mean in prayer that is consistent, concerted, and focused on specific issues of Kingdom importance. But prayer opens doors of opportunity. Walking through them is like walking from the burning bush to Egypt. When the ministry has been undertaken as far as God has opened that opportunity, returning to prayer is like returning to Mount Sinai and the bush. It is a process and a journey more than it is an event and an arrival.

Roger Ralston is a well-known icon in Redding, California. In 1984 he had a dream in which God called him (and his wife, JoAnne) to begin a ministry to pregnant women in crisis. God promised him in the dream that this ministry would one day operate in three counties—Shasta, Trinity, and Tehama. He also promised that they would one day possess the land that was then occupied by the local family planning clinic. The Ralstons regularly walked the land in prayer, claiming it for the Kingdom, at the same time they opened the first local Crisis Pregnancy Center (eventually called Carenet Pregnancy Center) in another location.

Fast forward to 2005, when Sharre Littrell has become the new director of Carenet Pregnancy Center. While driving she heard the voice of the Lord speaking that the Red Bluff chapter of the Salvation Army would partner with Carenet to open a facility in that Tehama County city. (Carenet was already operating a mobile unit in Trinity County.) At first she did not believe her ears, but the prophet who was speaking at that night's meeting—she was on her way to it when God spoke to her—singled her out and told her that God said she was to contact the Salvation Army in Red Bluff. The next morning a girlfriend who was not at the meeting called Sharre to urge her to call Salvation Army. Three times was enough.

Salvation Army lived in a small building on Walnut Avenue in Red Bluff. Like most urban ministries of care, they had barely enough room to house themselves. Yet shortly after her first contact, they called to say that they would empty two rooms for the use of Carenet—even if it meant trashing their own badly needed assets. One of the captains—Laurel—was a registered nurse who had been waiting for the opportunity to serve in a pregnancy ministry. The entire Christian community leapt into the parted waters to provide funds, volunteers, and spiritual support. Within a couple of months the center was open, training and deploying volunteers, and looking for a larger property to accommodate the already expanding clientele.

(A few months later, when Laurel and her husband, Dyrk, resigned their captaincies in order to better care for family members in poor health, Laurel avoided several attractive job opportunities in her nursing field for reasons she could not explain. When Carenet had the chance to expand into a three bedroom home on the main street of Red Bluff and their local directress resigned to better care for her own family, Sharre called Laurel. Only then did she know why the Lord had placed the drag on her acceptance of job offers.)

In mid-2006 Family Planning called. The government funding of that agency had dried up, and they were closing down. They offered the building—two blocks from City Hall and three times the size of the existing Carenet facility located well out of town—to the ministry God had placed on Roger's heart in 1984. Today Carenet operates in the new building and in the three counties God promised. But God always seems to give more than He promises—Carenet is today a fully licensed medical clinic equipped with ultrasound in both Redding and Red Bluff. People who come in with sick babies—in their wombs—receive prayer, and there have been several documented healings prior to birth. Decisions for life are up by 130 percent in Redding—Red Bluff shows a similar surge—as volunteers pray daily for the blessing and transformation of those involved in the deadly abortion industry.

Most of the hundreds of volunteers who have served in Carenet since 1984 know nothing about a dream given to

Roger or a revelation given to Sharre; they know only as much as they needed to know in order to play their part in the unfolding of God's plan. They answered God's call in their lives with faithful obedience. Yet their presence and their obedience were absolutely essential—each of them counted. Again, that is how things work in the prophetic community that God is building in our midst.

All that Roger and Sharre and Laurel and the other volunteers who sowed into this vision did was believe and act on the teaching that what is impossible for men is possible for God—when we obey what seems like foolishness to us. And they remembered that this God is a God of duration—One for whom a moment is a span of years and vice versa.

Jesus is forever referring to His followers as *leaven in the loaf*. Leaven is yeast introduced into the bread in the early stages of preparation and—once the bread is properly kneaded—it slowly begins to rise from the expansive action of the yeast. This yeast is the smallest part of the ingredients for the bread; yet without it the bread remains flat and relatively tasteless. Waiting upon the Lord—for purposes of personal growth or community transformation—is a dynamic process in which the yeast of the Spirit permeates the loaf of the Body with the cooperation of its members in consistent and concerted prayer and in the service to the King that becomes opportunity in its wake.

The process takes time—just as it took time for the Lord to prepare me to meet my wife and it took a lot more time for the dream of Roger Ralston to come true. The yeast was sown when Diana had that conversation with Him and Roger woke from his dream with a resolve in his heart. Every one of the people who worked with him and each of the folks who prayed for and witnessed to me were the expanding molecules set in motion by that yeast—and every one was absolutely essential to the process in the First Corinthians 12 partnership, which God does not need, but which He absolutely insists upon just the same. This process can be so unglamorous that Diana and I call it the ministry of the earthworm.

Earthworms are a central component in the productivity of the land. They aerate the soil so that it can support and encourage strong root systems in the crops that are planted in it. They pass nutrients through their own bodies so that the soil is enriched for the passage. And they do the job much faster and more thoroughly than any chemical or organic fertilizer ever can.

They express in their faithfulness to a simple calling the very essence of actively waiting on the Lord. The intercessors who carry us on their prayers right to the throne room during the outreaches to Fiji—and the warriors of Paah-ho-ammi who do the very same thing—are the earthworms of the Kingdom without which there is no fruit. Call them yeast bearers or call them earthworms—they are the often anonymous frontline infantry of spiritual warfare. They are the miracle that is so great in scope we cannot see the outlines of it. We can only remember how God used prayer in the Name of Jesus and the bold humility to give ourselves no rest as we give Him no rest—whether it is praying for Qaumaniq's cancer or Kaifafa's paralysis, feeding the 1,100 in Hoopa, or begging Abba to inhibit suicide in Shasta County. His personality is revealed in miracles small enough that we can see their outline. We can come to believe that what He writes small He is committed to writing large in the midst of us. But we have to wait on Him.

A Trip to Galilee

I have been personally waiting on God for the fulfillment of a word He gave me in Virginia since 1989. We had moved to the little city of Danville in the Piedmont region of the state the year before to pastor a church named for the visit of the Wise Men to the Baby Jesus. In my second year on the job, God spoke to me one day saying, "I want you to go to Galilee." Although I have wanted to visit Israel since I was a 20-something, I knew at once that He was not talking about geography. Galilee was the crucible in which the disciples served out their apprenticeship. The Spirit was telling me that we had been sent to Virginia to begin an apprenticeship—I thought we were there to make the next step in what looked like a fast-track for my ministry.

When I met the Lord Jesus in 1970, I was so much the product of the dysfunctional family in which I was raised that the last thing I would have been interested in was any sort of faith that played to the emotions—and I met Him just as the Jesus People revival was getting well underway in Southern California. A professor at San Diego State University—well-known for his non-directive and inconclusive answers to any and all questions—responded to mine for further directions by directing me to All Saints Episcopal Church at the corner of Sixth and Pennsylvania. There, he assured me, I would be told what to do next in my journey with Jesus.

They told me what I needed to do in both word and deed. On my first Sunday in church, I felt a compulsion I could not explain to receive Holy Communion. During those rare Sundays in childhood when my parents took me to church for unexplained reasons, I always felt that we did things that had no meaning outside of that building—we sang songs we never sang anywhere else, and the preacher talked about things we never discussed in any other setting. It was no different after my initial encounter with the Lord, and I attempted to respond by going to church—until I entered that very stuffy enclave of ceremony and ritual in which the priests even exchanged a kiss of peace during the service without ever making contact with each other. It made no sense to me until I received the piece of bread and the sip of wine before the altar; at that instant the dawn broke. As I returned to my seat I sang in my heart, "So this is why you go to church!"

In that moment God birthed in me the sacramental mindset that defines me today. In the rote learning of prayers and use of the prayer book to frame my prayer life, I found the solution to my shapeless life as a hippie of the '60s that I had always craved. (Before Jesus, I knew what I was against— I still strive against those things today—but only after Jesus did I know what I was for. And only in that repetitive and hyper-structured approach to faith that was the Episcopal Church did I find a way to move and grow toward God instead of merely away from the things I detested.) This style of faith set out to celebrate salvation history not as a series of episodes but as an eternal event into which we can step and stay if we choose.

In the meantime I was still a college student with a minor in religious studies. Over the next years, I was exposed more and more to the evangelical theologies of C.S. Lewis, Wolfhart Pannenberg, and that old father of Christian existentialism, Soren Kierkegaard. I came to love the stories of Martin Luther—who took Romans 10:9, that if you confess with your lips and believe with your heart you are saved, so seriously that he defied the Roman Catholic Church and the Holy Roman Empire with his words, "Here I stand; God help me, I can do no other" (see Rom. 10:9). I was overwhelmed with the reality of God's love for my country manifested in the sending of the Puritans to Massachusetts Bay and the clear creation of every political and social institution I held dear in the teaching of these evangelicals and those who followed them down the centuries of American history. My eyes would fill with tears as I read and heard of St. Francis—a dyed-in-the-wool albeit gentle evangelical of his day—who took his monks into the forest to teach them to preach, and when they had cut wood for a widow, shared lunch with a blind man, and played ball with a lonely boy. When he was asked when he would begin the preaching lesson, answered, "What do you think I have been doing all day?"

My frame of mind was the sacramental way in which I encountered the Lord Jesus on a regular basis, and my understanding of those encounters was thoroughly evangelical. But, although I've received visions most of my life and thought of God as someone with whom I could literally walk down the street, I rejected what charismatics called the "baptism in the Holy Spirit" until 1987, when I told the Lord that I was OK with His evident call to embrace that dimension of spirituality as well. When it came, it encouraged my all-the-way-or-not-at-all approach to just about everything. I was awakened at two o'clock in the morning by the sound of a rushing wind in our backyard. The moon was full and the stars were brilliant; I had a clear view of the trees that were holding perfectly still in what sounded like howling wind. I became conscious of a warm sensation in my belly that was rising in me. When it reached my throat,

I erupted in praise of my God in a language I could enjoy without understanding.

Fast forward to Danville, Virginia, and the church I began to lead three years after graduation from seminary and a stint as an associate pastor in San Diego. This church was not especially sacramental in mindset, nor seriously evangelical in outlook, and they thought of charismatic experience as being from another planet. But they called me to be their senior pastor as surely as the Lord called me to Galilee.

During our slightly less than three years in Danville, we learned to engage in deliverance ministry, and we learned the process of doing spiritual battle through sowing in the opposite (positive) spirit of engagement. I came to a lively appreciation of how God has blessed the various denominations with gifts that are to be shared rather than hoarded or lorded over the rest of the Body. I came to an enriched compassion for those who practice the idolatries of alternative sexual lifestyles—because I ministered to many and saw the great pain they wreak on themselves; I came also to the conviction that when we speak against those lifestyles we need to speak from the standpoint of a broken heart or else not at all. Diana and I began to speak prophetically.

Our next congregational assignment was in a San Francisco Bay Area bedroom community. This was my first experience of leading a Spirit-filled church, and I quickly learned how easily even so-called freewheeling Charismatics could sink into legalism and control issues. (I spent my first years there trying to liberate the congregation from the teachings of a cult leader in Christian clothing.) I came to know firsthand what it is to trust the Lord to supply need in the very hour of it—at one point we experienced such devastating losses to our membership base during a recession that it looked as though the church would have to let me go because they could not support full-time ministry. The Lord told me He would take care of the situation in one week, and that is exactly what He did; He also told me in the next month that, with the crisis past and the people celebrating the fact that we could stay, He was moving me anyway within the coming year.

Stuffed into the interim between Danville and the Bay Area was a year in post-graduate study leading to a doctorate in pastoral psychology. God called me to the Gilroy ministry before I was well into the three-year course—when I asked Him about calling me to the university and then seeming to change His mind, He reminded me that He had told me to begin the course but had never said a word about completing it. The experience I gained in ministering inner healing and in substance abuse intervention was just another season on the road in Galilee.

We arrived in Redding in 1996, and I began to pastor a church just down the road in Anderson. Our ministry there followed a 1995 visit to a gathering of 20,000 Christians in Orlando, Florida, from dozens of denominations. One day while praising the Lord for the privilege of worshiping Him in such a ménage—but noting that we really did do it a bit better in our Anglican style—He retorted that He was sick and tired of my denominational idolatries—in a loving way. While there I had the privilege of questioning Jack Hayford about his support of the Toronto Blessing—which was in full swing at the time—and he told me—also in a good-natured way—to lighten up and go see for myself. We did that in the spring of 1996, and I got a glimpse of what Holy Spirit transformation in whole communities might one day look like.

Once in Redding we quickly became part of the interdenominational ferment that had taken root there. We rejoiced in the opportunity to become part of a First Corinthians 12 expression of the Body of Christ in the city—one in which I was the Episcopal guy and Bill Johnson was the Assemblies of God guy and Bryan Blank was the Calvary Chapel guy and others represented the Presbyterians and the Methodists and the Catholics and so forth. We were privileged to be part of the radical visioning process for ministries such as Faithworks Coalition that built transitional housing and reduced welfare roles while sharing the Gospel with the homeless. We joyfully participated in the burgeoning prophetic culture and community that God was building before any of us had the vocabulary to really talk about it. We also embraced the heartache of bearing the gifts God had given to our own denomination as we watched that branch of the Body slide more and more into apostasy; He called us to grieve and witness but forbade us to write off people who He loves, even in their sin, and who He promises to resurrect in His time.

At the dawn of the new millennium He made it abundantly clear that He had been preparing us for a new and extra-congregational ministry all along. On February 1, 2001, we launched a ministry of "cooperation, encouragement, and proclamation" of what we saw God doing in the midst of our region to make it a province—eventually—of the Kingdom as Jesus demonstrates it in His Matthew 11 report to John the Baptist, and Paul describes in First Corinthians 12. In June of that year we left congregational ministry and PrayNorthState became our sole focus.

The point of all this is that I believed I had done my time in Galilee with the conclusion of each stage of the journey. The Lord did teach and prepare in me what He wanted me to know for the next step—as a good master will always do with an apprentice—teaching him in that very hour what he needs to do and say and know. But I was sure that He had taught me so much about deliverance and appreciation of gifts in Danville to prepare me for a ministry of counseling and intervention with individuals and families. I believed that He brought me back to San Diego for all of that training and internship in counseling and intervention so that I could apply it to congregations and communities struggling to become Great Commission people. I was convinced that pastoring in Redding was for the purpose of sharing my own personal and denominational giftings—and receiving the gifts of others—as a member of the mix of the larger Christian family. And I knew that I knew that He brought us into PrayNorthState as His way of summarizing all of the above in the context of the prophetic community and the vocabulary for that community that He is still unveiling. But reality is that we are still in the Galilean countryside as He brings more and more change and permutation to a ministry that was once about gathering the Body in our region (and still is) and that becomes more and more stretched into a ministry of writing and media and a ministry of launching and teaching about grassroots projects of prayer for the community in targeted ways —in more and more locations nationally and internationally.

Every stage of this Galilean journey has produced wonderful fruit in terms of lives enriched, bodies and minds healed, and men and women coming to know the Lord; it has been valuable in and of itself. And every segment has been an introduction to the one that would follow.

ABBA'S VIEW OF IT

Our God has always been a God of duration. He has never been a God of caprice. He does what He does out of the overwhelming love He bears for us in His heart, which is too big to be contained even in His Body. But He always has plans and ideas that operate in a scope and majesty that are way beyond our comprehension. This too motivates Him, and He calls us to appreciate His perspective and to enter into it through our faithful obedience, our honoring of His sacrifice even when we cannot see the sense of it in our present situation.

One of the most profound natural proofs for the very existence of God and His purposeful activity in creation is the Big Bang Theory. The theory is simplicity itself when it comes to verifying God and His intentionality—you cannot have a big bang without a big banger! And one of the prime pieces of evidence for the Big Bang—that orgasmic and conceptual moment when the universe exploded outward from the infinitesimally small to the astronomically vast—is its evident method of dispersing heat throughout the galaxies. Astronomers mostly agree that the method is about the same as what would happen if I turned on my oven, opened the door, and waited for it to heat my whole house. But there is a logical problem with it.

This method of heating is about as inefficient as any that one could devise. It is a stumbling block to many intelligent people who might be otherwise inclined to see the hand of an all-wise God in the creation of the universe. It is a stumbling block precisely because they cannot see how an intelligent Creator could be so much less efficient than they could be if heating the universe were their problem. What they fail to see is that God's intention was never to create a heating system that would satisfy the mind of a civil engineer or a building inspector. His plan was to heat the universe in such a way that He would be revealed at its core. His intention is always self-revelation. His idea is always to reinforce the idea that, "The Heavens declare the glory of God!"

His invitation to us is delivered in Isaiah 55 when He says,

Come all you who are thirsty, come to the waters; and you who have no money, come, buy and eat! Come, buy wine and milk without money and without cost...Seek the Lord while He may be found; call on Him while He is near. Let the wicked forsake his way and the evil man his thoughts. Let him turn to the Lord, and He will have mercy on him, and to our God, for He will freely pardon. "For My thoughts are not your thoughts, neither are Your ways my ways," declares the Lord. "As the heavens are higher than the earth, so are My ways higher than your ways and My thoughts than your thoughts" (Isaiah 55:1,6-9).

It comes again in Jeremiah 29:11-14 when He tells us that He knows the plans He has for us—plans for our prosperity, our hope, and our eternity. He adds that when we seek His face we cannot fail to find Him. We are invited to leave behind the myopia and distortion of our vision and step into His. Jesus does it with greater clarity when He says—in John 8—"If you hold to my teaching, you are really my disciples. Then you will know the truth, and the truth will set you free" (John 8:31). He is even more succinct in John 15 when He says that if we abide in Him, He will surely abide in us (see John 15:7). But the revelation of truth does not enable obedience—it is the other way around. We come to understand from inside faithful obedience to the counter-intuitive stuff He is forever calling out of us.

His challenge to us is to stop worshiping our inadequacies and start worshiping Him.

Every Christian knows and loves Second Chronicles 7:14, "If My people, who are called by My Name, will humble themselves and pray and seek My face and turn from their wicked ways, then will I hear from heaven and will forgive their sin and heal their land." This is yet another Scripture passage that calls for duration in the pursuit of the Lord, for it pre-supposes prayer that is both corporate and consistent. But the operant phrase in this passage, from the Lord's perspective, is "turn from your wicked ways." This is where the rubber meets the road.

The word we translate as "wicked" is really much more akin to inadequacy than to moral wickedness—yet the Bible translators knew what they were doing from the context of the Word of God. We understandably think of ourselves as limited beings—inadequate beings under God—and that is exactly what we are. There is no moral failing in that—unless we place our very inadequacy before God as an idol—which is precisely what we all too often do.

Have any of us ever heard an exhortation from the Bible and responded to the teacher with something like, "I would love to know Scripture like you do, but of course I don't have the time to study it like you do. My schedule is just a killer."

What we have done—every time we make that excuse—is to elevate our schedule as it is presently constituted into the ultimate reality of our lives. And whatever is ultimate reality to us is the thing that we worship. I am not suggesting that everyone should just change their schedule—by addition or subtraction—so that Bible reading now occupies six or eight more hours a week than it did before. If we succeeded in that we might replace the schedule with our ability to make executive decisions as the ultimate reality of our lives. The point is to put God in that spot—to worship Him and to depend on Him to make time for His instruction taken from His Word. That may involve changes to our schedule; it may also involve time standing still like it did for Joshua (see Josh. 10:13). The question is not, "What shall I do about it?" but "Am I willing to turn this over to God and go wherever He leads?" The fact remains that the commanding influence in my life is what I worship; it can either be the real God or one of my manufacture.

The process of placing God progressively in that spot of ultimacy is the very essence of a season prophetically spent in Galilee.

Another favorite dodge I have heard over 20-plus years of ministry is, "Pastor, I wish I had your gift for visiting the sick. You always make people feel so comfortable and you pray for them so well. I am so distracted by the machinery and the tubes they stick down people's throats—I'm afraid I might gag or even throw up if I went into some of those sickrooms. I just can't handle it." I am not saying that everybody is called to make the rounds of the hospitals, but I am saying that some people elevate their own gag reflex to the pinnacle of Godhead. And they bow and worship.

It is not about whether I can put aside my own revulsion at what we sometimes must do to one another in an exercise of medical tough love. It is about whether I am willing to go where God calls me and do what God calls me to do, trusting in Him to prepare my heart and mind and body for what He has in heart and mind and Body. He is the God who promises He will teach you in that very hour what you are to do and what you are to say. We are called to worship Him, not our gag reflex.

There is nothing so revealing of this human habit greater than your average stewardship education occasion—whether a class or an annual appeal for the church's budget support mechanism—which is what most stewardship programs are really all about. The revelation comes in the repetitive comment, "I would love to tithe; I know the Bible says to do it. But Moses didn't have a mortgage and taxes and kids in college and the rest of my bills. If you could see my bills every month, you would know that I am doing the best I can. When I am making more money, I will be glad to give more—until then don't try laying a guilt trip on me." Of course what we have here is the placing of our checkbook—or more to the point our monthly bills—on the altar that should be reserved for the Lord our God.

I knew a couple of brothers in Danville, Virginia, who both claimed Christ as their Lord. One tithed and the other did not. One had twice the income of the other, and was always in need of more money to meet his increasing needs, while the other brother—the tither—always seemed to have enough. The truth is that God loves a cheerful giver and nothing could be farther from His mind than to lay a guilt trip on even those of the family who do not obey His commands. But it is also true that He calls us to certain habits of life because they lead us more and more into His abundant life—not because He wants to see how much He can make us suffer. The greater truth is that God is the biggest party animal in the universe—that is why He sends Jesus into the world to invite all of us to the heavenly banquet that will run us into eternity.

Even back in Deuteronomy—when God is laying out the instructions regarding the tithe—He makes a point of calling on the people to bring their goods to the place He has designated and there to eat and drink and be merry in His Presence as much as in His Name (see Deut. 12; 14). He gives the option of converting the goods into money only when it is too tough to try transporting them—but the idea is to celebrate as we make provision for the needs of the Kingdom (see Deut. 14:25-26). It is for Him to sort out our affairs to make the tithe possible in the context of that celebration—once we give Him a free hand. And the greatest truth of all is what we have been saying all along—we need to worship Him and not what we think of as an inadequate income—or excessive obligations—for our purposes.

God does not create adversity for us—but He surely knows how to use it in such a way that we are actually better off on the other side of it than we were before the storm struck. When Paul and Silas found themselves in prison they waited upon the Lord—with singing and praise—and the Lord sent an earthquake that blew open the doors of their prison cells. They waited upon the Lord some more—knowing that their purpose in the city was not to escape prison but to bring people into the Kingdom—and the jailer and his family came to Christ and released them anyway when He saw their faithfulness and their peace in the face of many kinds of storms that night. (See Acts 16:25-36.) When I saw that I was headed toward unemployment as the church in Gilroy seemed less and less able to support me, I simply obeyed God's prophetic word that He would rescue us and that my job was to depend actively on His provision. (The good news is that He called me into an intimacy with Him that I had been avoiding in my busyness and worship of my own schedule.) The same process was repeated when He said that He was moving me in the year following His dramatic rescue of the church from financial plight; He told me that He already had a place chosen for me and that I needed only to cooperate with His process. I did not solicit another position, and I found myself as a finalist for three placements within three months of that word—it would take another three months before I would hear Him say, "This is the place I have planned for you." In the meantime He cured me of any doubts I had about His sovereignty. He also demonstrated that waiting on Him—in active not passive mode—is the way we enter into abundant life.

His parable about waiting for the harvest when we notice the wheat and the tares growing together is not just about patience for its own sake (see Matt. 13:18-30). Sometimes what looks like tares to us is really growing into wheat and vice versa. He called the disciples to keep quiet about the miracles—although none of them ever did—because they would not know the whole story they were to tell until they had witnessed death and resurrection in Jerusalem. Galilee is just the run-up for the main event—but what a run-up it is!

How We Wait

There are least two types of waiting on the Lord. One is just waiting out the fruit that is already in the bin but not necessarily visible to the eye for a time. The other is that pro-leptic waiting for an acorn that is still an acorn but in which we know the oak tree is prophetically present—the baby that appears to be just a jumble of cells but in which Beethoven—or Billy Graham—waits to spring forth.

At one of our conferences we prayed for a 70-something-year-old lady named Linda. She was legally blind, and Diana and I prayed for the complete restoration of her sight for about half an hour as the evening session closed out on the first night. Nothing happened that we could see, but we asked her to return for prayer during the breaks the next day and said that we would keep praying for her. The next morning she burst into the church and ran up the center aisle of the church screaming, "I can see! I can see! I woke up this morning and I can see!" God had done the job, and we just needed to wait and see it become manifest.

It was the same with Dallas, who had intractable pain in her back from an old injury. Implanted TENS units and max-imum dosages of medications hardly dented her pain, and our prayers seemed to have minimal effect. I didn't see her for about nine months after the night Diana and I poured prayer into her. When we did meet again it was at a conven-tion; she ran up to me and asked if I had heard that she woke up the next morning completely healed and pain free.

There was Patrick—whose wife asked prayer for the ma-lignant tumor in his neck from a friend of a friend in the parking lot of the post office. The friend heard of Patrick's healing 18 months later, but it occurred that very afternoon.

It is no different when we pray for individuals or gather the Body—or a cross-section of it—to pray for the city and for God's amazing outpouring of His grace into it. The unfolding of the three holiday weekends in which not a single traffic fatality occurred throughout the northstate in 2004—the first year of the Paah-ho-ammi project—was sealed in the first month of prayer although we did not find out about it until the first weeks of the new year 2005. The Inuit people worshiped the Father under the name of Sila, while Hawaiians knew Him as 'Io. The Inuits waited for decades after it was prophesied for the arrival of the missionaries who would tell them of Sila's Son, and the people of Hawaii waited for the coming representatives of 'Io's Son for centuries after their coming was prophesied—but they understood that He had already given His life for their sins and that He was only waiting to invite them into His Kingdom. It was simply a question of spending their time in Galilee.

God wants to know if we believe Him when He says to wait, for we know not at what hour the bridegroom will return—but we do know that He will ask His faithful friends to come inside and celebrate with Him long before those who are out buying oil or catching up on their sleep.

Proleptic is a word I have used several times; it is a wonderful Greek word that means, "present but not yet." It helps us relate to sacramental outbursts by reminding us that when the Lord speaks a thing into existence, He speaks it all the way but—like a pregnancy—its ordained and inexorable destiny does not yet exist—even though it does. The man is present in the child in terms of God's plans for him to give him hope and a future and a calling—but the child has not become the man and there is a journey to be walked. Birth always constitutes an outburst of God's grace and glory—but there is much teaching to sow and incorporate and much escalation to undertake before the baby is ready to shave and get married and raise babies of his own. Scripture teaches that the Kingdom is *proleptically* present in Jesus and in the Body even though Herod and the Romans are still in power and well able to tax and to crucify—even to this day. Anyone who checks the back of the book knows who wins.

Danielle, a newscaster at one of the stations on which I broadcast my weekly radio program, had a cyst on her wrist. Although she was not a believer she was happy to have me pray for her wrist each time we ran into each other in the hall. I prayed for her wrist a couple of times a week for several months. She always felt better—pain free—after prayer, but there was never a significant change in the cyst itself until one day—there was! She burst into the station that afternoon shoving her wrist in my direction and wearing the biggest smile I had ever seen on her face; there was no cyst. God is still waiting for her to receive Him as her Lord—but she has learned that He loves her with no strings attached. Her healing was promised, but it appeared and actually occurred only in the fullness of time.

Kevin was born with cerebral palsy due to a brain hemorrhage that occurred at his birth. He had seizures during and after the birth as well. Doctors gave him—at best—a year to live and the promise of blindness, quadriplegia, and minimal brain function. His grandparents—Keith and Trish Wright— would not accept the diagnosis. They raised him in the heart of the church they pastor. They brought him for prayer to any Christian gathering they could find, and they were tireless in seeking care for him from medical bureaucracies who told them they were wasting their time—until the bureaucrats came around like the unjust judge in Luke 18:1-5. Christians in medical care came to specially identify with Kevin and to take pride in giving him innovative care. Today Kevin is a teenager; he has returned from the brink of death five times. His body is untwisting with the aid of botox injections in his legs. He walks with the aid of a gate trainer walker, and his sight is coming to him in portions. His God-given intelligence is slowly revealing itself. Trish writes—in a 2007 letter to the author—"As we continue to learn to co-labor with Christ, we see a very intelligent child who is learning to overcome many obstacles. We have had many discouragements in our journey with Kevin, but all the obstacles have served to throw us at the feet of Jesus to find the answers from above." Their story is a case in point that God draws His most comprehensive miracles from the developing human beings of the prophetic community He is creating.

Jesus wants us to recognize that He uses all those agricultural parables for a reason. Transformation is a developmental process that can end only one way—but the details are still being worked out in the relations of you and me and the Lord we serve. King David waited many years for the kingdom of Israel to be his—as God had promised and ordained—and Saul had his way during most of that time. But David was being transformed into the kind of man who would not only want God's heart, but would know it when he found it. David was being grown into the man who could return to Ziklag (see 1 Sam. 30), find the Amalekites have burned the city, kidnapping his and his men's families, and—in the face of his men threatening to kill him—call for a worship service and hot pursuit of the enemy. His leadership has become such that the men obey at once and—while they are gaining victory over the Amalekites a couple of days later—Saul and his sons are dying on Mount Gilboa so that the promise might be fulfilled (see 1 Sam. 31–32).

The *how* of it is strikingly simple—although it is not necessarily easy. Acts 2 recounts the striking advent of the Kingdom of God in terms just as seminal and just as explosive as the Big Bang that started the universe at God's command. One moment the faithful remnant are huddled in the fragile protection of their upper room—getting ready for church—and the next they are wearing tongues of fire and engaging extravagant praise to the Father and the Son in the power of the Spirit. In a suddenly uncapped fire hydrant of living water, they have become a vanguard and—with a boldness and peace they have never known before, even in the company of Jesus—they step into the market place and begin to preach and minister the Kingdom. When it was over—for the first day—they "devoted themselves to the apostles' teaching and fellowship, to the breaking of bread, and to prayer," according to Acts 2:42.

They would be devoting themselves to these things for the rest of their lives—on earth as it is in Heaven—and they were devoting themselves to these things from the moment Jesus ascended into Heaven and the angel asked them what they were looking up into Heaven for when they needed to get back to Jerusalem and wait until they were clothed with power (see Acts 1:11).

The apostles' teaching is to steep—like a tea bag—in the Worship of God, the Word of God, and Obedience to what they already know of His Will for their lives. (Obedience wraps the other two in the context of ongoing prayer that has become as natural as breathing or the beating of their hearts. Paul was not introducing a new command when he told the Thessalonians to pray without ceasing (see 1 Thess. 5:17).) In Acts Chapter 1, that means being continually in the temple praising Him, searching the Scriptures they had in order to get the context for what was happening, and choosing a replacement for Judas Iscariot (see Acts 1:20-26). In Chapter 2, a new dimension is added as they receive the Spirit and head out into the streets—and it will be developmentally so for all of the time to come. But the principles in which they live and act do not change—they have not changed since the Exodus, and they will not change as the Second Coming draws closer and closer.

They are also called to steep in the fellowship—the First Corinthians 12 world—that God has provided—with special emphasis on embracing the Christians of other folds and other cultures and seeking to make converts of those who do not yet know Jesus—teaching one another to observe all of the things the Master has taught them. They are to party in the name of the Lord every chance they get—remembering that the breaking of bread is the sacramental deposit on the promise of the heavenly banquet. And they are to steep in prayer as a lifestyle that—by the grace of God alone—should become as natural and as continuous as the beating of their hearts. They are to continue these practices until the Lord comes for them.

In Isaiah 62, God tells the people to post watchmen on the walls, giving themselves no rest and giving Him no rest until He establishes Jerusalem (see Isa. 62:6). Jesus tells the parable of the widow and the unjust judge in Luke 18—and wonders aloud if He will find enduring faith like that of the widow when He comes to claim His Kingdom on earth (see Luke

18:1-8). He contributes the tale of the workers in the vineyard—in Matthew 20—who think they should work fewer hours or get more money than the ones hired near the end of the day—and He allows that they ought rather to focus on the generosity of their master and the reality that they are privileged to co-labor with Him (see Matt. 20:1-16).

Back in the Old Testament book of Zechariah, Yahweh promises the returning exiles a coming harvest that will blow their minds in the extravagance of His largesse—but He calls them twice to let their hands be strong for what is to come (see Zech. 8:9-17). He offers a foretaste of that largesse in the feeding of the 5,000 and the 4,000, in the baptism of 3,000 on the first day of the life of His Church, and in the rapid-fire spread of the Gospel throughout the known world in the first decades following Pentecost. But we are still awaiting fulfillment of the promise, and we wait with our tunics tucked into our belts and the unleavened bread in our hands.

Ken Greenlee made half a dozen trips each year to Fiji over several years—making the relationships and building the trust that was needed to make his ministry a success—before leading the first outreach in 2005. We prayer-walked the schools that later became California distinguished schools for a similar length of time before seeing that kind of miracle. The Puritans of Massachusetts Bay cast vision and practiced what they saw in ways both halting and vigorous for a fulfillment—when the United States would be a beacon of freedom and witness—that was more than 300 years in the future. And the Christians of Siskiyou County are still waiting on the fulfillment of their prophecy that when word of Pastor Gerry's healing gets out there will be revival in that county, just as we are waiting in Redding for the fullness of the prophecy re-naming us Abundant Springs. But we are waiting actively, and the fruit is good.

How should we be waiting on the Lord—celebrating His commitment to duration? Steep in His worship, Word, and will as we presently know it. Gather with Christians who know that what we do in church is meant to prepare us for what we do in the streets outside—and that what we do outside is meant to prepare the world to come back inside and dance again around that burning bush. Cross the lines and be agents of reconciliation; make prophetic acts with impact in your community, and shout from the rooftops what God has done in plain view. Do not wait for all of the leaders to get it; some will embrace the call and others will not. But do wait upon the Lord. Wait on Him, dynamically seeking for His peace and His joy that pass all understanding—on earth as it is in Heaven.

Chapter 6

⁓

WARFARE BY HONOR

The elder of one of the largest Northern California tribes was an invited guest of the Aglow International prayer conference in Redding that year. Leaders believed the best way to kick off their event was to honor the first stewards God had placed on the land. They invited the tribal council of the Winnemem band of the Wintu, honored them for their service and for their ongoing authority to bless the region, and gave small gifts. The Aglow leaders declared that they served the Lord Jesus Christ and knew it was His will for Native American leaders to be honored in this way. The woman declared, "If this is the way your Jesus treats people, then I want to know him." She received Jesus as her Lord and was baptized on the spot along with seven others.

The prophetic word I brought to the Fifth World Christian Gathering on Indigenous Peoples in Kiruna, Sweden, was a hard one. I addressed a plenary session of the gathering with God's commitment to begin worldwide transformation—in every corner of the planet—with the indigenous peoples. I pointed out that God had been doing just that in more than 500 communities around the world—all but one of which was a first nations community. I declared that God's love for the first nations was so profound that He leaves His fingerprints— the recognizable imprint of His Son—on each of their cultures so that the Son can be recognized when His missionaries come to tell of Him. I apologized for the ways in which representatives of my own culture had so often dishonored the peoples that God so loved, and I identified with my listeners in recounting how the first people of my own Caucasian race had been themselves obliterated—with no trace left of them—in the Caucasus Mountains in which we originated. I did this to honor my listeners before challenging them.

But I did share God's challenge that this prophesied worldwide transformation could only happen when they were as committed to repentance from their own sins of idolatry and abuse of one another as they were to seeking justice in light of the terrible things that people who looked like me had done to them. God's timing and preparation were perfect—it was His word and not mine, after all—and the master of ceremonies grabbed the microphone as soon as I finished, calling us to act on that word at once! We spent the rest of that day repenting to one another and to God, promising each other that this process would be continued at future gatherings of this body.

Daniel Kikawa is a cultural anthropologist who loves his people in Hawaii. He is numbered among the pioneer scholars who identify and celebrate the ways in which God has imprinted Himself on the many cultures of the world. In fact, his first book, *Perpetuated in Righteousness*,[1] was a starting point for my personal discovery of how God prophesied His Son's coming to the people of 'Io—and many more such discoveries as I read the works of Don Richardson and George Otis Jr. and heard the stories of such people as Dr. Ighlaliq Suuqinna and Chief Lynda Prince. But Daniel's highest and best contribution to the process of Holy Spirit Transformation was his leadership of the Spiritual Warfare Project of the 1990s. I learned of this project on Maui, where it was known simply as the 'Io Project.

Daniel had a vision in the early '90s to gather 10,000 Christians of all denominations and cultures. Their task would be to pray everyday for the establishment of intimate relationship between the living Lord Jesus with every citizen of the Kingdom of Hawaii. (In the Hawaiian language He is known as Iesu–Ee-ess-soo.) He and Leon Siu and a few close friends began to pray and meet with others in small groups, exhorting them to pray as well on a daily basis. Some of the intercessors were recruited supernaturally—Diana received a word from the Lord one day that she was to pray every day that everyone in Hawaii would come to know Jesus as Lord; she obeyed faithfully even though she had no idea why—or in what—she was a participant.

By 1996—between the leaders in Hawaii and the Lord's intervention around the world—there were 10,000 people praying every day for the Kingdom in Hawaii. They prayed blessing and forgiveness on the people—Christian and pagan, native and immigrant alike. They asked God to come among the people and make His own heavenly banquet. On March 14, 1998, Diana received another word from the Lord—she could ease off on the daily prayers because the Lord's will had been accomplished.

On that 14th day of March the intercessors who were in Hawaii and appointed for this climactic task marched out to visit every one of the pagan worship sites in the state. In each case they honored the landowners on whose land these sites were located with a knock on the door and a polite request to come onto their land and pray. In no case were they refused admission.

They had prayed for two years for a softening of the spiritual ground in Hawaii, and the universal permission to enter was the first fruit. As they approached the sites other miracles were in evidence—one site was only accessible by helicopter, and the cloud cover was so thick that a landing prognosis ranged from dangerous to impossible. As the intercessors prayed overhead, the clouds suddenly parted. The chopper landed, and the skies remained clear until it was time to return and pick up the prayer warriors; after that the skies lowered once again. Another site was accessible only from the sea, and the breakers were so strong and so constant that a landing through the surf was out of the question. Once again prayer was made from the boat, and the surf calmed and remained calm until the time for pick-up and return.

At each site the Christians blessed even those ancient Hawaiians who had conducted human sacrifice there—in the conviction that what God blesses He transforms. In each case they forgave the sin that had been committed there—acting as a cross-section of the Body of Christ to whom Christ has committed His authority to forgive sin and His warning against retaining it. During each moment of sacramental outburst the Supper of the Lord was celebrated according to the Eucharistic traditions of the people conducting the celebration—whatever they were in those particular denominational backgrounds. Within two days, a two-year drought was broken with a tropical deluge. Within two weeks, locations like Moo' Kini—once barren of life—were teeming with sea creatures—because our God is a God who loves it when we are willing to wait on Him. But the biggest miracle— from 'Io's standpoint—was that in the next few months many thousands in Hawaii did come into a life-giving relationship with the Lord of Life—His Son, Jesus.

And the biggest revelation? The intercessors who worked miracles in the Name of Jesus knew they stood on the shoulders of the two years of prayer by the 10,000 earthworms of the Kingdom—and said so. They said so because they were coming to understand that this type of warfare is not confined to a tactical exercise but is intended to the building of a culture of honor. In such a culture there is still both room and need for loving confrontation with sin, but there is the difference between saying to a brother, "You have disgraced yourself and the Kingdom; repent and get your act together," and "You are much too wonderful a person to behave in that way; let's repent together and go again for the image of God in which you are created." In such a culture we begin to practice looking at one another through the eyes of the One who thinks each of us worth dying for and worth mentoring into our Kingdom destiny. When it becomes a corporate habit to live this way, it becomes a culture in which we can live.

Warfare by honor is conducted in large venues and small. Sometimes it is about bringing a nation to know and love God; sometimes it is about building bridges between nations, as God decrees when He says that He has other sheep not of this fold. Sometimes it is just about blessing one another as He blesses each of us. It is always about honoring one another into the Kingdom and displacing the throne of the enemy—which is established in dishonor—as we lift up the throne of the Lord on our praise to Him and our honoring of those He loves.

When the native Hawaiians—the kanaka moile (kah-nahka mo-eely) in their own tongue—decided to build a war canoe of the size and range of the craft of their ancestors, they no longer had native trees of the size and strength that would do. They were in contact with an Aleut village in Alaska and the Aleut leaders agreed to provide two trees of the proper proportions. The Hawaiians had the trees shipped to Hawaii and the canoe was built. They then arranged to take the canoe to Alaska and enter the village by water so that the Aleut people could see the fruit of their generosity to the Hawaiians.

Nainoa Thompson, the canoe's navigator, tells of how the Hawaiian delegation approached the Aleut leaders and protocoled them with gifts from the Hawaiian homeland. The Aleuts—for whom protocol is just as important—then presented to the Hawaiians a hat full of money to aid them in returning home and maintaining the canoe in which the Aleuts felt that they too had a proprietary interest. The Hawaiians—knowing of the material poverty of the Aleuts—attempted to refuse the gift. The Aleut chief said, "You must receive this gift of our hearts. If you do not you impoverish us. Do not dishonor us by rejecting our effort to honor you."

The Hawaiians received the gift with thanks, acknowledging what many others know as well—that God has been building spiritual, cultural, and historical bridges between the land and peoples—native and immigrant alike—of Hawaii, Alaska, and California for two centuries.

GOD'S WORD ON WARFARE BY HONOR

Warfare by honor is the guiding principle for warfare of all kinds throughout Scripture. It takes the lead in establishing a Kingdom culture or economy.

Protocol is a commonplace English word that simply means "doing the right thing in the right way." Paul asks that all things be done "decently and in order" (1 Cor. 14:40 NKJV). In Genesis 14:18-20, Abraham and Melchizedek protocol each other in the aftermath of a battle in which Abraham has rescued both people and goods associated with the city of Sodom—before its storied fall (see Gen. 14:18-20). Melchizedek, identified only as a priest of the living God and king of Salem—a location no one can identify—shares bread and wine with the victorious shepherd, Abraham. (This event is often identified as an original type of the Lord's Supper and Melchizedek as a pre-incarnate appearance of Jesus.) Abraham gives a tenth of all of his goods as an offering to Melchizedek in an obvious precursor to the tithing principle.

The protocol does not end there. The king of Sodom asks Abraham to return only his people; he is welcome to keep the spoil since they have been won on the field of battle. But Abraham is well aware that his military prowess depends on his obedience and faithfulness to the Lord His God. He tells the king that he has taken an oath to retain nothing that belongs to Sodom and he cannot break it. In returning the goods to their rightful owner, he protocols king and Lord at the same time.

Later, Abraham again protocols God as he honors the three strangers who appear at his tent and are later revealed as angels (see Gen. 18:1-15). This passage makes clear that there is nothing extraordinary about protocol—the law of hospitality is universal in the Fertile Crescent region where Abraham lives and, really, anywhere in the world at that time. Abraham treats the strangers as his God has treated him—caring for their needs with food and a place to rest. In return they care for his needs, promising him the son for whom he has longed.

The biblical view of protocol has nothing to do with the worthiness of the recipient. The very reason we call it warfare by honor is that it is designed to help usher people into the Kingdom who might otherwise reject it. When Moses approaches Pharaoh with the storied, "Let my people go," it is in the context of protocol. (See Exodus 5:1; 7:16; 10:3-4.)

Although Scripture does not record gift-giving, it is likely that Moses and Aaron brought gifts to Pharaoh—it is what was done when the representative of one monarch visited another. What is recorded is an absence of threats during that initial audience. Moses and Aaron identify themselves as ambassadors of the God of the Hebrews and request permission to lead the people on a three-day journey into the desert that they might worship their God (see Ex. 5:3). Although the Lord is under no obligation to respect the king He has created over Egypt, He instructs His emissaries to honor that king precisely because he is the creature and officeholder of the

Lord Almighty—we serve a God who never expects us to do for Him what He has not first done for us.

When Pharaoh responds to the reasonable request of his guests with contempt and cruelty—and only then—we can expect things to get ugly. In Chapters 6 through 12, Moses returns to Pharaoh repeatedly. He renews the request for a religious holiday for the Hebrews each time—and each time Pharaoh denies protocol as he exercises contempt. There are consequences following that contempt in the form of the ten plagues; yet God gives Pharaoh another chance each time to simply be the king he was created to be before new consequences are unleashed in the face of the man's arrogance and pigheadedness. He liberates His people in this way for the same reason He does every other mighty act recorded in the Bible—"And the Egyptians will know that I am the Lord when I stretch out my hand against Egypt and bring the Israelites out of it" (Ex. 6:5).

The bottom line here is that the Lord cares as much for the Egyptians and their Pharaoh as He does for His own chosen people. (OK, He chose His people and fell in love with them first and most passionately for all time.) His desire is to get glory for Himself and revelation for all of the people concerned. Of course, what they do with the revelation is their option—as always.

The pattern continues throughout the Old Testament, and often with special emphasis on those who practice honor pitted against those who do not. David encounters Goliath, for example, and the giant roars his contempt for the Israelite and his God while David simply replies in First Samuel 17:45, "You come against me with spear and javelin, but I come against you in the name of the Lord Almighty, the God of the armies of Israel whom you have defied." When King Saul becomes jealous of David, sensing the anointing that is on him, he makes numerous attempts to murder his rival. David, on the other hand, releases Saul when he has the drop on him—in a cave in the wilderness of En Gedi—because Saul remains his rightful sovereign, even though he has lost the confidence of the Lord his God (see 1 Sam. 24:1-4). Honor is God's way, regardless of qualification, and history records not only who is approved, but who wins the contest.

The New Testament continues God's pre-occupation with warfare by honor. In Acts 4 Peter speaks respectfully to Caiaphas even though the high priest is clearly defying God in his effort to suppress the testimony of Jesus. This staunch resolution in the context of respectful confrontation is not something a fisherman is trained to do—Peter picked it up from watching His Master demonstrate the same resolve coupled with respect when the Samaritan villagers will not receive Him on the way to Jerusalem (see Luke 9:51-56); indeed, He demonstrates it for three years of ministry before the ultimate confrontation in Jerusalem with Pilate.

Paul waits for an invitation from the Jewish synagogue authorities before rising to speak in Pisidian Antioch (see Acts 13:14-16), and the people are so moved—by his eloquence coupled with his manner—that they follow them out of the meeting asking for more (see Acts 13:42-43). That pattern is repeated in Iconium (see Acts 14)—where the apostles perform many signs and wonders—because the Gospel is one of power and not mere words, but they do not neglect honor just because they can do powerful stuff. These events are what distinguish them from the sorcerers of Pharoah and the magicians of the Greco-Roman world.

In Athens Paul begins his address with praise for the Athenians as the religious people they are. Noting that they still worship the unknown God who had delivered them from a plague centuries earlier, he offers to identify this God in the person of His Son Jesus Christ. But the most dramatic—and radical—act of warfare by honor is performed by Jesus on the night of His betrayal and death.

The Lord of Life—knowing that each of His closest friends would betray him by their desertion in the face of danger—strips Himself and washes their feet before supper. This is the dirtiest and most humiliating task that can be assigned to a Jew—washing with his bare hands the feet that have walked through animal droppings in the road on the way to dinner. Yet Jesus knows that the crucial battles of ultimate warfare—although they may include the weapons of force and violence—are won by the invasion of heart that is a consequence of the radical and sacrificial love of God. He washes and then feeds them with His own hand as the opening shots of the greatest battle ever fought. And what looks like a vain exercise as He hangs butchered and deserted on an instrument of torture will bear fruit when He feeds them again on a beach of Lake Tiberias and sends them out as His ambassadors of reconciliation.

Resurrection and the coming of the Kingdom in power are the results of this kind of warfare—because this kind of warfare gives God absolute free rein in the affairs of His people. Other kinds of weapons—whether the whip with which Jesus clears the temple or the bombs and guns with which American forces seek to provide a platform for a republican form of democracy in Iraq—are useful only for clearing a space and providing an unimpeded opportunity. It is then that the real battle begins, and it is sometimes true that guns and bombs are of no real use even in that preliminary action—as when the innocent blood of thousands of martyrs brought down the iron curtain in Eastern Europe and the Marcos dictatorship in the Philippines. But whatever the circumstance, whenever God's people sacrifice their right to defend and attack—and to dictate the rules of engagement—God always does His best work through His best warriors.

The apostles of the Son of God are called to the exercise of bold humility in spiritual warfare. That means they are to be as nonchalant about their circumstances as they became following the initial expulsion from Jerusalem in the wake of Stephen's death. These men who cannot cast one demon out of one epileptic boy before Pentecost are preaching and cleansing cities while facing down crowds of religious men and hordes of demons after watching their friends stoned and beheaded on the other side of the harvest feast in Samaria and beyond. But it also means they must wait upon the Lord in humility until He gives them the order to charge the enemy and love on the enemy's victims even if their sores stink and ooze in the process.

I will never forget the man dying from AIDS in the Memorial Hospital of Danville who asked me for prayer one night. His sores—from Kapozi's Sarcoma—oozed and stank as he told me how he had contracted the disease in the years of his gay lifestyle and how the Lord had healed his heart and caused him to fall in love with the woman who became his wife—but had not healed his body of all the residue of a sin-filled past. He and his wife were at peace with letting him go, but he wanted me to lay hands on him and pray for his peaceful passing—and for the rest of her life here on earth.

I was frankly frightened of touching the man at all—I had two small children and a wife of my own at home. But I also heard the voice of the Lord in his voice, and I knew what I was called to do. I did something we are not supposed to do with the Lord—I bargained—and He cut me some slack, as He is always happy to do with His dependent ones. He knew I would obey Him, but He acknowledged that my ministry would be less than effective if my anxiety showed when I prayed. He allowed that, if it would make me feel better to wash my hands in as hot and soapy water as I could stand after the prayer, He would honor my obedience and protect me and my family at the same time. (We both knew that if the virus entered through a cut or scratch on my bare hands there was no way provided in nature to protect me.) I held the man in my arms as I prayed with he and his wife that night. I blessed them. I walked slowly from the room as we finished and after they blessed me and my ministry—right to the nearest restroom and the soap and water I could find there. Two decades later, I know I would behave in the very same way—in the boldness of His provision and the frightened humility of knowing my heart beats at any given moment only because He wills it.

This bold humility is the same equipment with which I prayed for Kaifafa's healing from paralysis in that Fijian emergency room—not believing that God would heal him but deciding that God cared more about what I did in obedience than what I thought and felt in a limited intellect as flawed as my emotions. It is the same thing to which He calls the woman of the streets who washes His road-soiled feet with her hair in Luke 7 and the guests at the feast in Luke 14 who jockey for position close to the head of the table (see Luke 7:36-50; 14:1-14). "For everyone who exalts himself will be humbled, and he who humbles himself will be exalted" (Luke 14:11).

In the Old Testament the children of Israel never lose a battle when they remember to exalt the Lord and practice preliminary protocol on their enemies. But let an Achan pollute the ranks (the anger of the Lord falls on the whole people in Joshua 7 when Achan disobeys the Lord and hordes some of the consecrated items from Jericho) and no good or victory ever comes of it. Let Gehazi, the servant of Elisha, exercise his greed to make a profit on the prophetic activity of his master when God has not called it forth, and leprosy will afflict him for a long time. (God passionately desires to prosper His people—and He does it across the board—but in His time and in His way.) And for a Jewish king—from Saul who falls on Mount Gilboa to Zedekiah who is captured and blinded after presiding over the fall of Jerusalem—when honor is not practiced, there is only suffering to come.

It never seems to matter whether Israel is numerous and well-equipped or no more dynamic than Jonathan and his armorbearer who take out the Philistine company in First Samuel 14. The only real difference between a successful king like David and a failure like Saul is that the one loved the gift of kingship—that he received from God—so much that he was willing to do anything to serve it, while the other loved the Giver of the gift so much that he was willing to do anything to serve Him. It is a difference of protocol—giving honor. That difference is decisive at any moment and in any circumstance throughout the Word of God.

GOD'S FINGERPRINTS LEFT ALL OVER

The best blueprint for warfare by honor that I have seen is in the first nine verses of Luke 10. Jesus sends the disciples out to serve in the towns and villages where He has not yet gone. He tells them to bless without prejudice the people they meet—because what God blesses He transforms. He tells them to hang out with the people and share their lives; for people do not hear wisdom when they have not grown accustomed to the sound of the speaker's voice and the beating of his heart in their midst. He tells them to meet the people's needs as He gives them grace in His Spirit to do that—knowing that His Gospel is one of restoration and revitalization before it is a message of instruction. (It has been so ever since the Father first led the children out of captivity in Egypt and then taught them His ways in the wilderness.) Finally, He tells them to bear witness to the faith that is in them—that is the essential purpose for which Great Commission Christians do everything that they do in the name of Jesus—but it is empowered and established on the shoulders of those Agape acts that precede it and make relationships for housing it.

This is just as true whether our task is prayer evangelism—what Ed Silvoso calls talking to God about our neighbors before talking with our neighbors about God—or the more direct evangelism that is actually illustrated in Luke 10. The one paves the way for the other as we are directed to pave a straight highway in the desert for our God, and if we function in prayer in a way that is inconsistent with God's game plan for ministry, we are building a house divided against itself. Prayer warriors who think their function is to tear down strongholds and curse the forces of darkness need to remember that God limits us to the weapons of Heaven.

When we practice warfare by honor we discover that God has been there ahead of us after all—leaving His fingerprints all over the culture in which we are called to serve. The first missionaries to Hawaii were appalled at the degradation of the pagan culture they encountered on leaving their ship. It was a culture that featured human sacrifice and a kapu system of such ferocity that a commoner could be executed for simply allowing his shadow to fall across the path of a member of the aristocracy. But because they came ashore in a spirit of bold humility, they soon learned that the traditions of 'Io included prophecy to the effect that 'Io had a son who had died for the sins of all mankind.

The prophets of 'Io told the people centuries before the missionaries arrived that they would recognize the people of the Son by their coming in a larger canoe than any Hawaiian had ever seen. It would feature square white sails (the Hawaiians used tan sails of triangular shape) and the canoe would anchor at a specified rock in Kailua Bay on the island of Oahu. The people would come ashore bearing the word of 'Io in a wooden box. It was just as the prophets foretold when the brig Thaddeus came into the bay in 1820. The ship was square rigged with canvas sails; the captain anchored alongside the prophesied rock, and the missionaries came onto the beach carrying a Bible in a wooden box. The Hawaiians who remembered 'Io and His prophecy welcomed the strangers—for whom they had waited nearly 1,000 years.

Even the Hawaiian language features the word, *aloha*, which in its original meaning says, "May the Spirit of the Living God be all over you." The word itself is a combination of three phonemes that represent Father, Son, and Spirit in Hawaiian. Just as He did in its most comprehensive form for the Jewish people in the Old Testament, God knew just how to prepare for His own revelation in the very fabric of a culture He created for the sheep of another flock.

God manifests Himself in and through non-Jewish cultures throughout the pages of Scripture as well. In Genesis 12:3, He declares His blessing over all the peoples of the earth through relation to His servant Abraham, and He is always as good as His Word. In that passage, incidentally, the Lord protocols or honors Abraham in advance with the blessing. Abraham's trusting obedience—his willing acceptance—of a fearful and completely unknown future returns the honor to the Lord.

The Wise Men who visit the manger in Matthew 2:1-12 are astrologers from Arabia and Persia by all respected accounts. God appears to them, in spite of their study of astrology, because their hearts were to seek Him in truth. And they walk across the desert, just as Abraham does, in the faith He gives them. (See Matthew 2:1-12.) Jesus heals the daughter of a Canaanite woman in Matthew 15 because she is so desperate for His love that she offers to lick the crumbs from under the table as the children of Messiah are fed (see Matt. 15:21-28). She knows enough of Him through prophetic revelation to recognize Him— but her pagan background does not inhibit her reach to Him or His to her. The Good Samaritan of Luke 10 would be thought such a renegade from the Covenant as to be a pagan and a foreigner in Jewish eyes (see Luke 10:25-37);

yet, he is commended by Jesus for following the same God-given law of mercy and hospitality that motivates Abraham to protocol the three angels back in Genesis. Peter's dream of the animals on the sheet (see Acts 10:9-23) prompts him to visit and baptize Cornelius and his family because the Roman centurion recalls enough of his own upbringing in the virtues of charity, piety, and service to care for the Jews in his district and to recognize Messiah by His signs and His wonders. When Paul speaks to the Athenians of God "in whom we live and move and have our being" (Acts 17:28), he enshrines in Scripture the words of a Cretan poet who wrote 600 years before the birth of Christ.

Jesus tells the disciples shortly before His death that He has sheep not of the Jewish fold—they are already His if we receive the implication—and He must bring them into the place of refuge as well. And He quotes His own prophet, Isaiah, in Mark 11:17 when He says that His Father's house is to be a house of prayer for all nations. The Isaiah passage makes it clear that—while we are called to read, learn, and digest the Word that is first given to the Jews—it is not a prerequisite for worshiping the Father, Son, and Spirit in His own house in spirit and in truth. Honoring the sheep of each fold that the Father claims is—on the other hand—a prerequisite for considering ourselves fruitful servants.

Reality is that we encounter a new culture each time we cross the street, let alone when we cross an ocean or a continent. The race we call human has been compartmentalizing since the fall of the tower of Babel—and more likely since Adam said of Eve, "It wasn't me that sinned; it was this woman you gave to me" (see Gen. 3:12).

Original sin is not a de-struction or a dis-integration of human nature; we lack the power to do that to what we have not created. But the original sin is the betrayal of trust—between the first persons and God—when they ate the one thing He told them to leave to Him—and between each other when they excused their own behavior by blaming the other.

Reality is that every sin partakes of betrayal to some extent. We substitute idols we can control for the authentic God who is beyond our control; we seek to manipulate Him (when we take His Name in vain); we trash His special day and dishonor the parents He gave. We murder, cheat on our spouses, steal, lie, and act on the envy in our hearts. Reflecting from this perspective we can see that the overwhelming spiritual pollution we call original sin is the accumulated weight of every betrayal in history under which we labor when we seek the face of God. It is not unlike trying to walk on the bed of the ocean—under the crushing weight of many miles of seawater. Our nature has not changed and our ability to walk is, theoretically, intact. But try walking under that weight. Or try reaching out to God when every moment of our history orients us to another direction and attraction.

The good news is He will not be inhibited by our history. He sent His Son to re-establish the connection between us by Himself bearing the weight of our sin—that ocean of inhibition between His righteousness and us. He says to Peter on their last night together before all things are made new, "Simon, Simon, satan has asked to sift you as wheat. But I have prayed for you, Simon, that your faith may not fail. And when you have turned back, strengthen your brothers" (Luke 22:31-32). He does not say that Simon will not betray Him by denying Him; He knows better. But He also knows that His Father will not let that betrayal be the last word or the end of the story. And even in the Old Testament times our sin was not the measure of our relation to God.

In that famous passage from Jeremiah 29, in which God claims that His plans for us are as marvelous as they are wonderful, He is speaking to the Jewish nation as it then existed—in the midst of apostasy and coming disaster at the hands of the Babylonians—not as it might exist if it embraces Messiah (see Jer. 29:11). He says in that same passage that when we seek His face we cannot fail to find Him (see Jer. 29:13-14). The fullness of our redemption will only come in the Son's incarnation, but the father's love for us is manifested every morning as the sun comes up, and He has left His fingerprints all over our lives as a reminder so that we can recognize Him when He comes. He has left behind gifts in each of our cultures—whether we are talking nation-sized, generation-sized, community-sized, or just plain old family-sized. Each of us has peculiarities that God redeems into particularities for His purposes.

But the fact remains that in every sin—every betrayal—we find what we found in Genesis 3 and that smarmy scene in the Garden. Adam and Eve dishonored God when they ate and each other when they blamed. The way back has always involved displacing dishonor with a renewal of honor. It took Jesus' death and resurrection to re-boot the system, but He expects us to act toward Him and toward each other like people made in that honoring image.

Jason was a great friend of mine when we both attended San Diego State University. He was everything I was not—a gifted athlete, a *lady-killer* of the first degree, and a young man full of confidence—or so I thought. He came from the beach culture of Southern California; our shared love of surfing was the touchpoint of our friendship. And—like me—he valued trust, honesty, and personal loyalty to friends above all other things. We shared an ambition to hitch-hike around the country—seeing it all—after graduation, but I had lost contact with him by the time I carried it out.

After more than two decades of occasionally wondering what ever happened to old Jace, I ran into him in the neighborhood in which my in-laws lived. By chance (if there is any such thing in the Kingdom) he owned a home about three blocks away from them. I went to his home that night to share some coffee and catch up on each other. When I arrived and he told me his story, I soon realized that the connection between us was both deeper and different than what I had always believed.

Like me, Jason had grown up in an addictive and utterly dysfunctional family. His immense self-confidence was a con he had been running all of his life, and he was deep in the throes of his own alcohol addiction. The culture we shared—for real—was still the attachment to the beach and to honesty—about everything except his terrible fear of life itself—and personal loyalty. He told me his wife and girls had left that very evening; they would no longer tolerate his drinking and the behavior that went with it; this night his commitment to honesty trumped his reliance on facade.

I had been doing substance abuse interventions long enough to know that you don't intervene on an addict alone. The process is a variation on the loving confrontation of a sinner depicted in Matthew 18:15-20, and it requires overwhelming but loving input from a number of people who both love and hold the addict accountable for the ways he will likely try to evade health. But I was all there was that night and the Lord seemed to be telling me to go for it with Jason. I breathed a prayer to the Lord to get me out of myself and into Him. I told Jason he was one of the men I would trust all of my life. I said that he was one of the best men I had ever known— and one of a handful that I would consider traveling the country with as a young man. I said that he was killing himself and that I wanted him to enter a recovery program the next morning. He said that he would—and he did. Two weeks later, we spoke again and I was privileged to lead him into abundant life in the Lord Jesus. It has again been some years since I have seen Jason. I know I will be spending eternity with him—and he will be drunk on the Holy Spirit, but not on wine.

How does this incident connect to warfare by honor, cross-cultural ministry, and all of that other stuff we are talking about in this chapter? It's not rocket science. My friendship with Jason was not based on what we did not have in common—his athleticism, for example. (It certainly was not based on his veneer of self-sufficiency.) It was based on what we did share—a love of surfing and personal trustworthiness— letting our yes be yes and our no be no. If culture is simply the values and habits and points of view that frame our lives—and it is—then we connected in those zones where our personal cultures would intersect. By honoring what I could appreciate of his culture—and by begging the Lord to draw me to those aspects of his person—I was enabled to reach him with the Gospel. And by addressing his immediate need for sobriety and hope first, I was merely following the formula laid out in Luke 10 to bless, hang out, meet needs, and share my faith in that order.

Looking for and acting upon the fingerprints that God has left on culture is a core method of engaging warfare by honor. The same principles were at work in the Native American children who attended the Kids Klub ministry that Diana and I began while still in the run-up stage of PrayNorthState. We hosted upwards of 50 elementary school aged children from a local public school on Wednesday afternoons at the church I was still pastoring at the time. (Some were Christians, but many were not.) About a quarter of the kids were of American Indian background. During the group time—before we tutored and helped them with homework—we would tell a story and lead them in three songs of praise. One week we returned from a conference led by Native people; we had a song in tow called "Gonoronkwa"—which is a Mohawk word meaning "good medicine." The refrain was "Yesu gonoronkwa," or "Jesus is good medicine." At least ten of the kids came up to me the first week we introduced and sang that song with them to tell me that they had never realized that Jesus loved them until He was singing to them in an Indian language! They told me they were proud of their heritage that day, and they wanted to know more about Jesus. I baptized several of them a couple of weeks later—and they began to tell their families about Jesus.

Warfare by honor is not always easy—or pleasant. Ask Moses—or Stephen or Paul or any of the apostles—then and now. Yet God always blesses us when we fight His battles in His way—His Kingdom come and His will be done.

Late in 2006 the Lord called me to attend the consecration of the new bishop for my division of my denomination. I was to stand in protest of the consecration of the new bishop—although there was zero possibility that my action would have any positive impact on the event or the process. The Lord told me to write out my statement and to observe courtesy and decorum however I might be treated.

The rules of procedure—of protocol—specifically provide for actions like the one I was called to perform. At a specified moment in the service the presiding officer asks if any present would like to object to the proceedings. When he asked I stood immediately and said that I would like to object. I was summoned to the platform and asked if I could make a brief statement. When I explained that I would have to read a statement that might require as long as two minutes to present there was a huddled conference off to the side and I was denied permission to read my statement—a clear breach of protocol. I left quietly, refused requests for interview from the press (reporters were welcome to copies of my statement), and wondered why the Lord had insisted on what was a waste of time and a sealer of my identity as designated irritant. I could not know until much later that my statement would be published on international web sites and would result in encouragement to many faithful Anglicans and an invitation to teach prophetic acts in an Anglican church in Glasgow, Scotland. I returned to Redding knowing only that I had done what God asked in the way He asked me to do it.

I still like it better when seeking and respecting the fingerprints God has left on a culture brings immediate returns that bless many—like the mission to Fiji in which my familiarity with the Hindu scriptures enabled me to respect the culture of my listeners at the same time I could tell them that—while Krishna gives them good advice in the Bhagavad Gita but offers no assistance in implementing it—Jesus will help them to do something that leads to abundant life.

I like it just as well when warfare by honor brings blessing like the time I was called to teach on a Native American reservation and I forgot to bring the protocol gifts I had planned to give my hostess as I began my first night's address. She and the elders were perfectly OK with my lapse, but I was so obsessed with making a proper presentation that I decided to drive home—for three hours—and return for the next night's teaching rather than remain in the home with the family that had planned to house me. A few minutes after I got home, made sure the gifts were in my car so that I could not forget them again, and settled into my own bed next to my own wife, there was a tap on our window. Our daughter, Malorie, had decided to make a surprise visit home from college. Had I not gone the extra mile to do proper protocol, I would have missed her visit. God always blesses us when we practice warfare by honor—one way or another.

A Kingdom in Pursuit

Jamie was a client of mine when I served my internship in marriage and family counseling during the year between Danville, Virginia, and Gilroy, California. He had been abused and molested as a boy, and when he took his anguish to his pastor, the man told him to keep quiet about it. He had developed a hatred for Jesus and for anything that reminded him of the Church; he made it clear in words of one syllable that he wanted nothing of me but secular counseling for the troubles in his marriage. His story made a great parable of reconciliation when I recounted it in *Living as Ambassadors of Relationships*; it is reprised here because it is a wonderful illustration of warfare by honor.

I pointed out—and he acknowledged—the word "Rev." on my business card that was just as clearly visible to him before he entered my office. I told him that I would respect where he was, but I would expect him to permit me to be who I was as long as I didn't whack him with the Word of God or lay some religious trip on him. He allowed that this was fair enough, and we began a seven month series of weekly visits.

I kept my word to him, but I would from time to time admit that I knew of no other way to make a point than by invoking Biblical imagery. I would proceed only with his permission at such times. We reached a point after a few months in which it seemed the best thing I could offer him was the ministry of inner healing; I told him frankly that I did not know how to do that without invoking Jesus as the author of that healing, and he gave me permission to proceed. It was another few weeks before he was ready to receive Jesus and begin a reconciliation process with his church—not because the institution deserved another chance but because Jamie needed to forgive for the sake of his healing. It is a moment of great joy when I led him—with his prior permission to even broach the subject—into an authentic relationship with the Lord Jesus Christ.

The sum of my contribution was engaging warfare by honor, respecting him where he was while holding out the prospect of being somewhere better. God's contribution was to chase him until he was ready to be caught.

When Jesus makes His first public pronouncement—it is found in Matthew 4:17—we read it as, "Repent, for the Kingdom of Heaven is near." But that is not what the Scripture says.

The Greek word we translate as "is near" or sometimes "has drawn near to you" is *eggiken*. It means "is pursuing you." Jesus says to the crowds who come out to see Him, "Repent, turn about, for the Kingdom of Heaven is pursuing you." Yet we know that God takes no one by force—He waits until we privilege Him with the Lordship He has earned on the Cross. That is why warfare by honor is His path to the transformation of our communities into provinces of His Kingdom.

Yahweh states clearly,

> *And foreigners who bind themselves to the Lord to serve Him..."These I will bring to My holy mountain and give them joy in My house of prayer. Their burnt offerings and sacrifices will be accepted on My altar; for My house will be called a house of prayer for all nations." The Sovereign Lord declares—He who gathers the exiles of Israel: "I will gather still others to them besides those already gathered"* (Isaiah 56:6-8).

Why do we imagine the Jews are called the firstborn of the Lord if there are not younger siblings to be treated in the same way? And why would we think the Lord would so emphasize the fact that He brought the firstborn out of Egypt when as yet they had not reached out to Him if He did not want us to know that the initiative to love was all His from before time and forever?

What would be the redemptive dimension of exile for the Jews as it is recounted in the Books of Daniel, Esther, and Nehemiah? Never mind the consequences of sin for their idolatry—God is not forced to change His plans by our behavior, however rich with consequences for us it may be. Yet, His plan for world evangelism is prototyped in the behavior of

Daniel and his friends—worshiping the Lord in crisis following emergency—as they demonstrate to foreigners in a foreign land what it means and what it portends to serve this Lord—even drawing the emperor of Babylon to faith. His plan to conduct warfare by honor all over the world is revealed and field tested in the behavior of Esther and Nehemiah toward their Persian masters as they bear witness to the faith that is in them after a time of blessing, hanging out, and meeting needs. And God thinks that time in Babylon to be of such surpassing value that He chooses to reveal His plans for the conclusion of history to Daniel and Ezekiel—His servants in exile.

The letter to the Galatians was written to sheep of other flocks. The Galatian Christians were falling for the teaching of some false prophets who had come from Jerusalem. Paul reminds them that they are children of the promise given to Abraham precisely because they have believed the promise. He says, "Understand, then, that those who believe are children of Abraham. The Scripture foresaw that God would justify the Gentiles by faith, and announced the gospel in advance to Abraham: All nations will be blessed through you" (Gal. 3:7-8). He follows it up in the next chapter with, "But when the time had fully come, God sent His Son…" (Gal. 4:4). The Galatians had no history of Law with God; He simply sent the Son to gather in as many as would come because the whole New Covenant can be summed up like this: Jesus has the last word and that word is, "I love you. I don't care where you have been or how long you have been there; I only want to know if you will come with me now."

The law and the prophets are the clearest fingerprints God has ever left anywhere—that is why we cherish the Old Testament as the Word of God that it is. But it has never been about worshiping Law or Prophetic utterance. It has always been about following the fingerprints back to the One who leaves them to draw us home.

One of my favorite films is *The Gods Must be Crazy II*. It tells the story of two children of the Kalahari Desert in Africa. The Bushman father of the kids has always taught them that God specially prepared the Bushmen to find food and water in the desert where others would not know to look. But the catch is that they are to stay away from things that clearly do not belong in the desert. (Sounds a lot like the Garden of Eden and that pesky tree of life.) One day a water truck is passing through and its drivers stop to relieve themselves. The children climb onto the truck out of curiosity and, when it moves, they fall into the tank.

The drivers take off, unaware of their uninvited passengers. When the father comes looking for his children, a quick check of the signs in the sand tell the story of what has happened. The father does not—however—respond to the news with, "I told those kids to stay away from what does not concern them!" Neither does he hang his head and say, "Oh well. They're gone now, and who knows where they'll end up. There's nothing to be done now." In fact, he doesn't say anything. He simply begins to run down the track left by the wheels of the truck. He runs for three days and three nights—without stopping until he finds them— because it is his children in danger. He behaves just like our Father in Heaven, Who says through His Son, "Repent, for the Kingdom of Heaven is pursuing you." Nothing will ever change His passion to pursue us until we permit Him to catch us.

Warfare by honor is nothing more or less than our cooperation with the Father's pursuit of the lost. The more we cooperate, the more thoroughly He finds and retrieves and
transforms us as well as the others after whom He is chasing.
That is the beauty of it.

Every story I tell in these pages—from miracles in Fiji to
FaithWorks Coalition, from praying on the Custer Battlefield
to Jesus Culture on the streets of Redding—is a story of God
with warfare by honor at its core. Yet, one of the most
poignant honor stories I know happened at a 2002 Christian
concert event in which local businesses brought in top flight
nationally known bands alongside local ones—the criterion
for inclusion was whether you could draw a crowd and
whether you would witness while you played. More than
3,000 young people were touched that weekend—including a
small group of satan-worshiping musicians who set up outside the convention center with amps—just to disrupt us if
they could. We walked out to them, singing "His Name is
Wonderful," and asked them how we could bless them. Their
shocked response was, "You aren't angry. We thought you'd be
angry. This is the first time Christians have ever loved us."

Transformation is a process, and it is radically incomplete in all of the places I describe—but it is underway by
the grace and provision of Almighty God. And it begins
right where God told each of us to abide way back in
Micah 6:8: "For He has showed you, O man, what is good.
And what does the Lord require of you? To act justly and
to love mercy and to walk humbly with your God." Jesus
puts it even more simply when He says, "I give you a new
commandment, that you love one another" (John 13:34).

It begins with honoring one another as we earnestly seek the face of the Lord our God.

Endnote

1. Daniel I. Kikawa, *Perpetuated in Righteousness* (Keaau, HI: Aloha Ke Akua Publishing, 1994).

Chapter 7

A SEASON OF UNUSUAL

MIRACLES

On a recent trip to New Zealand I was awakened from a sound sleep by the sound of my wife, Diana, saying, "Oh no!" It was not a dream, or telepathy, or even a prophetic revelation; I heard her cry out and it woke me up. When I reached her by phone and asked her what had made her cry out she said, "Let me tell you about that." It turned out that she had simply over-slept—it was five hours later in California—and said, "Oh no!" when she saw the clock by her bedside. But the Lord's purpose in connecting us in that way was simply to reinforce the reality that He is our connection; distance does not matter. It was a miracle—albeit an unusual one—with a message.

When Diana and I were in Scotland we rented a car and re-turned it the next day. When I attempted to pay for the fuel we had used the agent said, "But Sir, there is more petrol in the tank now than when you took the car out." Agencies don't make mistakes like misreading gas gauges, but God has an agenda to remind us that—like the 12 when Jesus first sent them on mission—we should expect to be provided for as we seek His Kingdom. And because we need constant reminding He showed me a bottle of anointing oil—the one I had used in Scotland—twice as full when I took it from my car's glove compartment in California as when I put it there on our return to the States. These are not the sort of miracles we usually expect, but we are in a season of miracles as unusual as they are incidental to what seem like larger issues and concerns. God is getting glory for Himself through these miracles while we get a message.

Unusual miracles are most easily described in terms of what they are not.

They are, generally speaking, unsolicited. During our time in Scotland we had planned to gather a team and visit the battlefield at Culloden—the Scottish equivalent of the Little Bighorn. Our plan this year was to assemble a team of British and Scottish prayer people and fulfill the instruction of the Lord to make reconciliation by blessing the English who fought there. When the team unraveled and we found ourselves preparing to worship with only our assistant, Elizabeth, to accompany us, we were at peace with it. Yet without our asking, God orchestrated our lodging; we were hosted by a direct descendant of the English soldiers of Culloden. David went with us to the battlefield representing a family who—unlike those who merely pillaged after battle—remained in the Highlands to serve the people over two and a half centuries.

I did not ask the Lord to awaken me at 3:00 in the morning so that I could hear Diana's voice—had I thought of it, I would have requested a daylight connection! But these miracles come as an unexpected token of God's overwhelming love for us—and His unspoken inquiry as to whether we are paying attention.

Unusual miracles are usually uncompelling—we can explain them away if we are so inclined. In Fiji, when I was called to the hospital to pray for Kaifafa after his paralyzing accident, I had also planned to pray for a woman recently blinded by diabetes. I believed that visiting hours began and ended an hour later than was actually the case. When I got to the hospital, it seemed as though the Lord wanted me to visit the blind woman first, although the injured man was clearly the greater emergency, and I thought I had plenty of time for both of them. I followed the nudge and went to see the woman; she was healed instantly after prayer. But it turned out that visiting hours were nearly over; I would not have been permitted on her ward later.

After praying with her I went to find the young paralytic. When I arrived he was about to be taken to x-ray; half a minute later and I would not have been permitted to see him either, but two minutes earlier and I would not have found him. Kaifafa was so thoroughly healed within ten minutes that the x-rays showed no indication he had been injured at all. Clearly his healing—and that of the blind woman—are miracles of the most dramatic kind. But the incidental and unusual miracle was God's ordering of both visits without which there would have been neither praying nor healing on that day.

God's timing of both visits was as precise as it was perfect; my role was to obey the Lord's prompting even—and all the more—when it was counter-intuitive to the max. My choice was to explain away the nudging as coincidental, or to depend on God by acting in the incidental and unusual prompting He placed before me.

Just as undemanding—unless we are predisposed to see God's hand at work—is the sign of an inch-and-a-quarter rainfall in my home city of Redding in the middle of July—where everybody knows we are in severe drought and rain never falls in the summertime even when we are not. Anyone could rationalize the fact that our mission team in Fiji sounded like a professional choir each morning as we sang the Doxology at worship even though we had never met or sung together before. Message received: God really wants us at this time to be seeking first His hand in all of our adventures.

A third feature of unusual miracles is that they are frequently unspectacular. We all love to shout from the rooftops when God heals blind eyes and deaf ears; it is wonderful to watch a leg grow out or a tumor disappear. Not so dramatic are signs like the level in a speaker's water glass that does not lower after fifteen or twenty big gulps—that happened in a recent Northern California conference—or the fact that some pastors in Scotland thought it important that we meet their leadership even though we were not scheduled even to be in the country at the same time—and suddenly we found that we and they were arriving at Glasgow Airport at precisely the same time on different flights. Message #1: Are we seeking God's face only in the speaker's teaching or in every dimension of the time and place appointed? Message #2: Are we leaning on God or on our own understanding of what can be orchestrated for His Kingdom?

More than three hundred people prayed daily this summer for a reduction in traffic fatalities and—while fatal bike crashes are skyrocketing around the state—there were at least three NorCal collisions during this period in which the bike was totaled and the riders walked away with minor injuries. Supernatural prevention of the crashes would have been spectacular; handling them as He did was simply God telling us softly that He is calling each of us by name. (He might be telling the bikers to slow down as well.) The message is the same as that given to Elijah three millennia ago—listen for the still small voice and recognize in it the Word of God.

All of this asks us to reason against the logic we have invented in our fallen state. It requires us to keep our eyes on Him instead of on our project—even if we really did consult Him at the beginning. He wants us to keep in contact, continuing in His fellowship moment to moment so that we can come to know truth and be set free.

DOING A NEW THING

In Scotland this year Diana and I saw an unusual miracle played out on a strategic Scottish moor. As we prayed for the revival of our ancestral homeland we saw two male deer grazing and hanging out together. The older looked for all the world as though he were mentoring the younger. It was unsought, uncompelling, and unspectacular—and it is a phenomenon that does not normally occur in nature. (Bucks come together during the mating season and only to fight over the females.) Our hearts were drawn to Malachi 4, in which God connects calling the hearts of the fathers to the children as a precursor to revival and transformation.

On our return to the States, one of our intercessors related that she had seen the same miracle on the road from Redding to Weaverville, a town in the next county. Since then I have heard a similar report on the same road heading out of Redding in the other direction, and while writing these chapters, I personally witnessed two bull elk—fully racked—hanging out together in a field in the Scott Valley of Northern California. I have long believed that God is linking the calling forth of His Kingdom in regions like Scotland and Northern California. His promise in these signs is real, and it is clear.

But what is God doing, and what are we called to do about it?

The Letter to the Hebrews tells us that our God is the same yesterday, today, and tomorrow—and the Word is true (see Heb. 13:8). But God tells us in His Word over and over again that He is doing a new thing (see Isa. 43:19)—and that word is also true. Paradox is what we get when we live in the space held by two equally true statements that appear to contradict one another. It is the reality that can only be expressed in that space. The Father dwells outside the creation in light inaccessible from before time and forever. He is fully present on earth to all who truly seek Him; He invades time to meet with His people who call upon His Name. The Son is fully God and fully man. He truly died, and yet He lives. The Spirit is 100 percent God and 100 percent complete when we receive—yet not at full potency in us at that time. God loves paradox.

The Lord shows His commitment and delight in doing a new thing over and over again in Scripture. In Psalms 40 and 98, He calls His people to sing a new song to Him and to each other about all His marvels. He raises the first kings of Israel—Saul and David—from the least of the Hebrew tribes, and He brings His Son forth from the most insignificant of their cities. In Isaiah 42:9, He declares the coming of Messiah with a shout that the former things have come to pass; now comes the new; He announces that His people will be called by a brand new name in Isaiah 62, and in Isaiah 65, He calls for the creation of a new heaven and a new earth—but He promises that this new heaven and earth—and the new name for His people—will endure and not change in Isaiah's last chapter. Jeremiah 31 and Ezekiel 11 promise a new covenant and a new spirit for the people, and the best news comes in the New Testament on which this covenant is grounded.

In John 13:34, Jesus issues a new commandment to his disciples—that they should love one another. (Never again will the people of God be able to get by with simply doing no harm to one another.) In Acts 5, the angel who releases the apostles from a Jerusalem jail orders them to stand in the temple courts and proclaim the new life in Christ Jesus; in Second Corinthians 5:17, we learn that in Christ we are a brand new creation; and in Colossians 3, we find that new self is to be worn like a garment as we are progressively re-made into the image of our Lord and King. The Jews used to enter the holy of holies—in the person of their high priest—through the blood of dead animals, but Hebrews 10:20 says that there is a new way through the living Body of the Messianic High Priest. But as new as all this will be—and is—it is ever and always the same with God.

All of the heavens and all of the earth have been proceeding toward this climax of creation since the beginning. When God called Abraham to go to the land He would show him, it was the beginning of the same Galilee journey on which God has taken me and every other Christian who will come when he is called; it is the same journey on which Jesus took the 12 when He first said, "Come, let us go to Jerusalem." When God told the Hebrews to mark their doorposts with the blood of a lamb so that they might be spared when the angel of death came, it was a clear foreshadowing—in retrospect—of His plan to mark our bodies with the blood of the Lamb and to lead us into abundant life—with plenty of time spent with Him in the desert into the bargain. And when He led them through the water of death into new life on the other side of the Sea—with the Egyptians in hot and deadly pursuit—it was their first taste of a baptism of repentance (which means turning away from the old and into the new) for new life in covenant.

God has been building the prophetic community of His Body and Blood since the first Pentecost after the resurrection of the Son; this is not new, but the vocabulary with which to talk about it is decidedly new. Revivals in various parts of the world, and in various epochs of salvation history, are not new—averaging about one in every generation—but averaging at least one in every decade is radically new, and it is just what He has been doing for the past generation. Outbreaks of demonstrable and documentable miracles are not new—but the ease and the speed with which God is distributing His gifts without regard to Church pedigree—are we charismatics or evangelicals or liturgical types—do we pray in tongues or just plain English or in dance or in silence—is astoundingly new.

Let me say again that I don't know whether the Lord will return in a few weeks, a few months, or a few centuries. But clearly the intentionality and variety of Holy Spirit activity is rising exponentially. Just as clearly this can only be due to the fact that the Lord has been waiting for His bride to prepare Herself—with fruit in keeping with repentance—for 2,000 years. He is saying in as many ways as He knows how, "I am coming soon—as I understand soon—and you need to be ready as though I were coming tomorrow—as you understand tomorrow." In this season of incidental miracles, He is trying to prepare us for glory—and asking if we are paying attention or setting the alarm clock and taking a long winters' nap.

One of the things He is calling out of us—if the signs of the deer and the elk planted in two regions are any indication—is a commitment to partner with Him and with each other— with the other—whoever and wherever the other may be. It is First Corinthians 12 activated and actualized way beyond the limits of our imagination.

One of the new things God has been doing in my life that is the same old thing He has called out of me for years concerns my relationship with the author, Thomas Cahill, a man I have never met or contacted. Cahill has written such modern classics as *How the Irish Saved Civilization* and *The Gifts of the Jews* with a scholarship that is both massive and completely accessible alongside a style that is engaging. The former title put me onto the track of my ancestry as a field of ministry as well as the joy of finding lost roots; the latter triggered many of the paradigm shifts I try to explore in this book. But the thing that most entirely blows my mind about Cahill is how much I respect him even as I complain about his penchant for judging the authenticity of the Word of

God coupled with his profound belief in a real-time and real-world God who is indeed revealed in that Word. The new thing God calls of me that He's been saying for years is to judge not lest I find myself being judged.

Cahill will tell me—and his other readers—that much of the Genesis narrative is indebted to the earlier epics of Sumeria because of—for example—the shared traditions of a great flood followed by the rescue of a righteous man and his family, instead of believing (as I do) that the flood narrative so many cultures share is simple evidence that the flood happened pretty much as the Bible describes it. He seems almost smug when he informs that the parting of the Red Sea was really set in a marshy area—location unknown—and that loss of life on the Egyptian side was probably much lighter than the Exodus narrative claims after filtering through many generations of story tellers. Yet he can turn around and speak with profound conviction that the song of Miriam—danced after Yahweh's great victory over Pharoah—can only be a historically real experience. He writes of giving Torah that the commandments are so rational, simple, and compelling that they can only be the blessing of an almighty and completely just God—one who is not infected with human sin. He is convinced and convicted that God indeed spoke to Moses and the prophets and they relayed pretty much what He said.

He tells me things about the God we both serve that I have never before known. He believes our God is a God of miracles, even if he wants to re-write some of the details—and he believes from within the very textual criticism that so often debunks them. He reveals to me that the Jews—through their covenant relationship with Yahweh—literally invented history as we know it today. Before Abraham left Haran all mankind knew life as a turning wheel; nothing ever changed because no one ever moved away from the bondage of existence. After that departure at the command of the Living God, life has become an adventure and a journey—with room for both triumph and disaster—and Cahill argues that—with all of the errors and conflicts he ascribes to the Bible—only an authentic encounter with an almighty God who actually loves us (no pagan god ever did that) could account for such a sea change in human understanding. He says that Abraham's departure, and Moses' acceptance of call, are the most courageous things he has ever seen—and only an authentic God above all Gods could inspire them. He says later that these facts alone should bring believers and unbelievers to their knees—and he has access to pre-believing people who would never open a book written by a man like me. It is an unusual and incidental miracle to know his work and be blessed by it.

We used to think in the Church that the peoples of other lands and cultures needed us to bring them the Gospel—and it is surely true that those who have are called to give to those who have not. But we also believed that since we had received the Gospel before them God must somehow favor our culture over theirs. We believed our own translation of the Great Commission that we were to be "teaching them" rather than the more correct rendering of the Greek as "teaching one another" to observe all things that He has commanded. God is showing us more and more of our mutual need to hear and to share what He has lavished across the cultures.

The Great Commission—as we find it in Matthew 28—is actually a narrative in three parts. First the disciples do as Jesus has told them, going to the mountain and worshiping Him when they see Him, despite the fact that some have doubts. The

Son of God has no problem with honest doubt of the kind displayed by Thomas; He calls us to bring our doubts to Him so that He can resolve them as He did with the man who first addresses Him as both Lord and God. He objects only to those who hide their doubts in a mask of pretended piety and so place themselves beyond healing. Thomas Cahill, like his namesake of the apostolic band, plays no such games with King Messiah.

The second section holds the call to now go out into all the world and make disciples—learners and followers—of all nations and tribes. This is to be accomplished in the mutual immersion of baptize-er and baptize-ee in the water of life which was the exclusive method of baptism in the first century, and in implementation of the word *edukos*—teaching one another—all things that Jesus has commanded. For the Greeks all learning emerged from a mutual drawing forth of what God has planted in the souls of His children. While the teacher indeed orchestrates the process, it is a process of relation and sharing of gifts.

The third and final part holds in it the best news of all—Jesus' promise that He will never ever—and that means ever—leave us alone as we walk out His vision for a Kingdom set up in the midst of our participation in Him and in the community of which He is the Head.

I hope to meet Thomas Cahill some day. If I do I hope I will praise God for him and for his value to the Kingdom before I begin to tell him of all of the mistakes he makes in his analysis of the Word of God. That too would be an unusual miracle.

When God tells the returning exiles to let their hands be strong as they prepared to build the new temple with their own hands instead of the hands of the slaves that built the first one (see Zech. 8:9-17) it is the same thing He does when He permits the apostles to be expelled from Jerusalem so that His strength can be perfected in their weakness and they can bring the Gospel to Judea, Samaria, and all the world. And so when He calls two buck deer to commune together on a Scottish moor—or on a Northern California meadow—in the sight of some of His little ones—He is doing a new thing, a thing not seen in the very nature He creates and has created. But He is also doing the same old thing He promised in Malachi 4 when He said the precursor to His coming would be turning the fathers' hearts to the children and the children's hearts to the fathers. The fulfillment of promise that is new and yet old comes in the midst of a culture that increasingly denigrates the central role of fatherhood—due in large part to the many failures of fatherhood—and so it comes not a moment too soon.

A History of Unusual Miracles

The first time I began to use the vocabulary of unusual miracles was during the first reading of the Bible over our city in 2003. Diana and I took the first site captain shift—the one beginning at 6 A.M. on the Monday preceding the National Day of Prayer. We were sure we had prepared everything for success—we had lined up site captains to oversee every three hours of the event, we had our permits, and the porta potties and snacks were ready for the people reading during the wee hours. We had readers signed up for every one of the 312 15-minute slots over the three and a half days. But would any of them show up? It was the first time, and there was no one at City Hall at dawn besides us—and eight Canada geese foraging for their breakfast on the lawn in front of where we had set up the lectern. I stepped to the lectern at the appointed hour and began to read, "In the beginning God created the heavens..." and it happened.

The eight geese marched over to stand at attention about a dozen feet in front of where I was reading the Word of God. For the next 30 minutes they stood and listened to the Scriptures being spoken over their world, and then they flew away. I found out later that—in terms of biblical numerology—the number eight is significant for new beginnings; I certainly thought of this reading as a new beginning for our ministry and for our city. But the plain teaching of this miracle is a trumpet blast from the Lord. "If they keep quiet the stones will cry out," said Jesus when He made His triumphant entry into Jerusalem (Luke 19:40). God used a donkey to speak His word (see Num. 22:23-31); surely He intends for us made in His image to proclaim it! "The heavens declare the Glory of God," says the Psalmist (Ps. 19:1); surely we can do this and do it with joy.

From that moment Diana and I were determined to sow that teaching back into the escalating miracle by making the proclamation of God's good news as public and as frequent as we could—in any and all venues. The expansion of our radio and television programming, the conduct of September 11 commemorations in the Name of God at the county courthouse, the annual seeking—and receiving—of Culture of Life proclamations from our County Board of Supervisors, the rallies for life in the city hall plaza, and the facilitation of a GodTalk feature in a regional secular newspaper are just some of the ways we have tried to sow this teaching back into the Kingdom.

The Bible reading was the first time I found the vocabulary for these unusual miracles; it was not the first time I encountered one. A year earlier PrayNorthState facilitated a visit to Northern California of some Messianic Jewish people from Israel. As a climactic moment in that visit we gathered with our guests and leaders and intercessors from across the Body in Shasta County on the bank of the Sacramento River in Redding's Caldwell Park. We worshiped the Lord, listened as His word was spoken over our land, and we celebrated His supper together. We poured a bottle of water from the Jordan River into the Sacramento, and we gave our guests a bottle of water collected that day from the headwaters of the Sacramento River. We believed the connection of Northern California with Israel was especially ordained by God—at least in part—because Israel sits above the largest natural aquifer in the world and Northern California sits over the second largest.

Arnie Klein—who at that time, with his wife, Yonit—operated a 24-7 ministry center for worship and prayer in Tel Aviv—the center of communication in Israel—told us that a few weeks prior there had been a gathering in Israel of 40 Messianic rabbis. Their purpose was to generate a full-page ad for the Jerusalem Post expressing the solidarity of the Messianic Jewish leaders with the government and people of Jewish Israel. Klein pointed out with laughter in his voice that it was a major league miracle getting agreement on the wording of anything from 40 Jewish rabbis. But the unusual miracle became evident when I did a quick head count of the group on the river bank—there were 40 of us worshiping the Lord and praising Him for His people Israel.

God says in His Word that He cannot and will not forget His people Israel as He comes to possess His own and what He has earned as His own. The teaching in this event is obvious—God wants the younger brothers to reach out to the older, and the time is short—whatever that means in God's idea of time. We need to sow seed with our brothers the Jews, and that begins by honoring them before we begin to exhort them—just as God spoke to me about Mr. Cahill.

Two of the most profoundly unusual miracles we have seen were displayed for us in 1998 within a month of each other. Diana and I made our first trip to Maui that spring, although it was by no means our maiden voyage to Hawaii.

We spent our honeymoon there in 1975, and I fell in love with the people of Hawaii—the kanaka moile who inhabited the Kingdom when Captain Cook arrived in 1778. They were not the original Hawaiians—known today as the menehune—but 14th-century immigrants from Tahiti who wiped out the worshipers of 'Io and introduced the gods of Tahiti. With their gods, they introduced Tahitian practices that included human sacrifice and the kapu system. The people who welcomed the missionaries in 1820 were a small and fragile remnant of the original settlers and keepers of the prophecies regarding 'Io's son. I fell in love with the people on that first trip, but Diana had loved them since she was a little girl listening to a radio program called *Hawaii Calls* in her home in Illinois—long before she ever laid eyes on the people she loved and prayed for.

It was a heartbreaking thing to love the people of Hawaii as we did. They have legitimate grievances against fair-skinned people like ourselves—not the least of which is that we have exploited and crushed their culture for centuries through whalers, merchants, soldiers, and—after the first glorious wave of servant-hearted people—missionaries. In 1893, backed by a U.S. Navy cruiser and a company of marines, we stole their country and made a prisoner of their queen. The Hawaiian people—who need our tourist dollars and our business and military interests for the support they bring—hold us at arms length in their personal lives. They wait on us hand and foot when we stay at their hotels, but they largely shun our efforts to enter close relation with them.

Knowing some of Hawaiian history as we did, it was even more frustrating to love them and at the same time believe that they had squandered their assets and set themselves up for the 1893 takeover through the greed and debauchery of their leaders. The sandalwood forests that had all but disappeared by the 1850s were sold by the son of Kamehameha the Great to pay for his parties; and their most beloved king of memory was an alcoholic who essentially turned his palace into a casino. But the fact remained that American business interests—with the collusion of our government—stole a kingdom that had never shown anything but kindness to our people. And the larger fact remained that Diana and I knew we were called to love and pray for a people who rejected our love and prayer simply because we represented a despised people in their eyes.

All of that changed dramatically in April 1998. On that trip we encountered Suuqinna in the airport and obeyed God's command to meet him only when God called the time and the place right. We answered God's call to go out and meet Jill and Tia at the mall—just because God said to do it now. And Diana was given a vision of the angel who guards Maui and instruction to paint the angel and present it as a gift to the people of Maui. A series of events had been set in motion by God—partnering with us in obedience to some of His more oddball instructions to us—that would bring us into the Hawaiian *ohana*—immediate family. Learning of the 'Io Project alone would transform our understanding of the nature and power of corporate prayer. The extended journey on which we had embarked when we thought we had been sent to Hawaii for rescue from burnout would permanently constitute us as ambassadors of reconciliation and Kingdom transformation.

The unusual miracle God sent on our last day in Hawaii confirmed all that we hoped and believed about this trip. It was well past the season for whale watching, as the driver informed us on the way to the airport and return to California. (I had mentioned that the only disappointment for me was that we had seen no whales.) We rounded a bend and there—in an offshore spot where the whales were never spotted—were two humpbacked whales leaping clear of the water. It was God's way of saying the vision and calling we received were indeed from Him and not the product of our grandiose imaginations—and we praised Him for it.

The message in the miracle was simplicity itself—none of them are rocket science. When we obey God just because we know it is God, everything really does change; until we do that, nothing will ever change.

The other unusual miracle that blasted my understanding of the Kingdom came a few weeks after our return to Redding. I was the master of ceremonies for the March for Jesus that year, and the organizers were concerned that we would have a small turnout for this opportunity to lavish public praise on our Lord and Master. The issue was heat—the march was scheduled for the middle of May, and weather forecasters were predicting an unseasonably hot 99 degrees for that day. Redding people are used to high heat in the summer months; they just deal with it. But in the middle of May!

Diana and I made up a small prayer vanguard team to walk and pray the march route from the parking lot of the downtown mall to the grassy area in Caldwell Park where we would hold a rally and picnic following the march. We begged God to bless the day and get glory for Himself as we wrapped ourselves in the Scripture from Joshua 1 in which the Lord promises Joshua that every place his feet fall will be given to him and to the people. We sang praises to the Lord and left the coming day in His hands.

The day of the March for Jesus dawned bright and fair. Temperatures all over Shasta County were just as the weatherman predicted—and without a hint of breeze to make things easier to bear—except on the march route. Temperatures for that mile and half strip leading from downtown to the park were in the mid-80s with a cooling breeze, and when we got to the park the river flicked up a better breeze and lower temps for us. It was a glorious day to give public praise to our Lord, and everyone who came out for it was treated to a much more pleasant day than were those who stayed home or did other things that day. The catch was that attendance fell from 1,500 the previous year to about 300 this time out. God showed up, but many of His people did not—and by not showing up they did not get to see Him showing off.

The teaching for this one is just as simple—and just as direct—as for the miracles we saw in Hawaii. You need to come out looking for God and His miracles—in season and out of season—if you want to experience them.

These unusual miracles have always been with us, but they are coming fast and furious in the past few months. Some have been very personal—like the coral pieces the Lord always enables me to find as a token for Diana when she is unable to come along to Fiji and even on one trip to Hawaii. If I don't have snorkeling gear that will enable me to see the pieces underwater, He has placed them literally beneath my toes as I leave the surf. Some have been just the encouragement needed at a time of crisis—and the medium in which doctrine is transformed. My friend, Larry, is the dentist on the Fiji missions; on our last trip he scratched his head in frustration over a tooth that broke as he was pulling it; he did not have tools to remove the twin roots staring up at him. Had there been only one root, he explained, he could have gotten to it, but two required special equipment that was unavailable in the ghetto in which we work. He looked at the ceiling—this man from a stream of the church where they just don't believe God works miracles today—and prayed, "Lord, I don't know what to do; you have to tell me." He looked down at the woman's mouth, and there was only one root to remove.

Some are meant to telegraph God's plan for a relationship. When two close friends of mine were recently married in another state, it rained all day on their special day and for a week before and after. They are both hardheaded and intense people, and their relationship has always been volatile. On the day of the wedding the bride was concerned that her hair and the hair of the bridesmaids would fall because of the rain. The groom was worried that the 75 monarch butterflies they planned to release after the service would not fly because of the rain. We all prayed for God's grace and mercy before heading to the church. When the car carrying Maria and her attendants stopped in the driveway of the church, the rain abruptly stopped; the moment they were safely inside, it began again with gusto. When Daniel led the wedding guests, stepping to the porch of the church to release the butterflies, the rain again stopped. All of the monarchs flew, and—once they were clear of the church—the rain came again like turning on a spigot. The God who graced a wedding in Cana for His first public miracle in human flesh had clearly spoken His heart over the marriage that was begun.

But the really unusual miracle comes later in this season of unusual miracles. Their relationship proved to be as intense and volatile as it appeared to be on the day they were wed. Within two years, they were actually meeting at an outdoor coffee shop to discuss their impending divorce when— out of season—a monarch butterfly landed on Maria's shoulder—an eloquent reminder of God's will for their marriage. There has been no further talk of divorce.

Most of these unusual miracles concern themselves with facilitating the Kingdom. From the deer spotted on the moor— and in the meadows back home—to the whales confirming our call to Hawaii, to the weather on the March for Jesus, God is calling the prophetic community to link arms and hearts and watch for the approach of the bridegroom. From the placing of Diana and me in the home of a direct descendant of the English soldiers who fought at Culloden—and who needed to see God's prophetic direction and activity for himself—to the water glass that would not empty in front of 800 people at a conference in Redding, God is saying that His miracles are for our edification and exhortation, but not for our entertainment. He wants a response—and we can't respond if we don't notice the call.

God wants to know if we are paying attention and if we are following up on the messages He is sending out wholesale in the signs and wonders He displays in our presence. Even—or especially—in the unusual terms of this time, His Gospel is one of power and not of mere words.

THE AUTHORITY OF THE UNARMED MAN

One of my favorite movies is the 1986 Peter Weir film *Witness*. It stars Harrison Ford as a Philadelphia cop investigating the murder of a fellow officer in the men's room of a train station. The only witness is an Amish boy whose own life is endangered when it turns out crooked cops may be the perpetrators of the crime. Ford hides the boy and then is forced to run with him when an attempt is made on his life as well. They reach the Amish community that is home for the boy, and the people agree to hide the wounded Ford at least until he can make some sense of the predicament they all share.

The plot develops as it becomes increasingly clear that Ford's character—John Book—cannot leave behind his life as what one Amish calls "being a basher," and he cannot understand how they can live so out of touch with the world as he understands it. The climax comes when Book beats a man who is abusing his Amish friends, thus drawing attention to himself and enabling the crooked cops to locate him. They corner him in a corn elevator and—after gunshots are exchanged and two men die, the crooked police captain has the drop on Book. But the Amish community has been aroused by this time and hundreds have run across their fields and through their groves to stand in silent witness as the captain threatens to shoot Book if he does not come along. When Book points out that there are too many witnesses and it is over—finished without the violence both Book and the captain think is absolutely necessary—we are treated to what Jesus might have called the authority of the unarmed man. The witnesses have expressed what Corazon Aquino achieved in the Philippines and millions of Eastern Europeans accomplished in their struggle to throw off the yoke of dictatorships of the right and left.

The authority of the unarmed man is not the only kind of legitimate authority—on this the Amish are mistaken. But it is the ultimate authority for which all other kinds must ultimately make way—it is the authority Jesus wields from the Cross.

Jim Lovell tells the story of the closest shave he ever had as a pilot prior to commanding Apollo 13. He was flying off a carrier in the Sea of Japan and on high alert because of instability in the region. It was night when his radio and all of his navigational equipment went non-functional at the same time. The carrier was darkened because of the high alert, and so there was no way to find his way back home using the technology on which modern warriors depend—and he would soon run out of fuel. While trying to figure his way out of the quandary, insult was added to injury—his cabin lights went dark. And God gave him an unusual miracle.

In the artificial brilliance of his electrical lights, he was usually unable to see the trail of phosphorescence kicked up by the plankton through which the great aircraft carrier passed as it tore through the sea. But without those lights, Lovell could see the path home laid out by the agency of some of God's humblest creatures. He also got a quick course in the authority of the unarmed man—in which God makes His strength perfect in our weakness.

One of the clearest scriptural pictures of this authority comes in Matthew 8:5-13. Jesus has just arrived in Capernaum and a centurion approaches him with a request to come and heal the soldier's servant who is paralyzed. Jesus agrees to go with the centurion, but the centurion allows as how that is not what he meant. "Lord, I do not deserve to have you come under my roof. But just say the word and my servant will be healed." He goes on to explain that he understands authority because he is a man under it. He then details not how he submits to it but how he exercises it, telling one to come and another to go—all without raising a weapon or even his voice. He can only know this because he submits in the same way to the authority of his cohort commander who submits to his general who submits to his emperor. There is power at the end of this chain of command; the foot soldiers have swords and spears to place at the disposal of their officers, but the authority is wielded as a matter of right and cultural disposition. It is the authority of the unarmed man—and Jesus marvels that before that moment he has not found such faith in the nation of Israel.

We make much of the planes and guns and tanks that wrenched Europe from the Nazis of Germany and the Pacific basin from the forces of Imperial Japan. But they were the power wielded by the authority of the unarmed men and the voices God gave them—men like Franklin Roosevelt and Winston Churchill. Silence those voices and the military machines and the peoples they defend lose their will and their skill to fight. Silence the voices of Ronald Reagan, Margaret Thatcher, and Pope John Paul and the Cold War continues today—or perhaps is ended in nuclear holocaust.

It is this authority on the part of God that enables the intervention of His miraculous signs and wonders—including the unusual ones that are the subject of this chapter. It is this authority imparted to God's servants that makes possible the recognition and application of the miracles God sends—in the same way that Peter walks on water in obedience to His master who walks on water. It is this authority that God exercises to heal another paralyzed man named Kaifafa when God's servant—me—does as he is commanded even though he doesn't believe the miracle is going to come. Talk about an unarmed man and strength made perfect in weakness!

This authority that His servants are called to wield as we make a straight highway in the desert for our God first came to my attention in the story of St. Magnus. Magnus was a Norwegian earl—a warlord whose father ruled the Orkney Islands off the north coast of Scotland in the Middle Ages. The father left the family estate to his son and to a nephew—leaving the stronger of the two to resolve the obvious dilemma of who really gets to rule. After several years of jockeying for position and raiding one another's holdings, Magnus contacted his cousin and asked for a parley. On the condition that neither would come with more than one ship or men at arms beyond a personal entourage, they agreed to meet at a cove known to both of them. Magnus came as promised, but the cousin sailed around the point with several ships and a small army. The outnumbered bodyguard told their lord they would sell their lives defending his, but their lord would have none of it. "It ends here," said Magnus, and if that means I go to be with Jesus, so be it. I am not going to be the cause of any more bloodshed."

When the cousin landed, he ordered Magnus' execution, but he had to go through several soldiers who refused to murder a man in cold blood before he threatened his cook with death if he failed in the beheading of the earl. Even at that, the cook was only willing to proceed after Magnus told him in advance that he would forgive him. The cousin ruled the islands until his death—and today the islanders barely remember his name while they celebrate Magnus—known for his care of the weak and the poor long before his martyrdom—every April 16.

Think of Peter and John before the Sanhedrin, exercising that authority as they honored the men who threatened them with death and left the meeting having said, "You will have to do what seems good to you and we will have to obey our Lord who said to proclaim His Name" (see Acts 4:18-20). They are acting in the tradition of Daniel and his companions who told the King it was alright to place them in the fiery furnace—they would worship the Lord their God whether He came for them or not (see Dan. 3). The Lord of both Daniel and the apostles— the one who said we must give up our lives if we would save them—is not looking for people to protect Him or His sheep from His own; He seeks only those who would serve Him.

The unusual miracles we see in the life of Paul come in his decision, when he is released from prison by the earthquake, to remain and minister to his jailers (see Acts 16:16-40); in his rejoicing in his chains because they afford him an opportunity to witness with his voice and with his pen (see Phil. 1:12-18); and in his enthusiasm for witnessing to the Roman governor and the Judean king when he could have been set free had he only not appealed to Caesar (see Acts 24–26). We can call them miracles because they witness so thoroughly to the supernatural transformation that has overtaken Paul's heart since the day he held the clothing of those stoning Stephen (see Acts 8:1). This is the authority of the unarmed man, and the Lord reveals it in a new way for such a time as this. We exercise that authority every time we pray for suicides to cease.

THE KINGDOM COMING—UNUSUALLY

Most of these unusual miracles have a bearing on preparing the straight highway in the desert for the coming King and for His Kingdom—although they are delivered in the most personal way and serve always as a sign of God's personal favor and concern.

What general revelation about His plans is God sharing in this season? Among other things, He is clearly changing the guard of leadership within the Boomer generation—which is currently stewarding the Body for the most part—at the same time He is raising up a Genesis Generation of teens and 20-somethings who have a passionate heart for their own generation first and for the whole world after.

These signs are for the most part being shown to and testified by a new class of prophetic persons. The buck deer and elk I described earlier are a gender and intergenerational phenomenon not seen in nature unless God plants them there. Likewise, they are clearly all about the Kingdom promised to Northern California and Scotland—and the fact that the Lord sends the same sign to be witnessed by members of the same ministry speaks volumes about His intention for linking the regions. But we need to pay attention to what God is doing outside of the box we have made for His miracles so that we actually see the deer and note the news.

The phenomenon of 40 California intercessors gathered on the river bank to bless the 40 Messianic Jewish rabbis—let's remember that 40 is considered a generation in Biblical parlance—is just as clear a telegraphing of God's plan for linkage on the Kingdom Highway. But what if no one saw anything suspiciously God-incidental about the event and decided to count the worshipers on the river bank? God is not playing games with us to see who strikes out first—He is revealing Himself in this way for a reason that will bless us if we cooperate and stay alert.

We have never been called to put our faith in our ability to hear His voice; it has always been about putting our faith in His ability to speak, from when God walked with Adam in the Garden to the moment He sounds His own trumpet on the last day. He is training us for a larger life than we can imagine, even as He looks after us with all the tender loving care that only He can express. While He is at it, He is asking not just whether we are paying attention to the teaching He reveals, but whether we are making a point of sowing it back into our life with Him so that we can partner in its escalation.

The Lord has shown a great interest in sprinkling the signs of His coming and His presence across the streams of the Church without regard to whether they have a vocabulary for revival and transformation—He is providing that vocabulary in what He is doing in our midst. From disappearing dental roots that plague a Presbyterian dentist on the mission field to healing a cancer through the prayers of a non-charismatic catholic to drawing latter rain type charismatics and Holiness-rooted evangelicals into a deepening appreciation of Holy Communion as the central event in which His disciples recognize Jesus, our Lord is crossing and re-crossing the lines we have drawn between us and making His revelation more and more of a composite phenomenon.

He is calling up unlikely prophets and making ethnic, denominational, generational, and all other kinds of reconciliation a burning priority—and He is insisting on mutual repentance for all of the idolatries and betrayals and dishonors we have heaped on each other over the centuries.

Matthew 25 contains three of Jesus best-known parables. The parable of the virgins calls us to remain alert—setting our alarm clocks will not do because we have no idea when He will return and He seems to like it that way. The parable of the talents reminds us that investment in the Kingdom is for its own sake—the one who risks and gives His life for the Kingdom, whether he has a lot or a little to give, is the one who will receive his life back in much greater measure than what he gave. And the parable about the sheep and the goats displays the fruit of relationship with Jesus against the fruit of a mere awareness of who He is and what He expects. But the story of the virgins goes in first because if we are not awake when He comes for us—at any time and in any measure— we will never have opportunity to invest or relate in these unusually apocalyptic times.

He says, "Therefore keep watch, because you do not know the day or the hour" (Matt. 25:13). He really wants us to pay attention to Him at this time and not to what we think we know about Him. May we have eyes to see and ears to hear.

Chapter 8

PRACTICING THE PRESENCE

Nearly 20 years ago a woman entered my office to say that she needed serious inner healing. She claimed that Jesus told her, "There is healing in the Eucharist," and that my church offered Holy Communion every Sunday. The woman remained to worship with us for about three months of Sundays, seeking healing prayer during the week. When the Lord had completely healed her heart, He also healed her knee—which had been scheduled for arthroscopic surgery—and she returned to the church from which she had come.

I alluded earlier to one of my favorite passages from the Gospels; it's in Luke 24 when two of the disciples are walking from Jerusalem to the little town of Emmaus on the afternoon of the first Easter Sunday. The newly risen Jesus falls in with them on the way, and they do not recognize Him as they talk. He opens the Scriptures to them as they walk so that they come to see how His every move and happenstance is predicted—they will say later that their hearts burned within them as they listened to the Word of God from His own mouth—but they still do not recognize Him. When they arrive at Emmaus they persuade their new friend to stay the night. As they begin the evening meal Jesus breaks the bread—as He did on the night before His death and as He has doubtless done on countless other evenings—and they finally see Him for who He is.

There is nothing magical about the Supper of the Lord and no guarantee that all of our illnesses will be healed when we partake of it—either instantaneously or over a period of months. But the supper is a profoundly iconic practicing of the presence of the Living Lord—because of His promise to be present whenever we do this thing for the remembrance of Him—and it is in practicing His presence that we come more and more into our destiny as people made in His image and likeness. It is His presence that heals.

I am blessed to be able to say I have never been afflicted with a dependency on alcohol or any substance, although addiction runs deep in my family of origin. So I was surprised when the Lord spoke to me a number of years ago and told me that He didn't want me drinking alcohol on any occasion other than celebrations of the Holy Eucharist—the Lord's Supper. He answered my question by telling me that He was not criticizing my social drinking, nor was He making a new law about liquor—abuse but not use is prohibited in Scripture—He was just saying that in our personal relationship He wanted no use of it except in remembrance of Him. I was happy to obey, and He has downloaded everything I now understand about a sacramental worldview and such things as His sacramental outbursts in the intervening years. The wedding of my friends Daniel and Maria (cited in the last chapter) was the first exception He made to that ruling—and I can count the others on the fingers of one hand.

The wedding was in another state, and as Diana and I were on the plane winging our way to it, I asked the Lord about my duties as best man. I allowed as how the best man was supposed to offer a toast to the bridal couple in champagne, and I wondered if He would permit me an exception to the personal ban for this occasion. (I admitted to Him that I knew I could do it in 7UP or even water; I just thought it would be nice to do it in the traditional way.) He gave no answer, and I approached Him again—this time acknowledging that I knew I could only drink on sacramental occasions, but wondering if this wedding were a worthy exception. It is incredibly rare for me to get an audible response from the Lord, but this time I distinctly heard a deep and growly voice, with just a touch of laughter in it, saying, "This is a sacramental occasion."

Sacraments are deposits on His promise to keep us with Him forever if we claim His Name on lips and in heart. They require His presence to become authentic deposits, and we need to practice His presence in order to recognize Him in these events—as Paul exhorts the faithful in First Corinthians 11:29-30. That is to say we are called to place ourselves regularly in His presence and to seek opportunities each day for that practice of the presence—the Eucharist (it means Great Thanksgiving) being an archetypal expression of the concept. Sacramental moments are always moments of worship, but they are also moments of reciprocity—when we can be as aware of His presence as He is always of ours—whether in the prayer closet, on the field of ministry, or in a cathedral. The Bible has no space to describe every conceivable sacramental moment, but it does offer us models—and ample direction on how important these moments are to the abundant life we are offered. John goes further than Paul, quoting Jesus to the effect that if we do not eat His flesh and drink His blood we have no part in Him (see John 6:53). Now that is practicing the Presence!

Daniel and Maria's wedding was sacramental to the max— the joining together of a man and woman to become one flesh and to take their place in the fabric of creation itself—as Jesus points out in His Mark 10 statement about the sanctity and centrality of the marriage covenant (see Mark 10:6-9). They practiced the Presence to the max as well—although they have failed to do so just as often as the rest of us since then; they have to keep coming back for do-overs—by committing everything to prayer—even rain and butterflies.

Jesus offers the first recorded sacramental moment in John 2:1-12—at the Wedding in Cana of Galilee. The party has run out of wine, and His mother asks Him what He intends to do about it. He tells the servants to bring several jars able to hold up to 30 gallons apiece, and by the time they have set up the vessels, the water has become wine—and not just wine, but the finest wine the steward has ever tasted. He exclaims—after he has drunk from it—"Everyone brings out the choice wine first and then the cheaper wine when the guests have had too much to drink; but you have saved the best till now" (John 2:10).

Jesus has not prayed over the wine; there are no gestures or incantations. His presence alone has brought about the transformation. And the catch is just as evident: the guests who made themselves drunk on what came before will be sleeping it off when the best wine is served—the wine of the presence of the Lord. Abundant life is available to all who confess Jesus as Lord—but it gets a whole lot more abundant right here on earth when we practice dynamically waiting on Him instead of indulging our own impatience.

What we need desperately to understand is that Jesus is at the wedding whether we see and interact with Him or not; that is Paul's point in First Corinthians 11. The guests have the choice to recognize Him—His identity is never veiled except to closed eyes and hearts—and to behave accordingly, or to see nothing but their own agenda and to behave according to that. We have had unlimited access to this God—even the One who says that His thoughts and ways are not ours—ever since Jesus died and rose for us—and the Old Testament prophets allowed as how we had pretty good access before that. (For we know what He expects of us in the way of loving justice and mercy and walking humbly with Him, says Micah, and when we seek His face we cannot fail to find Him, says Jeremiah (see Mic. 6:8; Jer. 29:13).) The question is always to what degree we will give Him access to us—Behold, He stands at the door and knocks. He is knocking on each of our individual doors, and He is knocking on the door of each congregation of the Body and—always—He is calling for the whole of His Body to become One as He and the Father are One.

On a family vacation some years ago we stopped in Pittsburgh en route to another place—just long enough to visit

Fort Pitt and look at the three rivers that intersect there. We were carrying much of our luggage in a cartop carrier, and the locking mechanism was two tiny padlocks without which we could not secure our belongings. As we prepared to leave I had to do something with the carrier before reclaiming the driver's seat and taking off through the bumpiest road I had ever driven inside a city. (It had been dug and scraped and trainwrecked prior to reconstruction—which had not yet begun.) Our teeth were bouncing around inside our mouths, and it was perfectly clear that anything not well secured would bounce away—never mind anything I had been careless enough to leave loose on the roof. And the Lord chose that moment to give me a vision.

I saw—with eyes wide open—the two little locks sitting loose on the car roof where I had left them when we set out. There was no way I could even pull over for several blocks, and so I decided that it was either entirely my imagination and I should let it go or it was indeed a vision from God and He would secure the locks until I could retrieve them. When I was finally able to stop, I went immediately to the place He had shown me on the roof and there were my locks—as steady and secure as if we had floated and they were bolted down. It was practicing the Presence in a very small way.

It was practicing in a bigger way when I was elected to Diocesan Council—the equivalent of a board of elders for an entire district—some years later. I was the only member of that council committed to a biblical worldview, and as the lone conservative, I was far more effective at influencing policy than any skill of mine could ever account for. The terms were for two years, and as mine was drawing to a close, I went before the Lord to see if I should run for re-election—which promised to be an easy task if I chose it. My concern was that I believed my congregation was in a season of needing my full attention, and I was not at all sure I could be faithful to them and still serve on this council. When I prayed about it I thought that was the direction the Lord was heading, although I saw neither burning bush nor tablets of stone. I believe in giving whatever I think is a word from the Lord what I call the 4-way test—and that is what I did.

The test is simple. Do I have peace about a decision I think the Lord has made? Have I consulted someone whose judgment and maturity in the Lord—usually Diana—I respect, and does that person also have peace? Does the opportunity come as a gift, or have I manipulated it into being? And—last but certainly not least—has God brought to mind a Scripture passage that is consistent with what I believe He is saying?

I told the Lord I would not run for re-election and waited. The reaction bordered on violent. "How can you think of bailing out on your brothers and sisters across this diocese just because they don't attend your little church? How dare you be so parochial in your thinking?" I sat back with the wind thoroughly knocked out of my sails and told the Lord I would seek His face on this some more. But over the next couple of weeks He still seemed to be leading me to give up the council seat, and so I told Him again that I would not seek re-election—and once again was hit by the arctic blast of what sounded like His anger. And then I remembered to ask—when had He ever spoken in hateful tones to me before? He has confronted me with many sins and stupid decisions in the 40 years I have known Him, but His voice has always been the voice in which I could hear and receive His love. Something was very wrong with this picture.

I spoke out loud that I was addressing the Lord my God and no one else. I commanded all voices other than His to be still and depart in the name of Jesus. I said one more time that I was not planning to run for re-election to the council. There was nothing there but His peace and—a few days later—His judgment, "I have called you to spiritual warfare, not administrative tinkering." I have profound respect for those who are called to political office—inside and outside the Church. But my vocation is different beyond those two years when I too was called to serve in that capacity. And His presence—whatever else it may bring—always brings peace because He comes in peace.

C.S. Lewis reportedly said that it is what we do in our solitude that makes us fit for company. That sense of being in company is illustrated in one of the rarely recognized Kingdom images—the one in Luke 11:5-13 where the friend comes in from out of town and pounds on the family door at some ungodly hour wanting bread. What we seldom pay attention to is the initial response of the patriarch who is rousted from sleep. "Then the one inside answers, 'Don't bother me. The door is already locked and my children are with me in bed. I can't get up and give you anything" (Luke 11:7). (Of course he does get up and meet the need standing at his door.) There are two crucial Kingdom lessons to be learned from this parable aside from the often preached one that God is never too busy to help us in need and neither should we be.

The first is that the intimacy of the shared bed is what the Kingdom is supposed to feel like. God really does want all of

His kids snuggled together with Him, and He does not enjoy leaving the fellowship for anything. It is this for which we prepare when we practice His presence in solitude—and in community. But the second lesson is just as important—God is never willing to write off any of His lost sheep. When one of us is knocking on the door He may wonder out loud why we weren't home when we were told to come in, but no power in Heaven or earth will keep Him from coming to the door and gathering us into His presence that we might practice along with the other kids.

What has this to do with transforming our culture into His Kingdom?

HOW WE PRACTICE

The Jewish people have always looked back on the wilderness experience as the pinnacle of their relationship with the Father—as rugged as it got and as often as they had to be disciplined during that time. It is in the Sinai wilderness that they are always perfectly aware of His Presence and can practice it—except when they willfully ignore it in favor of whatever golden calves they prefer at that moment. They still commemorate this time—when the Kingdom was promised but not yet present—with the Feast of Tabernacles, the name coming from the tents in which they lived.

There are actually three bases of emphasis in the Feast of Tabernacles. The second basis the Jews commemorate is their return from Babylon when the exiles rebuild the temple with their own hands—they had slave labor to do it the first time—and Ezra rediscovers and proclaims Torah from the steps of the new center of worship. The third is their own sense of helpless dependency on the Lord their God. This oblation of neediness is expressed in their fervent prayers for early rainfall; without it the crops will be neither good nor abundant. It is not rocket science to see that each of these foundations for the feast is grounded in an intimate practice of the Presence of God.

In the wilderness they were so dependent that they had to gather fresh food each day in a land that offered no food supply. The Lord promises in Exodus that He will send a substance they call manna (it is Hebrew for "whatcha-call-it") everyday, to be gathered from the ground. They are forbidden to gather more than a day's supply; when they try to store it they find that it rots by day number two—the one exception being when they gather on the day before their Sabbath and the extra day's supply remains fresh until the day following Sabbath (see Exod. 16:15-36). Water comes from rocks that Moses strikes (see Exod. 17:1-7), and they follow a pillar of cloud by day and a column of flame by night (see Exod. 13:21-22). They camp only when the pillar stops and they must move when it begins to move or lose their way in the trackless waste. In other words, they stay in the Presence or die in the desert.

The Babylonian Exile counts as the most serious corporate identity crisis of all time. The people of Yahweh knew that He had promised to establish the Kingdom with an heir from the family of David on the throne for all time and forever. They also knew—if they thought about it—that Moses offered life and death in terms of their adherence to Torah way back in the time of Deuteronomy. Had they remembered the death of virtually the entire generation that marched out of Egypt before seeing the promised land, they might not have needed the reminder of John the Baptist half a thousand years later that

God could make children for Himself from the stones beneath their feet. Had they remembered all of the revelation that was already theirs—including their Father's love of paradox—they would not have needed Paul's statement from Romans 8 that God brings good out of all things for those who love Him and are called according to His purposes to give them a clue that Jesus is in fact the unexpected King from David's loins (see Rom. 8:28). As it is they know only—and weep and wail only— that the land of their promise and their identity has been wrenched from them. They know that they have committed repeated idolatries, but this is a disaster beyond comprehension. In other words, they return to the Presence or die as a people.

Their need for early rains—like the poor—will always be with them. In the feast they celebrate that perpetual neediness, because at some level they know they need even that neediness to remind them to practice the presence of God on a daily basis. And so they practice and commemorate every year—and it is not enough practice to bring life.

Only John 7 records Jesus' appearance at the Feast of Tabernacles. It is an incognito appearance until halfway through the feast, for His time has still not yet come. He stands and acknowledges the power and the quality of their gathering— He is after all a Messiah who engages warfare by honor—before telling them on the last day that if they come to Him they will receive a spring of living water that will never run dry. This spring will—of course—enable them to practice His presence every day and for all time.

Tabernacles is considered a harvest feast—what the Greeks would call a Pentecost. Christians are called to celebrate Pentecost itself, and we need not confine our celebrations to the one great day on which the Church is born into but not of the world. When we celebrate Pentecost we are called to remember and renew that moment of being blasted by the Holy Spirit out of the upper room onto the balcony from which Peter spoke and out into the marketplace of Jerusalem. We need to remember that the events celebrated in the Jewish feast were and are a sacramental outburst—just as our Pentecost is such a burst— and that we are called into escalation of that outburst into Samaria and all the world. We are to practice becoming Christians of the Great Commission every day of our lives. Escalation is one of the prime features of Kingdom.

We are expected to practice that process of escalation in the context of the Lord's commitment to duration. Do we find ourselves in the midst of a prophetic act like Paah-ho-ammi, Jesus Culture, or the building of a ministry like Carenet from the vision of a Roger Ralston to the still escalating reality presided over by Sharre Littrell? Wherever we are and in whatever process the Lord has landed us, we are to rejoice over all of the things we see Him doing at the same time we are watchers on the wall—giving Him and ourselves no rest—or widows approaching injustice until it is transformed—or centurions exercising the authority of the unarmed man in submission. We are on the road from Galilee to Jerusalem with our brothers and sisters in the culture of First Corinthians 12 and the straightest line between the two points is our route only if it conforms to Bible math (see 1 Cor. 12).

We are privileged with the opportunity to speak the language of those to whom we are called (whether that means we pray literally in incomprehensible prayer language for guidance we can implement without necessarily understanding it before we do it), or sometimes we are simply called to sit and mingle as God sovereignly reveals the fingerprints He has left on the culture of a nation, a community, or even the family from down the block. The gift He gives in the upper room that is packaged in tongues of fire is the gift of reaching out as He reaches out—in terms and symbols that can be understood and embraced by the other. And the more we practice the culture of honor—that warfare by honor of which we see countless examples in the Word—the more we come to see and touch the ones to whom we are called as Philip touched the Ethiopian eunuch and I am privileged to touch the Indian people of Fiji. Honoring the people God loves is the release point for the Kingdom.

How do we practice the Presence? We seek His face as a lifestyle—but not solely for our own comfort and companionship. We are already in the bed with the Father, if we will have it, due to the unlimited access we have enjoyed since the first Easter. If we would go all of the way, we will be as passionately concerned for those knocking on the door—and for those standing on the doorstep without knowing how to use the knocker—as is the King. This is the essence of spiritual warfare—whether as prayer or practicum.

The principal effect of spiritual warfare is to modify the atmosphere over the place of battle in such a way that God has readier access to it—this is clearly the impact of Daniel's 21-day prayer effort prior to the arrival of Archangel Michael and it is just as clearly the value of a prophetic intercession project like Paah-ho-ammi or Arrowhead. These activities certainly satisfy the criteria of escalation, duration, and honor.

Moving to the New Testament, we recognize that Communion comes as fulfillment of the Passover meal and sacrifice.

Jesus prepares the atmosphere around His people for the greatest battle ever fought on earth—His own crucifixion and subsequent resurrection—with the sharing of His body and blood in Matthew 26:17-35, Mark 14:12-31, and Luke 22:7-22. But the most explicit expression of the communion as an act of spiritual warfare comes in First Corinthians 10 when Paul asks, "Is not the cup of thanksgiving for which we give thanks a participation in the blood of Christ? And is not the bread we break a participation in the body of Christ? Because there is one loaf, we, who are many, are one body, for we all partake of the one loaf" (1 Cor. 10:16-17). The breaking of bread, which is one of the big three continuing acts encouraged and exhorted by the apostles in Acts 2:42, is not the only way to militantly practice the Presence, but it symbolizes the twin poles of recognizing and participating in His Body in such an elegant and pragmatic way that we can make it the principal icon of our efforts. We can keep asking through its lens if we are combining scriptural consistency, preparation for the Kingdom in both a seminal and summary way, and serving the prophetic community as an expression of the vision of First Corinthians 12 for the Kingdom.

HOW NOT TO PRACTICE

There are some fairly serious ways in which we must not claim to be practicing the Presence of God. They all involve idolatry of one form or another. Idolatry always comes as a shortcut to the presence of God in the same way as the golden calf was produced in the Sinai because the people grew tired of waiting for Moses to return (see Exod. 32). It will manifest itself as the worship of some inadequacy of ours—something that we never imagined as an object of worship but which does serve as an excuse for not doing God's will in God's way. Whenever we put something that is not God in place as the ultimate and governing reality of our lives, we have created an idol—and it needs to go from us.

We know that our God is a God of promise and of deposit on His promise that becomes an escalating process of fulfillment. In the Scriptures we can cut right to the chase with the promise in John 14:12-14 that the disciples will do the things they see Jesus do and even greater things than those they have witnessed because Jesus goes to the Father. A quick read of Acts reveals that Jesus brought about 120 into the Kingdom during His earthly life—that is the count of the saints gathered in the upper room as Pentecost dawns—and the harvest on that day alone is about 3,000. We see acts of faith like the casting of the net on the other side of the boat in Luke 5 and John 21 met with the promise of catching men and women for the Kingdom on the one hand and the commissioning of the disciples to begin doing just that on the other (later) one. We know Paul— who went from being a Christian hunting vigilante to the most prolific and productive apostle of them all after being knocked to the ground by a vision on the Damascus Road—started a process that toppled a pagan empire and re-made the world.

But there are consequences when people who claim to serve the Lord rebel at His call to enter this process of escalating grace and glory. We don't have to look any farther in the Word of God than to the leaders of the Sanhedrin in the time during and after the coming of Messiah for a gut-wrenching portrait of that reality. The full fruit of the leaven of the Pharisees becomes visible as early as the aftermath of raising Lazarus from the dead—recounted in John 11. The Pharisees—who have substituted the Law for the kind of intimate encounter with God for which they pray in the annual Feast of Tabernacles—are alarmed at the reports of Lazarus rising. They have already decided that Jesus represents a threat to their idea of law and order, and they are so committed to their decision that they begin plotting His death by the time Chapter 12 opens. Their high priest, Caiaphas, prophesies a legitimate word from God to the effect that it is better for one man to die for the nation than for the nation to perish (see John 18:14). But they don't realize it is their rebellion against God that makes the sacrificial death a necessity and that will eventually blast the Jews into a Babylonian exile that will make the first one look tame.

In a more contemporary crucible we come upon the Azusa Street revival of 1906. The denominational heirs of the Reformation had in many ways devolved into societies for the propagation of good morals and manners on the one hand, and merely political justice on the other. They deeply needed a fresh wind of the Holy Spirit—and one that could encompass the classes of society who were unsure which fork on the left was for salad and which for the entrée. This fresh wind came into Los Angeles and triggered an outbreak of dynamic Holy Spirit activity that had not been seen in the last 100 years. It had all of the markings of the first century about it—from people speaking in strange languages to the wholesale appearance of healing miracles. Most important was the fact that many thousands who had never heard of or accepted Jesus now came into the Kingdom with dancing and peace.

Several denominations came to birth in this time period (see Chapter 1), and the process has continued to escalate with the Latter Rain, the Evangelical Awakening (led by Billy Graham), the Charismatic Revival, the Jesus People,

the Toronto Blessing, and Brownsville Revivals, and the Transformation Movement. Each of these revivals came on the heels
of their elder siblings in the mid to late 20th century; some
were of Pentecostal flavor while others were more evangelical,
and some stood astride more than one stream of the Church.
But the denominations that were birthed in the Azusa caul-
dron have—for the most part—declined to participate in these
escalations. (The Vineyard was actually itself birthed out of
the more evangelical Jesus People movement; yet they refused
to accept Toronto as an escalation of their own adolescence.)
Although they—and others—continue to do much high quality ministry and to win souls, they are missing out on much of
the exciting fulfillment that God is presently revealing; they
will either turn again into the wind or be relegated to the
backwaters of God's river like so many other denominations
before them.

Jack Hayford said it best when he taught on the Toronto
Blessing in the mid-1990s. "Everybody thinks the way they got
filled with the Holy Spirit is the only way it can be done. But
God is always doing a new thing that better fulfills what He
was doing before with a fresh revelation." Denominational
leaders who refuse to embrace their destiny in the escalation
of the call from the Lord that brought them into existence
will—like the Sanhedrin before them—cite their commitment
to order and their distrust of the messiness of new birth as
their reason for sitting out the new work of the Spirit. They
make idols of their own ideas as they worship what they have
developed.

Scripture is clear about the value God holds for waiting
until His time is ripe. Abraham was forced to wait a century
for the first child of the union of his body and that of Sarah,

his only wife. God's promise was for children to Abraham as many as the stars in the sky, and it is a repeated promise, coming in Genesis 12 and 15. Isaac was indeed born of their union, and his birth sets in motion the escalating cycle of what we might call births to the unopened wombs. Isaac becomes the second patriarch of Israel, Samuel becomes her first great priest and prophet after Moses and the initiator of the Davidic monarchy, John the Baptist becomes the greatest prophet of them all and the announcer of the coming of Messiah, and Jesus Himself is the product, not of a long barren and then supernaturally ripened womb, but of a womb that has never been penetrated by the seed of a man. (We could argue that Jesus is the product—spiritually—of Israel's long-barren womb.) Abraham's promise becomes the human source of the Son of God and the Kingdom of Heaven. Unfortunately, Abraham did not adhere to the promise as faithfully as he could have, and the resulting catastrophe is shaping the world of today.

Genesis 16 tells the story of Hagar and Ishmael. Abraham and Sarah know the promise of God, and they know how He has supernaturally cared for all of their needs and manifested Himself in their lives. They also know of the times they have taken shortcuts to meeting their needs—like when Abraham passed Sarah off as his sister before the Egyptian king out of fear instead of trusting in God's word to him (see Gen. 20:2)—and the chaos that resulted. They become impatient again, reckoning that God has promised them a child and Abraham an heir while (perhaps) leaving the means and methods to them. (When does that ever really happen?) Sarah gives her slave woman, Hagar, to her husband—who goes along with it as surely as Adam ate the apple when Eve supplied it. When the slave becomes pregnant, she shows contempt for her mistress, who treats her cruelly out of both outraged dignity and simple jealousy. Hagar and her son flee the camp, have an encounter with God, and bring back a promise that Ishmael too will father a great people. Even so, when Isaac is born and begins to grow, the mistreatment begins again, and Hagar and Ishmael make a permanent departure (see Gen. 16; 21).

Ishmael becomes the father of the Arab peoples. God loves and shows them favor as well as the Jews, although He will always claim the seed of Isaac as His children of the blood covenant. But the conflict between Arab and Jew continues to this day; it all finds its own genesis in the failure to wait upon the Lord displayed in Abraham and Sarah. Of course, they imagined they were acting from necessity rather than idolatry.

In a much more localized setting, many congregations use the rule of unanimity as the model for decision-making in their leadership boards. This means simply that measures are adopted on a unanimous vote—in the style of the Acts 15 apostolic council in Jerusalem—or not at all. Issues lacking that overwhelming consent are still under or eligible for discussion—even if until the Lord's return. Of course the rule is grounded in a covenant with a particular board of elders; it must be re-agreed by a succeeding board and—inasmuch as congregational by-laws are usually based on Robert's Rules of Order with their emphasis on majority rule—it depends on the good faith of the committing board to remain in force.

In a church with which I am acquainted the senior pastor went to the elders with a request to bless a vision for ministry not unlike PrayNorthState. The elders discussed and prayed over the proposal, finally voting nine to two to endorse the vision and make the necessary adjustments to the pastor's responsibilities. Although the vote was a large majority it was not a unanimity, and so the measure was not adopted. All concerned agreed to think and pray and continue to hold this up to Heaven. The pastor made no effort to claim that this issue was some sort of exception to the covenant of unanimity.

As the next few months passed by new leaders were elected; they also committed to the rule of unanimity, but the atmosphere regarding the vision became more acrid with each passing week. Some elders wanted to never mention it again, although the pastor pointed out that the covenant required continued freedom to discuss and pray over items that had not been adopted. The time came for bi-annual evaluation of his performance as the pastor, and there were dark mutterings from some corners that he would now be held accountable for neglect of the flock in the pursuit of some interdenominational dream. Things did not work out that way; in fact the congregational survey conducted by the board gave the pastor high marks in every area of ministry. This did not satisfy all of the leaders—if anything it seemed to stir the pot. There came a moment of supreme confrontation a couple of weeks later; a motion to refer the pastor to district authorities for investigation and possible discipline passed by one vote.

The one-vote margin was hardly a unanimous vote, but those in the majority insisted their denominational rules permitted the consignment with a majority vote. The dissident leaders were unwilling to wait out the process and see where it might lead, and they placed the non-binding denominational rules ahead of their covenant with the Lord. The chief administrator—when he saw the congregational survey—recognized that something was seriously wrong with the whole process and offered the pastor a chance to resign and receive his full salary and benefits for six months while he established the new ministry. This God who draws all things together for good saw to it that he was launched with abundant blessing as the pastor waited on Him. But the congregation that failed to wait and worshiped their own impatience has never recovered the vitality it experienced during that pastorate.

Scripture places a premium—without exception—on what I have come to know as warfare by honor. From God honoring the first man with His company on their nightly walks in the Garden of Eden, to Daniel beginning each address to the emperor of an empire that had tortured and oppressed his people with the words, "O King, live forever," (see Dan. 3:9; 6:21), to Paul addressing the Sanhedrin as his brothers and the Roman Governor Felix with, "I know that for a number of years you have been judge over this nation, so I gladly make my defense…" (Acts 24:10), the heroes of the Bible are courteous to their listeners even when it is clear that these listeners have been a disgrace to the Lord our God. Even the Jewish authorities who accuse Paul look for ways to compliment the hated Romans for the peace and order they have brought along with their harsh measures when they make their formal accusations against Paul—this is not boot licking on their part but a remembered code of conduct placed in their hearts by their God.

But the times they forget that code of conduct stand out like beacons over decay. The failure to practice the culture of honor is not so much a cause as a symptom of the coming of death—to the individuals and the communities that root in that failure. Goliath falls under the weight of his own arrogant self-assurance that no shepherd boy bearing pebbles can threaten his status as champion of the Philistines, and Saul is already hearing his own funeral music by the time he begins making serious efforts to kill by treachery the man who will succeed him. Legend has it that Judas did what he did out of a desire to force Jesus' hand into an uprising; his commitment to this kind of manipulation of God's Son is only reflected in his failure to repent along with the other disciples whose passive and cowardly behavior is just as much a betrayal of their Lord—but Judas preferred death to restoration. And the Sanhedrin itself—able to treat their Roman overseers with honor in the Book of Acts—resorts to insults and beatings for the prisoner who has not yet been tried but is already convicted in their minds when Jesus stands before them. In their arrogance they hear and act on the prophecy about one man dying for the nation, but they cannot see to act on His resurrection which—coupled with His sacrificial death—was to be the salvation of their nation—and still is.

I will always remember the young man in my developmental reading class who had been labeled by his parents, grade counselors, and past teachers as learning disabled. They all urged me to go easy on Jesse because he simply could not keep up with even the remedial section of my class into which he had been placed. I came to believe that Jesse had a whole lot more on the ball than these other authorities would admit, despite the fact that he routinely failed to even attempt assignments and was generally a disruption in my class. I spent time talking with him and encouraging him and the day of the final—which was a make-or-break proposition that would determine whether he would have to put up with me for a repeat semester—came upon both of us. Jesse knew that if he aced the final he would pass with a C grade; he also knew that I did not give D grades in this class. He actually studied and turned in some of his last assignments, and when the papers were graded and returned, he had earned a strong B on his.

It was enough for a D—if that grade existed in my grade-book—but it did not. I told Jesse that I was proud of the work he had done in the last two weeks of class—his performance had fully justified the faith I had in him—so proud that I would not cheapen it by giving him a C that he had not fully earned.

There was a hue and cry from parents, counselors, and from the principal of my school. I was pressured for several days to pass Jesse with a D, and we closed the last conference with his snarled, "I'll show you, Mr. Wilson!" The next time I saw Jesse was four years later. He ran up to me to let me know that he had graduated from high school a year ahead of the rest of his class. He had taken the tough honor I had shown him and he *had* showed me. The incident taught me the value of honoring people in truth—and especially when to show honor is not necessarily to give immediate gratification. This is why my heart aches and grieves for the way some denominations treat the issues raised in their midst by the gay rights movement.

It is a fact that drug addiction, domestic violence, suicide, and sexually transmitted disease (including, but by no means limited to, AIDS) occur at much higher frequencies in the gay community than in the straight world. At the same time, the projected lifespan of a gay man is much lower than that of his straight counterpart.[1] To pursue the gay lifestyle—whether by inclination or compulsion—is to invite suffering and early death. It is just as true that Jesus Christ gave His earthly life for the sake of each and every human person—hetero or homosexual is of no concern to Him when the time for the sacrifice has come. He came to us because He loves us, not because our lifestyles please or displease Him. He is just as determined to set us free— whatever that may mean from one life to another. Yet, many of the mainline churches—and some others—turn a deaf ear to the ring of deadly statistics and look for ways around the clear scriptural prohibitions against homosexual activity. They want to think themselves compassionate and so they sacrifice honor—tough honor of the kind that set Jesse free—on the altar of the leaven of Herod. They ask what Jesus would do if He were here, and they forget that He is here—understanding the situation far better than we do.

In my own denomination a formerly gay man stood in the congregation of the church with the reputation for being the most militantly anti-gay in the Diocese of Los Angeles just one week after the general convention voted to begin openly placing practicing homosexuals into positions of high leadership and to pursue blessing their domestic arrangements as though they were marriages. The decision was reached because leaders believe that a homosexual lifestyle is not chosen and therefore must be blessed by God. They are convinced they can do nothing to help people who practice it, and so they are committed to doing nothing to hinder it—such as lovingly confronting people over what passes all the tests for addictive behavior. (They forget that compassion implies identification and engagement, not benign neglect.) But the formerly gay man stood and said, "You may not remember me. I was a member here about nine years ago, and I was flamboyantly gay. You loved me and confronted my behavior. I want you to know that today I am whole by the grace of God. I am a doctor and happily married with three healthy kids. I came to thank you and to thank God for loving me the way I was and for refusing to leave me that way." The story was front-page news in the Los Angeles Times.

He was—at bottom—thanking the people for practicing the presence of the Living God by engaging warfare by honor—tough honor—over him. That church is today a leader in the larger community in which it lives and worships and ministers. The denomination that practices a shortcut to God at the expense of honor has lost nearly two thirds of its national membership in less than a decade according to some accounts.

PARABLES OF THE PRESENCE

In keeping with what C.S. Lewis said about what we do with our solitude making us fit for company, some of the best parables of practicing the presence are experienced in the isolation of one mind and one heart seeking the face of God and finding Him.

Jacob DeShazer was bombardier on one of the planes of the World War II Doolittle raid. Captured after bailing out over China, the man who brought the Gospel to Japan after being brutalized during his three years as a prisoner of war had no presence but that of the Lord to practice. He was held in solitary confinement after a Japanese tribunal convicted him and fellow raiders of war crimes during the bombing of Tokyo. He received Jesus as His Lord after reading a New Testament only because he believed he would lose his sanity without some stimulation for his mind—something already happening to George, down the hall. When Jake gave his heart, he gave it all the way.

When the Lord appeared to him in his cell, Jake knew nothing of classic worship and prayer practices—he had been reared in and out of a mainline church but had been out much more than he had been in. He had no spiritual resources beyond his own intense need for companionship and hope and the immediacy of God's Holy Spirit there in the cell. There were many days when he would hear a Voice and wonder if it was really God or if he had finally slipped into a merciful insanity like his buddy, George, down the hall. But the Voice did tell him the exact day on which the war would end; it did bring him comfort that changed his behavior and mind from something full of hatred toward his captors to something full of compassion for the darkness in which they lived without Jesus Christ. And a few days before his release from prison, Jake heard the voice say that he was to become an ordained pastor and return to Japan—as Patrick returned to Ireland 1,500 years earlier—with the good news of that same Jesus Christ. And Jake was not the only one whose solitary practice of the Presence would impact the nation of Japan.

Fuchida Mitsuo was one of Japan's most honored war heroes. He led the attack on Pearl Harbor and was the Japanese air wing commander at the Battle of Midway. He had staked his life and every dimension of it on his practice of Bushido—the warrior's code. He was a lot like Jake DeShazer, except that he was not taken prisoner, and he was completely disillusioned with all that he held dear when the religion of Shinto and the code of Bushido led his people into a defeat as identity-crushing for the Japanese as the Babylonian Exile had been for the Jews. Fuchida would come to partner with Jake

DeShazer as a Great Commission Christian and practitioner of the presence of God—but only after encountering another practitioner—a daughter of missionaries to the Philippines by the name of Peggy Covell.

Peggy's parents had been suspected of spying for the Americans when the Philippines fell to the invader. She was forced to watch as they were executed. She was then placed in a concentration camp where her skills as a nurse were badly needed by hundreds of people. But the experience of watching her parents' murder completely undid all of her previous training in the things of spirit. Her only hope of retaining sanity—and of remaining in relation to her Lord—became an act of forgiveness for her captors because of her certainty that this was what her parents would have done—and what gave meaning to their deaths. Peggy practiced the presence of God in the only way she could—by going from day to day, from need to need, from prayer to prayer.

After the war Fuchida heard of her lifestyle of forgiveness, mercy, and compassion and went to see her. He was astounded that anyone could respond in the way that she did; in Japanese culture one greeted such a trial with either suicide or vengeance. He was moved, but decided that a military man did not have the option of doing what Covell had done. Then he heard of DeShazer, and read Jake's pamphlet titled *I Was a Prisoner of Japan*. He knew that the missionary would be speaking in a nearby city, and he went to hear what he might say. They met after the presentation. Here was a soldier—as committed to cause and code as Fuchida had ever been—who had chosen the way of Peggy Covell.

Years of spiritual struggle lay ahead for Fuchida following that meeting. There was a time before he would accept Jesus. There was another time before he would abandon his mistress and become a faithful husband to his wife. There was still another time of struggle before he would acknowledge the authority of the Great Commission and accept God's call on him to evangelize his people. He practiced the presence in the solitude of his farm and his study of the Bible. He practiced with Jake DeShazer and with the memory of Peggy Covell. Between the life and witness—and the practice—undertaken by the three of them, Japan was impacted with the Gospel as it had never been before. And three human beings were not merely rescued from eternal death; they were set free into eternal and abundant life. Transformation comes in many forms and at many levels—the common denominator being, *His Kingdom comes.*

Jake DeShazer became the most successful evangelist ever to minister in Japan. His partnership with Fuchida was instrumental in the founding of some 125 churches in that nation. Practice of the Presence was all they ever had.

I have deliberately avoided offering any formula for practicing the Presence of the Living God. It is prayer. It is dedication of this project or that occasion. It is immersion in the Word of God, and it is spending as much time in corporate worship as the Lord allows. (That may mean going to the Catholic Mass, a service with guitars and drums, or even what we used to call four bare walls and a sermon.) It is sitting quietly and asking the Spirit to overshadow us; it is taking up a ministry challenge for the least of these—just because He says we can. It need not be on the grand scale of taking the Gospel to an entire nation. One of my most intimate moments came when a friend asked me to play pool with him (knowing I was one of the worst players on the planet), and I prayed that he would drop the eight ball into a pocket so that I might win by default. When he did "scratch" and I revealed that I had prayed, we both grew in our walk and our understanding of how much God wants to hear from us regardless of the subject—as soon as we picked our jaws up from the floor. The Lord our God really wants to be in conversation and in company with us—all of the time.

There are some types of practice that Jesus gives in the parables of Matthew 25.

The first parable in that chapter is that story of the Ten Virgins, which I mentioned as paramount in an earlier chapter. The whole point of the story is waiting upon the Lord, but the place where the rubber meets the road is in the realm of active preparation—they went out to seek Him and the wise ones took extra oil. The wise virgins had been hanging out with the Master long enough to know that His arrival was often unexpected. In their relationship with Him they had learned to place their faith not in their ability to hear, but in His ability to speak—they could depend on the crier to awaken them if need be. They understood the saying, "Therefore, keep watch, because you do not know the day or the hour" (Matt. 25:13). Preparation is not a set of learned behaviors; it is proximity practiced.

The second parable is the one about the Ten Talents. The point of the story is investment in the Kingdom practiced as a lifestyle. The man entrusted with five talents is not revealed as well versed in finance or securities exchange. It is the same with the man given two talents.

We know only that they made unspecified investments of the money they had and that the investments turned out quite well—the money was doubled in both cases. The third man knew he was in a bear market and did what many would think the prudent thing—he held onto what he had and took no chances. Yet, the master commends the first two for their faithfulness (in a bear market) and is livid at the report delivered by the other one (see Matt. 25:14-30). The Jesus we know—if we are people who hang out with Him—is always and forever taking risks for the Kingdom—from touching lepers to staking His Kingdom on the faithfulness of 11 men who have been pretty disappointing prior to the Resurrection. Yet any of us who put this to the test find that the more we invest and risk on the Kingdom the more we are filled with His abundant life. That life may or may not coincide with material wealth and well-being—but it is as rich as it is exciting.

The third and final parable in the chapter concerns the separation of sheep and goats at the end of the age (see Matt. 25:31-46). It is crucial to note that all of the characters sincerely intended to serve the Lord. Some of them had been hanging out with Him long enough for His character to rub off on them while the others were going to start hanging with Him as soon as they saw that His time was close. It is that simple: we don't know when the time is coming, and we don't know who will be delivering the message. But the more we practice doing what we see Jesus doing, the more we become like Him and so prepare ourselves for His coming. The doing of what He does is what constitutes the hanging with Him until His character rubs off.

The parable of the virgins is about internalized waiting, and the sheep and goats parable is about externalized waiting—

with the one about investment and risk nestling right in the middle where it belongs. Waiting for these purposes is just another word for practicing the presence.

Anskar of Scandinavia is probably my favorite saint. Sometime in the eighth century he was sent out from his native Germany by the pope of that day. His mission was to bring Jesus to the Vikings. Over the course of a 20-year ministry he was able to establish only two small congregations in the land of his assignment. When he returned to Rome to report and retire, he felt compelled to apologize for his poor showing. Yet his practice of the presence of God in his faithful caring, stepping out, and simply being with his people so inspired them that men and women from those two struggling congregations went out and brought the whole of Scandinavia into the Body of Christ. Anskar is today considered the patron saint of the region—not for what he achieved but for who he was in Christ and in town.

God asks nothing more from any of us than that we practice blessing, forgiving, and supping with Him. He calls us to be on the lookout for opportunities to escalate, to hang in and hang out, and to honor one another as we honor Him. He wants us to be on the lookout for His coming from an unexpected direction—and He is sending a lot of unusual miracles our way for both practice and discipline. He says He is on His horse and on His way.

Endnote

1. These statistics come from the following sources:

A. Steven Bryant and Demian, "Relationship Characteristics of American Gay and Lesbian Couples," *Journal of Gay and Lesbian Social Services*, 1.2 (1994), 101-117.

Maggie Gallagher and Joshua K. Baker, "Same Sex Unions and Divorce Risk: Data from Sweden," *Institute for Marriage and Public Policy: Policy Brief*, May 3, 2004, http://www.marriagedebate.com/pdf/SSdivorcerisk.pdf (accessed 7 June 2008).

Horwood and Beautrais, "Is Sexual Orientation Related to Mental Health Problems and Suicidality in Young People?" *Archives of General Psychiatry 1999*, 56:876-880.

Susan Jones, "Domestic Violence in LGBT Relationships Targeted," *CNS News.com*, October 20, 2004.

Patricia King, "Not So Different After All," *Newsweek*, October 4, 1993.

C. M. Rennison, "Intimate Partner Violence and Age of Victim, 1993-99," Bureau of Justice Statistics, Special Report, October 2001, http://fl1.findlaw.com/ news.findlaw.com/hdocs/docs/doj/usdojipva93-99.pdf (accessed 7 June 2008).

Sandfort, et al., "Same Sex Behavior and Psychiatric Disorders," *Archives of General Psychiatry 2001*, 58:85-91.

Jeffrey Satinover, *Homosexuality and the Politics of Truth* (Grand Rapids, MI: Hamewith Books, 1996) 50-60, 66-70.

Paul Strand, "Cause and Effect: The Benefits of Traditional Marriage," CBN News.com, http://www.cbn.com/CBNNews/News/ 040510a. aspx (accessed 7 June 2008).

True, et al., "Sexual Orientation and Suicidality: A Co-Twin Study in Adult Men," *Archives of General Psychiatry 1999*, 867-874.

Chapter 9

TESTING THE SPIRITS

In spring 2005 I received a call from Ken Greenlee of Teach Us to Pray International. Ken was planning an outreach in Fiji that would minister primarily to Indian people of Hindu background. (Ethnic Indians are a large minority in Fiji and are under-emphasized in the present transformational fervor in that nation.) He had recruited a pastor friend to lead the evangelism team, but the pastor's congregation was in crisis, and he decided he could not leave California at that time. Ken and the pastor met and prayed together; they believed that the Lord gave them my name as an alternate evangelist for the outreach. After prayer I too believed that God was calling me to go, and I have described elsewhere the spectacular fruit that God has grown in the annual mission to Fiji since then. "By their fruit you will know them" (Matt. 7:16,20), says Jesus, but we could hardly review the fruit of the mission before going on it; there had to be some other way to vet the prophetic word on my participation—and indeed there was.

Neither Ken nor the pastor had any way of knowing that I had studied Hindu sacred books in college prior to coming to know Jesus Christ as my Lord. I am uniquely suited to respect the wisdom in those books—in the sense that even a stopped clock is right twice a day—and preach from personal conviction that Krishna gives good advice, but only Jesus will actually help you to do anything about it. I was the only person known to both of these men with this qualification—and it was clear to me that God had begun preparing me for such a time as this when I was still a teenager. Prophetic message received and confirmed.

Diana and I enjoy ministering among indigenous peoples as much as we love to serve in our own culture; we know we were born for such a time as this and for such a ministry as well. But I was not thrilled when the Lord laid a very confrontive word on my heart in late 2003 and told me to deliver it at the World Christian Gathering on Indigenous Peoples in Kiruna, Sweden, when they met in 2005. We count many of the leaders of this worldwide movement as personal friends—but we are not numbered among that leadership ourselves. I knew that it would be presumptuous, at best, to seek a place on the speakers' schedule for that gathering. Add to that the fact that I would be coming from the background of a white middle class surfer guy from California attempting to instruct tribal people who have every historical reason to resent people like me, and it went all the way to insane to deliver that message. I decided that the Lord meant for me to find the right person to speak in Kiruna.

Over the next two years I prayed often with friends—leaders and workers—in the movement. Each time my friends would re-affirm that I was to give the word myself. I began to believe—and at the same time doubt—that this word was indeed for me to speak. Diana and I made our reservations for the conference and prayed for the funds to come in—we had never before needed thousands of dollars to appear as quickly as we needed it now, and we wondered as we prayed if stories we heard about money showing up in a missionary's mail were true enough for our benefit. In the meantime, I decided that I would simply approach the leadership when we arrived in Sweden and ask for about 15 minutes to address the gathering. If it was the Lord, my request would be granted—and the funds would arrive—we hoped.

Three weeks before the event I received an e-mail from one of the organizers. She asked if I had a word from the Lord that all of the participants needed to hear. When I wrote back that I did have a word, she offered me the keynote spot on the last day of the conference. When we arrived and met Hakon and Marie, she explained that she had heard a word from the Lord three months before the conference that a man from Northern California would come and deliver a word they needed to hear. Diana and I were the only people from Northern California to register, and she concluded that it had to be me. And the funds came in almost without effort; in one case, a family we did not even know sent a portion of the proceeds from the sale of their home. This word looks like a duck, quacks like a duck, and waddles very much like a prophetic duck. It is indeed by the fruits that we know the word—and He is quite capable of delivering fruit in real time.

Clearly, the prophetic dreams and visions given to Roger Ralston and Sharre Littrell about the ministry of Carenet expanding to three counties were living and active expressions of the Word of God. The word that God gave to me about calling our prophetic prayer project Paah-ho-ammi was just as right on. (The call to begin to pray over the promised clinic property was a good test for identifying God in the method of the first instance; the fact that 135 people of some 40 churches heard God's call in Paah-ho-ammi, despite my lack of detailed information was just as much a validation in the second.) Yet, we recounted some prophecies in Chapter 1 that were patently false; we also spoke of scribes masquerading as prophets who are just as false. Simply declaring a vision or a word authentic does not cut it. Paul says that we must test the spirits in First Thessalonians 5:21, even as we celebrate and hold onto whatever passes the test—however out of the box it may be (see 1 John 4:1). How do we do that?

PROPHECY WHERE YOU FIND IT

In the classic Walt Disney film, *Twenty Thousand Leagues Under the Sea*, we are blown right out of our old wineskin as we grapple with the notion that the castaways are the prophetic ones, as opposed to the captain and crew. (I know many are thinking they are stretched just thinking of an ac-tion-adventure yarn with only passing mention of a generic God as prophetic in any sense.) Disney and his director, Richard Fleischer, made the film as a classic jailbreak story, but God wove much more into the tapestry.

Nemo has built a wonderful craft that can take him any-where in the world without fear of the clumsy men who hate him from their terminally limited position on the surface of oceans that cover three quarters of the planet. While they struggle to light their hovels with oil and gas, he cruises beneath the storm on atomic power. He and his men seem able to antic-ipate any difficulty. If the rudder breaks they don diving gear and fix it, under water and under his all-knowing direction. If a giant squid attacks, Nemo knows the kill spot is right be-tween the eyes. If cannibals try to board the Nautilus, he expels them with a harmless electrical charge to the deck—installed in his wisdom for just such a purpose. And he alone knows the proper timing to share his knowledge with a waiting world. He alone has discovered the peace that passes all understanding—beneath the waves where he alone is master, as he explains to the very gullible Professor Arronax. Is not his kingdom the peaceable kingdom we are promised in Scripture—in which God takes vengeance on the unjust ones and cares for those who care for Him?

But wait. Is not the vision we are promised in Scripture a Kingdom in which every one of us becomes the best that God created us to be? Does not David, the shepherd, un-dergo transformation into David, the king who shepherds his people? Does not Paul, the scholar, become Paul, the vision-caster who takes the transformed knowledge of God to a world of many flocks under one shepherd, Messiah? Does not Peter, the fisherman, become Peter, the fisher of men in this Kingdom? The crew of the submarine Nautilus is not like that at all. Nemo has indeed become all that he can be, but his crewmen live only as extensions of his being. They have chosen to live under his rule, but it is the rule of a cult leader. Most of them never even speak; those who do either report to Nemo or respond to his orders. They have no life of their own; he does not marvel at the infinite variety of the people he loves. God comes into the world to give abundant life, not mere protection from evil; He plants that we might bloom. If prophecy is the word of the living God bathing the world that He is creating from moment to moment, then the Nautilus cannot possibly be a prophetic community. In the sense that Christians understand the concept, the submarine is not a community at all—a First Corinthians 12 world in which all members are honored for their unique contribution as they become their truest selves in Christ.

Consider the three castaways: Ned Land, Arronax, and his assistant, Conseil. They fuss and fume at one another constantly. They are the seeming victims of circumstance across the board—recruited to hunt a sea monster that isn't an animal at all, blown off the warship and onto the deck of the submarine, permitted to live by the caprice of the captain, and clumsy as all get out when they attempt to adapt to their new underwater home. One is obsessed with escaping along with some of the gold Nemo uses for ballast, another prattles on about how his life means nothing unless he can pry Nemo's secrets away from him and turn them over to a world that can only imagine using them for war, and the third is along primarily for comic relief. Is this a prophetic community? But wait again.

The three of them, in their clumsiness, live for each other as opposed to for themselves. Conseil was not blown off the warship by the collision with the submarine; he jumped in to save the professor. Ned works tirelessly to help all of them escape, although he knows all too well what Conseil points out to him—that he is far more likely to succeed on his own from a purely fleshly standpoint. The professor is glad to sacrifice his own life for the sake of the possibility of making life better for millions of people he does not know and who do not care about him.

During the climactic moment of the film—the fight with the giant squid—Ned even risks his own life to save Nemo. Nemo proves to be not as omniscient as he would have us believe and Ned—driven by impulse more often than thought and as quixotic as they come—kills the monster and dives into the water with it to save a man he has every reason to despise for imprisoning him. When the submarine is defeated by castaways, who have cast messages in bottles into the ocean as their most sophisticated weapon—it is their community that comes into larger life for having lived the adventure and survived it. Although they have grown (some) in wisdom and grace over the course of the story—and the captain and crew have not changed a bit—it is not their wisdom that makes them prophetic. It is their self-sacrificing love. In that love they endure to the end and are saved. In that end they look a whole lot more like people of God than do Nemo and his people. They resemble the people in whose weakness God's strength is perfected.

In Matthew 25:31-40, Jesus describes the people of God as those who feed the hungry and visit the sick and imprisoned and care for those who cannot care for themselves—whether or not they recognize Jesus in the ones for whom they care. In the moments following the battle with the squid, Nemo tells Arronax that Ned Land would regret saving his (Nemo's life) as much as Nemo would regret saving Ned. "The difference is

I wouldn't have tried," says the captain. Arronax responds that the difference between them is the humanity that Nemo no longer possesses. The castaways look a whole lot more like the people of God. And that resemblance is the very essence of prophecy.

Of course, prophecy is wherever you find it. When I preached a message recently based on this material, people in the congregation broke out laughing. Then one of the elders showed me the congregational newsletter that had just been published that morning. An anecdote is reprinted in which a parent who has just taken her child to see *Twenty Thousand Leagues Under the Sea* asks the child what made the submarine sink. The child exclaims, "Mom, it was the twenty thousand leaks!" Spiritually speaking, the kid was right on!

But the bottom line in testing the spirits is the degree to which the word or vision resembles the Author of life. There are some fairly simple criteria for checking out that resemblance. The test we applied to the movie is the one Jesus Himself commands—by their fruit we will know them.

SOME SIMPLE SIGNPOSTS

Just as important is whether the prophetic word stands scriptural muster. Is it consistent with the Word of God? My own denomination has taken some major league left turns in terms of doctrine in recent decades. Although issues of human sexuality have made the headlines, it is really the authority of Scripture that is challenged, and sexual issues are not the only places of challenge. The denominational leaders have proclaimed loudly that they are being prophetic in leading the flock into new understandings of God. If we have heard a word that sounds very much like whatever we think the voice of God sounds like, but it says that "she" is an appropriate pronoun for the first person of the Trinity, we have only to search Scripture to see whether God ever refers to Himself that way.

If someone wonders aloud—as a seminary classmate of mine did once—whether Jesus has already returned to earth without fanfare, we have only to see if there is any ambiguity about the trumpet blast in apocalyptic passages from the synoptic Gospels: Revelation, Daniel, Ezekiel, or First Thessalonians. If we believe that God has called us to particular action in order to display His mercy, we need to be assured that His justice is satisfied as well in that action—and vice versa. And if our sympathies are aroused by a group—from gay people to patients suffering with Parkinson's Disease—we need to recognize that when God calls something sinful—from gay marriage to destroying embryos—it is only because of His unlimited sympathy for people tempted to seek a shortcut to the life He has planned for them.

It is crucial to avoid what is called proof texting—the taking of a verse out of context to justify what we want to do or believe. If we believe that a word conforms to Scripture, we need to know that it is typical of what God has to say. There is the incident in Second Kings in which Elisha calls a bear to devour some boys who made fun of his bald head (see 2 Kings 2:23-25). The Bible actually tells that true story, but it is by no means typical of how God deals with the immature, and there is no parallel in the New Testament of any kind. We are looking for norms, not exceptions, when we evaluate an alleged prophetic word. But we are also looking for existing guideposts, not an excuse to write a new map. Everett "Terry" Fullam liked to say, "I dare not judge this book, for this book judges me."

I've not mentioned anything about whether the word comes true or not. Obviously if they do not—like the Iraq War prophecies from the first chapter—that is a deal breaker. But remember that most prophetic statements are interpretive rather than predictive—and the predictive ones usually have not had time to come true by the time we are evaluating them. We need to look for other fruit for our testing.

A criterion we should check out is whether the word has a Kingdom focus. The issue is simplicity itself. If we act on this word, will it advance the Kingdom of God where we stand? A few years ago I was driving past a beautiful place called Castle Crags in Northern California. (Many people have reported God speaking to them at this spot.) As I passed the turnoff, God spoke and told me that He was renaming Redding Abundant Springs. The word was a call to prayer for the prosperity of our city, and when I began to report it, people began to pray for Redding in light of the new name. This word was given during the prep time for the first Paah-ho-ammi, and it informed much of the prayer and process for that project. I believe that much of the new economic growth the city has experienced in the past few years is connected to this sustained prayer and testimony. The fruit is good and the Kingdom is advanced because people are strengthened in their faith, as well as given direction for its practice in prayer and anticipation.

At least a decade before that, I got lost on the way to lead a substance abuse intervention. God literally showed me every twist and turn of the road that I needed to take to get to the location. The intervention was a success and the person was ultimately set free of alcohol dependency—but nobody is running around testifying, "When Jim got lost the Holy Spirit gave him new supernaturally delivered directions." What I received was a bona fide word of knowledge, but it was not a prophecy. It neither advanced nor impeded the Kingdom in that community.

I don't want to give the impression that a word or vision is only prophetic if it impacts multitudes from the first shot out of the bag. Actor Stephen Baldwin describes the run-up to his acceptance of Jesus as his lord in his autobiography, *The Unusual Suspect*.[1] Baldwin says that his wife, Kenya, wanted to hire a housekeeper from her native Brazil. Her extended family in Brazil located—and the Baldwins hired—a woman named Augusta. The woman was a good worker, but her constant singing about Jesus began to annoy Kenya, who asked her one day if she knew any other kinds of songs. The woman burst out laughing and told Kenya it was very funny to her that she seemed to believe that their maid had come into their lives to clean their house. In fact, when she was considering the job back in Brazil, her church had prayed for her; and a member had given a prophetic word that she was to bring to Stephen and Kenya Baldwin a prophetic word about their coming life and full-time ministry before God— several years before they had even met Him! Today Stephen Baldwin considers his primary role to bring Jesus to the younger generation—as God spoke through a prophetic word given in a Brazilian church. If the word is life shaping, it is Kingdom significant.

If it has a Kingdom focus, does it also participate in a process of sacramental outburst? Is the prophetic word a lamp post we can lean against—an alarm clock we can set and satisfy ourselves until it goes off; or is it a foundation on which we can stand—a pad from which we can launch. One of the tragedies of the charismatic renewal of the '60s and '70s was that so many became filled with the Spirit of God and began to walk in the gifts such as healing and tongues and even prophecy but utterly failed to take their gifts to the street and call the lost into the Kingdom. There were far too many holy huddles—for members only. The Jesus Movement, on the other hand, was a primarily evangelical movement that knew little about the awesome power of God to intervene directly in every human crisis from disease to drought to depression. But their passion was to tell everyone they could about the new life they had discovered in Jesus. When they went on the mission field, which thousands of them did, they saw soon enough that stuff they thought God only did in Bible times was what was saving their bacon in the jungles today.

Our God is a God of the progressive revelation of His will and purposes. That is why Jesus uses so many agricultural images in His parables. He wants to illustrate the developmental dynamic of the Kingdom. The whole fabric of Scripture testifies to that dynamic. It spans from the beginning of His people in a shepherd named Abraham, who can barely grasp that his wife should be honored as his wife instead of passed off as his sister when danger threatens, despite the clear message of the first chapter of Genesis that the two are one flesh. God never upbraids Abraham for the sin he commits against Sarah when they were in Egypt (see Gen. 12), but Jesus has especially harsh words for His contemporaries over the issue of divorce. God was not ready to deal with it with Abraham;

He was ready to deal with it 1,400 years later; the people had so much to learn in the beginning, and we are still working on it.

When we blessed the churches in Los Angeles that were struggling against the attempt to confiscate their property, we could have simply testified that God would protect their interests. It would have come true, and we did have a word of knowledge to that effect, even though none of their peers had ever won in such a lawsuit. But to stop there would have short-circuited all that God meant to perform in them. He wanted us to speak to the dysfunctions in their history and to pray that they would become a great blessing to their community as they were healed. It was not a question of blaming the victim so much as claiming all that God had for them. They received all of our word, and they have all become lighthouses of blessing in their communities, as the oil in the bottle that multiplied has become a model for the oil of gladness they are splashing all over the southern region of their state.

The words given to Roger in 1984 and to Sharre in 2005 clearly partake of this sacramental dimension. That is, they came as deposits on God's promises, they contained teaching that has been sown into them for more than two decades, and they are still escalating in impact. The word given to the Baldwins' prospective housekeeper is bearing increasing fruit as they go out and sow the Kingdom from their celebrity vantage point in a Hollywood that is increasingly open to the Gospel and a younger generation that is increasingly open to Baldwin himself.

My own practice of intentional celebration of Holy Communion on land needing redemption was grounded in a word

God gave to me when we went to the bedroom community outside of Chico where the satanists had wreaked such havoc. He simply told me to address the bloodguilt on the land with the Blood. But this word was itself an escalation of a word given by a woman who came to me for prayer in 1986. The Lord had told her that there was healing in the Eucharist—which is what many traditional churches call the Communion service.

Another thing I don't want to encourage readers to think is that a word must be held up until every criteria mentioned in this chapter has been applied. No one would ever act on or utter a word of prophecy without consulting the manual, and I don't want that kind of responsibility—or ego inflation. We do the best we can to apply the tests that do apply. We put our faith not in our ability to hear, but in His ability to speak, and we rely not on our skill, but on His grace. This is true for people giving or receiving words.

Whenever we operate in the Prayer Vanguard ministry, I encourage our prayer warriors to speak out—in humility—whatever God seems to be speaking to them. They deliver their message, and then they let it go. If it is a word from the Lord, it will not fall empty to the ground; our host will either resonate with it immediately or be unable to forget it. That is between the host and the Lord. The vanguard person's job is to share what he has been given and let it go. Remembering back to a couple of stories shared in Chapter 1, I would hate to think of what might have been lost had the woman held back on her word about division in the congregation over the plan to open a school—that congregation is now a leader throughout its region. And what if I had kept silent about the gas leak in the 300 building of the high school we visited with Prayer Vanguard? That principal was enabled to guard his school against a real and physical danger, and God drew him into a larger appreciation of the Holy Spirit at the same time. The fruit of bold humility is good to embrace—and we have it when we are willing to risk.

Reality is that God frequently comes to the rescue when we act on our misunderstandings—through either lack or excess of imagination—to advance His Kingdom. Stephen Baldwin loves to tell the story of what he calls a bone-headed decision to star in a really bad movie; although universally panned by critics and audiences alike, it is a great favorite with people for whom God has given him a burning passion and an open door for ministry, especially teenagers, who begin to connect with Baldwin because they saw him in that movie. It is why Paul says that God makes His strength perfect in our weakness and later that we need to work out our own salvation in fear and trembling. My friend, Bill, likes to say that it is OK that God never told David to build a temple for Him; the temple was not God's idea, but David was God's idea. He is teaching us every moment we will permit it, and He loves it when we spread our wings and try to practice what He is teaching without a net.

God only gets really bent out of shape with us when we defy Him or don't care enough to seek Him. King Saul is such a case. The biggest difference between King Saul and King David—both of whom hit many a foul ball when they were at the plate and hit a few more out of the park—was that Saul was so impressed with the gift of the kingship that he loved it more than anything, including the Giver of the gift. (And he was sometimes numbered among the prophets.) King David was so impressed with the Giver of the gift that he loved the

Giver more than even the gift. When we seek God and His Kingdom at the expense of everything else, He will give us all that we need—including a little slack when we take a word as prophetic when it is not or fail to see His hand in a word that is.

Having said that, let me say that another good way to test prophecy is to ask if the word points toward a corporate act— a shared activity—that partakes of reconciliation, release, repentance, or all of the above. These are the three R's of the Kingdom. In it—whether we read the Kingdom description in Matthew 11:2-6 or the Luke 4:16-30 proclamation by Jesus in the Nazareth synagogue (quoted from Isaiah 61) or the appeal of Paul in Second Corinthians 5:16-20 to become ambassadors of the reconciliation we have been given in Christ—we find that the activity of the Kingdom is release and the population of that Kingdom are the people who repent and become its ambassadors. It stands to reason that a bulletin from the Kingdom would be recognizable in terms of sticking to the Kingdom identity and mission.

Any of the prophetic acts with impact that were discussed in the chapter bearing that name will work to illustrate this one. Paah-ho-ammi focused prayer on identified release points in the county such as crime, the economy, and public health and safety. It required that we be people of repentance because only then could we wholeheartedly employ the weapons of warfare—blessing, forgiveness, and the Lord's Supper—that we stressed in both training and exercise. In our sin we are no more capable of blessing those we regard as enemies than we are able to fly; in the confession of our inadequacies, we find that we have not been caught but have been ourselves released. When we proclaim the results as the fruit of calling on the name of God simply because He has named us for

Himself, we function as His ambassadors and free up our own personal witness as well.

The same dynamic holds up for the other acts—the Bible reading over the city, the prayer vanguard ministry, and most especially the walking and blessing and celebrating of Communion on the land. When we repent in identification with the people who sinned there—the satanists outside of Chico for example—it is difficult to accept responsibility for the sin of another; it is hard enough to accept it for our own. But when we permit the Lord to convict us of our own personal involvement in what may have happened when we were hundreds of miles or years away, it is an event of personal liberation without parallel. I will never forget the explosion of both freedom and joy when the Lord convicted me of my own hardness of heart toward Native Americans as He called me to join in His process of reconciliation with them—in the living room of some Native Hawaiians who have become family to Diana and me. The spiritual liberation of indigenous peoples in which we get to play a small part at home and abroad was all set up by allowing Him first to set us free in an escalating process that is far from finished. Each time we minister in these settings, we have to ask the Lord what He wants to set loose in the earth of our bodies at the same time He is loosing it in Heaven. If we don't ask, He will volunteer it sooner or later, but the whole process is a lot smoother if we are the ones volunteering.

HEART TRANSCENDING BODY

An amazing astonishment swept California in the fall of 2004, and it just happens to make a great illustration of what I mean to convey in this chapter. Intercessors and prophetic types from all over the state were getting words and visions about God's immediate plans for the state. They were seemingly contradictory words, and yet they all seemed righteous—and that was a major league puzzlement to many of us. At the time I was leading a statewide listening team, and one of our functions was to evaluate and recommend action on prophetic words that we received. The words that crossed our path were basically divided into three categories. One said that God was fed up with a state that led the nation in abortion, pornography, and the most violent forms of suicide—His judgment was coming. Another gave the same impression of patience that had run out, but indicated He was going to stay His hand of judgment if enough intercessors prayed consistently, in concert, and with focus on the spiritual state of the state. The third echoed that the Lord was so in love with California that He could do nothing in His heart but bless us. Yet we were inclined to accept them all as authentic.

We recommended—and the board of the statewide fellowship agreed—that we would call for a season of 40 days of sustained prayer for California. We asked only that people pray as they were led but that it become a daily exercise. And then—almost 30 days into the season—God gave me a vision.

I was on my way to Mt. Shasta City for a monthly pastors' meeting when I again passed Castle Crags. As I mentioned earlier, local and regional prayer people say that God really likes to engage them at Castle Crags, and He has met me there before. This time the Spirit literally came into my car and sat in the passenger seat. As I looked over, He showed me His beating heart for California—a heart so big it could not fit in the confines of His ribcage. As I watched the raw flesh of His beating heart that would not be contained, He spoke simply, "You think that my heart is contained inside my Body because that is how your heart is. But my ways are not your ways. My heart contains my Body."

I wept at the overwhelming love He displayed in that beating heart—and at the revelation of how the Church fits inside the heart, instead of the other way around. I knew then that the three strands of prophecy were indeed all true and that they were really one composite word from three strands of the Body. California—which has released legislation re-defining marriage, hosted more than 80 percent of the pornography in our nation, celebrated the devastation of land and people that is the legacy of the gold rush, and glorified drug addiction and all sorts of destruction through the entertainment industry—is indeed past redemption in terms of God's justice. Our God says that without a vision the people perish (see Prov. 29:18), and at this time we have no vision other than more of the glut we already produce. But California is also the birthing place of more revival culture and more innovation of caring for people in the Matthew 25 sense than anywhere else on the planet. Our state is the golden state in the sense of its opportunity and willingness to embrace the people God loves—and God's overwhelming love has never been a consequence of our behavior in any case. Finally, God has always said that if the people called by His Name will humble themselves and pray and seek His face that He will hear from Heaven and forgive sin and heal land (see 2 Chron.7:14). There is no termination point for His mercy.

The New Testament is indeed a portrait of a prophetic community in a First Corinthians 12 world, and God gives a piece of His thought to this one and another to that one, and it all comes together in a kaleidoscope of His glory.

This prophetic episode was simply one more expression of that reality.

It also brings to center stage the last criterion that comes to my mind—but certainly not the least important. Does a prophetic word or act partake of the one commandment against which there is no law in Jesus' mind—the one He gave to the disciples after He washed their feet and fed them from His own hand on the night before He was betrayed into the hands of the enemy and his servants for that time? Jesus orders His followers at all times to love one another—and to be known by that love they bear.

Most modern-day authentic prophets and trainers of prophetic people will stress that prophecy should be positive—sowing in the opposite spirit of the destructive situations that often confront us. This is indeed a central rule of thumb, and I teach our intercessors to pray in this way virtually without exception. (When we pray for the sick, we don't even curse the disease; we simply say that it has served its purpose in bringing the person to prayer and now it must depart to make way for the peace of God.) But the criterion for evaluating the prophetic word or deed must not be its sunshine quotient. It has to be the participation of the word in God's call to love at all times. If a confrontive word is given, we need to determine if it calls the recipient back to God's vision for them or simply upbraids them for failure. Tough love is still love—when it comes from God.

Do we pray that a smoker, for example, would come to see the degradation of his life because he serves the idol of tobacco, or do we pray that our brother who is in bondage would be set free into the destiny that God has planned and still holds open for him? Do we prophesy—as seemed to be the case at a time when God was calling me to a shift of focus in my ministry in Gilroy—that God would punish me severely even if I attempted the shift—or do we prophesy God's vision for redemption in the shift? At the time, more than a decade ago, I recognized God's voice, not in either of the specific directives on competing words, but in the presence of His love in one and its absence in the other. I made the shift and the fruit was good.

God gave me another vision early in my own ministry as a member and leader of the prophetic community He is creating as we live. It brings to mind even today His amazing co-mingling of the obligatory side of opportunity and the overwhelming love of Father, Son, and Holy Spirit for each of us and all of us.

In this one I found myself imprisoned in an old-fashioned root cellar—the kind found in so many mid-western farm houses. There were many of us in the cellar, and it was dank and sweaty and cob-webby—an invitation to advanced claustrophobia. Suddenly, in the midst of our despair and mounting desperation, the outer door was flung open to the sky and there was Jesus Himself—framed in the doorway and smiling down at us as He beckoned us out of the prison. We climbed the ladder as fast as we could and breathed deeply of the sunshine and the blueness of the sky.

We looked around and saw that we were standing on a vast lawn that was lined and marked with flowers and flowering shrubs. There were leafy trees but nothing to block the magnificent view of the sky. Jesus told us to play for as long as we liked, and we found as we romped and rolled on the grass with Him and with each other that we could even fly. I began doing the breast stroke about four feet off of the ground and having the time of my life. This went on for what seemed a couple of hours before Jesus called us all together to face Him near the edge of the lawn—an edge that gave on a long slope that was as barren as the lawn was lush.

At the bottom of this slope and many miles away was a dark and dingy city—a place so polluted that we could smell the harshness of its atmosphere from where we were, if we concentrated our senses in that direction. Jesus said that He had set us free from the cellar because He loved us. But He told us that He loved the people trapped in that city just as much and that His plan was that we should go down to that city and do for the people there what He had done for us. Everyone began to pack and prepare for the journey except me.

I said, "Lord Jesus, I can't do this. I love you and I cannot thank you enough for what you did for me. But I spent I-don't-know-how-long in that root cellar, and You rescued me when I was at the end of everything. I can't go to that city because it will be like going back to the cellar, and I can't do it. I can't believe you rescued us just to send us back there."

Jesus answered, "I love you. I rescued you because I love you. But I also want you to love Me back, and you demonstrate your love by obeying Me. If you do not obey Me, you cannot tell Me that you love Me. And I am telling you that I want you to go to the city and share My love with the people there."

"Jesus you don't know what you are asking. That place is no different than the cellar. You are just sending me back to the same claustrophobia and suffocation. It's no different than where I was before."

"But it is different, Son," He answered. "Now you can fly."

The bottom line is that prophecy—alive and well in the Church today to a degree it has never known before—is not given solely for evaluation, but for action. Prophecy is not entertainment for the people of God. When we get a sacramental outburst, we need to recognize it for what it is and act on it for the sake of the Kingdom and the abundant life, of which it is a deposit on the promise. We need to seek the teaching and the promised escalation and bear the incredible fruit that befits our ongoing repentance as we pave a straight highway in the desert for our God and King.

Endnote

1. Stephen Baldwin, with Mark Tabb, *The Unusual Suspect* (Nashville, TN: Warner Faith, 2006).

Chapter 10

WORSHIP AS WARFARE

One day a few years ago Diana and I were taking a carload of kids to the top of the Haleakala Volcano on the island of Maui. We had a wonderful time viewing and even walking in the moon-like landscape inside the magnificent crater, marveling at the change in temperature from the high 80s to the high 40s on what seemed like the top of the world, and praising God for the 19th-century Hawaiian princess who defied her gods and her culture when she accepted Iesu—Jesus—as her Lord and Savior. Kapiolani had seen men and women sacrificed to the volcano goddess; she had also seen terrible retribution poured onto those who did not please her. Yet, she took her new life so seriously that she stood on the lip of the crater and defied Pele—the goddess—to take her and prove that she was stronger than Jesus. When nothing happened but the peace of God—just as it was when Kryon failed to show up in Redding—many came to Christ.

We also thanked God for our borrowed vehicle as we started back down the corkscrew of a road that would return us to the valley and the sea. That road was legendary for its curves and the steepness of its incline, and I was being unusually focused on hugging it as we went. Suddenly something was not good, and it must have shown on my face because Diana looked at me and said, "Something wrong?" I whispered, as matter-of-factly as I could, "We have no brakes." Without skipping a beat or a breath she turned to the children behind us and said, "Let's sing *What a Mighty God We Serve.*" The kids broke into one of the favorite praise songs of Hawaii—not knowing why, but certain that it's always a good time to sing praises. Within half a minute the brakes came back online, and I pulled the minivan to a stop by the side of the road. Once we were securely stopped, with wheels cramped on the curbing, I tried them again—there was nothing.

Now it just did not make sense that one moment I had no brakes, the next moment they worked fine—just long enough to save our lives—and the moment after that we again had no brakes. It came to me only then that while I struggled to control the vehicle, Diana led the children into battle. The fight was against principalities and powers, not brakes and brake lines. She led the children to fight when she led them in worship, and the battle ended in victory for the Kingdom.

Some of God's greatest victories have been won solely on the basis of worship—whether the field of battle is physical or spiritual or both. When Joshua led the people to defeat an Amalekite army (see Exod. 17), the principal dynamic of victory was Moses' arms raised in worship throughout the battle. Joshua and his troops did no more to invest the walls of Jericho than to march around them—at the Lord's command—and offer musical worship to the Lord before He brought the walls down (see Josh. 6). God commanded King Jehoshaphat to send out the choir ahead of the troops when a much larger army attacked Judah (see 2 Chron. 20), because the Lord intended to fight in Judah's place; the people's task was to worship first and watch the enemy troops kill one another.

Daniel worshiped his way to victory (see Dan. 10) for 21 days, while angels fought over the Jewish people living in Persia in what was primarily a spiritual battle. In the last chapter I shared the story of Jacob DeShazer, Fuchida Mitsuo, and Peggy Covell being supernaturally linked for the bringing of the Gospel to Japan through their practice of the Presence of God. Their practice consisted—at ground level—of decisions to worship the Lord in the miserable conditions into which they had been thrust, and the fruit impacts a nation even today.

In early 2004, prophetic prayer warriors gathered on multiple Interstate Highway 5 overpasses on an appointed day to pray for God's blessing over California. We covenanted with each other to pray during a specified four-hour period while Tibetan Buddhist monks readied a sand mandala for deposit in the Pacific Ocean off the city of Santa Monica. The purpose of the mandala was to establish spiritual authority over California when the thousands of Buddhist gods (really demons) imprisoned in the sand would be released. The prayer warriors were instructed to utter no curses; they were to worship only while using the weapons of blessing, forgiveness, and communion as they were led. They were positioned on at least one overpass in every California county crossed by Interstate 5. Other intercessors worshiped on the pier itself, and in the museum where the mandala had been constructed. When the time for release arrived, the monks were astonished and disappointed: they were unable to contact their gods to release them from the mandala. They were afraid to step on the pier for reasons they could not explain, and when they tried to release the mandala into the water from the beach, a gust of wind blew the sand right back in their faces. We worshiped while God won.

Nate and Angelica were married in a church not long ago. Their guests were a mixed bag of serious believers, believers without a major league commitment to Jesus Christ, and a scattering of other spiritual types. The wedding party members were utterly convicted of their faith in the Lord Jesus. Nate and Angelica were determined that their wedding vows would draw more than the two of them into covenant. Their prayer was that this joining would leave one and all of the guests knowing they had been in the presence of the Living God.

At the rehearsal, one of the pastors involved gave a detailed account of the symbolism in each act that would take place—from the walk down the aisle on a carpet never before used to the giving of the Lord's Supper to bride by groom and to groom by bride. The couple planned to make it an interdenominational affair because they came from different backgrounds—but they were quite clear that their plans were more about First Corinthians 12 as a worldview, than about just letting all of the interested parties have a turn at doing something. They discussed the vows themselves with the guests, and they invited everyone to receive the Lord's Supper from the hands of the bride and groom—in the understanding that this was their first meal as husband and wife. The wedding party gathered before the ceremony to pray for the touching of every heart with the presence of God. And when the reception was well under way, the most popular comment seemed to be that the presence of God was pervasive in the church and could still be felt in the hall in the midst of the party. Worship was conducted as warfare that day—and everybody knew it.

Three things need to be said about worship—whether on a Sunday morning, in a brakeless vehicle on the slope of a Hawaiian volcano, or in the midst of the celebration of the joining of a man and a woman into one flesh. Worship is primary; authentic worship escalates; and worship frames our existence.

WORSHIP IS PRIMARY FOR GOD'S CREATURES

Reality is that in worship we reach the crescendo of our humanity, for only in the intimacy of worship do we most fully exercise the image of God in which we are made; at best it is as though we walk with God in the cool of the evening like Adam did. It is axiomatic in the behavioral sciences that behavior impacts brain chemistry. When we make a statement such as, "Love is not a feeling that leads to an action; it is a series of actions that lead to a feeling," we are stating a scientific verity. Likewise, when we worship God in spirit and in truth, over time we become more and more like Him.

It is neither accident nor act of extraordinary piety that men and women of faith—inside and outside of the Bible—

come to worship before, during, and after great crises in their lives. They may or may not comprehend the centrality of worship for framing their very being, but they surely know through the eyes of faith that they are drawn to worship the Lord as a moth is drawn to a flame. From the early Hebrew tribesmen who erected an altar at each passing of their journey, to Gideon throwing himself down to worship outside the Midianite camp as the Lord shows him the visionary strategy of coming victory, to David dancing before the Lord as the ark is brought into Jerusalem—and worshiping with all of his heart when news of his baby's death arrives—worship is as normative as it is primary.

In our own time, American presidents from Washington and Lincoln to both Roosevelts, Reagan, and the two Bushes have called Americans to prayer for aid and in thanksgiving—not so much in a civil action as in recognition that we are not the source of our own lives and we need to turn to the One who is. In the days following September 11, 2001, as in the days following Pearl Harbor, the churches and synagogues of the nation were crowded to the bursting point. (It could be argued that if they were that crowded prior to these days the events might not have occurred, but that is for another time.) Lieutenant Carey Cash, a chaplain with the Fifth Marine Division and one of the first Americans to cross into Iraq in 2003 tells story after story of miracle preceded and followed by acts of worship in his book, *A Table in the Presence*.[1] War brings out the worst in humankind, but it also brings out the best and most basic in us.

God's presence is so prevalent in war that many are tempted to decide that He is on our side—whichever side that may be—and against our enemies. But God makes it crystal clear in Joshua 5—when Joshua encounters an armed man on the road to Jericho and asks if he is for the Israelites or the other side—that the only question on His mind is whether we are on His side. "Neither," says the man with drawn sword, "but as commander of the army of the Lord I have now come." We have unlimited access to God through the blood of the Lamb and the love of the Father; the question is to what degree we give Him access to us. Joshua worships.

Richard Foster wrote that in real prayer we come to think God's thoughts after Him. He was writing of prayer, but inasmuch as prayer connects us to God, expresses our longing for Him, and places us in a relationship of looking up from where we are, there is no way I can imagine to distinguish real prayer from real worship. It all comes from the same neediness and the same gifting.

This primacy is on earth as it is in Heaven. Before Neil Armstrong placed the first human footprint on the surface of the moon, his companion in space, Edwin Aldrin, made the first act of worship on that surface in the service of Holy Communion—brought from earth so that man's time on the moon could begin in the proper way—just as the Apollo 8 astronauts felt compelled to read from the book of Genesis and broadcast it all over the world as they became the first men to orbit the moon at Christmastime 1968. Worship defines who we are while at the same time assisting us in becoming who we are called to be.

AUTHENTIC WORSHIP ESCALATES

In Acts 1, the disciples are instructed to steep in both word and worship, to pray, and to obey the instructions God has already given. Their primary activity is to be in the temple daily praising God as they study the Word and seek a replacement for Judas. (Waiting and replenishing the apostolic band are the only orders they have yet received.) In Acts 2 the tongues of fire fall and everything shifts into high gear. They are now called to continue in the apostles' teaching and fellowship, the prayers, and the breaking of bread—words may change but the instructions have not. They still spend time in the temple daily, offering their praises to the Lord in the heightened sensitivity and authority that are the gifts of the Holy Spirit post-Pentecost.

The first six chapters of the Book of Joshua are an extended narrative of escalating worship as warfare. In the first chapter, Joshua is at worship and the Lord speaks great promises to him—wherever the feet of Israel falls it will be given them—and reminds him to never fail to meditate on and obey the Law, which has been given in Sinai. By Chapter 3 the people are ready to cross the Jordan, which is in flood; God tells Joshua to put the ark on the shoulders of the priests, because when they enter the river carrying it, He will stop the flow.

I am certain the priests must have grumbled to the effect that God was perfectly able to stop the flow before they entered and risked drowning, but they do step into the river, and God does enable them to cross on dry land at that point. They build an altar to mark the spot and decide they are now ready to head for Jericho, but God says, in effect, "Not so fast." He points out that the men of military age have not been circumcised, and this must happen before they can go out on behalf of the Lord their God. (See Joshua 3–4.) I am just as convinced that they must have told God about how dangerous it was to be recovering from surgery for a week while camped in enemy lands—how will they defend themselves if attacked? But the Lord is adamant, and they do as He commands, hoping He will protect them as He has promised. The week passes without disaster and they are again ready for Jericho—they think—but the Lord again says, "Not so fast." It is time for Passover, and He expects them to remain in camp—unarmed—for another week of worship. They undoubtedly grumble again about how easy it is for someone who cannot be speared or struck, and how likely it must be that the Canaanites have by now located them, but they remain in camp and celebrate Passover. Another week passes without incident and they are quite sure it is time to attack Jericho. But the Lord says, "Not so fast," one more time. (See Joshua 5.)

The Lord their God now expects the children of Israel to march around the walls of Jericho each day with worship as their sole weapon. They are to blow the trumpet on the seventh day and watch God bring down the walls of the city that He has promised to deliver into their hands. Once again, there must have been anguished cries of, "Within bowshot? What is He thinking?" (See Joshua 6.) They may grumble but they are beginning to get the hang of this escalation thing; they do as they are commanded, and God does as He has promised. But the point of it all is that the worship of God—and the intimacy that both accompanies and constitutes it—has been escalating chapter by chapter and week by week. God is always calling us deeper and closer; it stands to reason that worship as a practice would be taking us there.

WORSHIP FRAMES OUR EXISTENCE

Sacrifice and *sacrament*—whether called by these names or some other—are the twin pillars of life with Yahweh. To *sacrifice* is "to make holy by giving to God." It need not always include death (we refer to the sacrifice of Isaac rather than of the ram, even though Isaac does not die), but the death and accompanying blood of the sacrifice is certainly the norm that pictures the irrevocable quality. *Sacrament,* as discussed in an earlier chapter, is "a deposit on God's larger promise." Sacrament partakes of the fulfillment in the sense that the act of baptism is done in real time with real water even as it symbolizes the eternal river of living water in which God wants us to swim. The Supper of the Lord is a symbol of the heavenly banquet delivered in terms of food that is both real and sacredly partaking of the one bread and the one cup that Jesus blessed and gave. Pentecost is a deposit on the promised harvest of all souls, which is promised in every one of the Gospels, rooted in prophecy of Holy Spirit poured out on all flesh (see Joel 2) and demonstrated in the 3,000 who enter abundant life on that morning.

These three sacramental moments occur during times of worship and are grounded in sacrifice.

Baptism—whether public or private—is an act of sacrificing the right of self-determination for the person receiving the sacrament, and it is a rite of initiation and inclusion for the Lord and the witnesses. Holy Communion is, of course, the worship time of which Jesus commands its frequent repetition, "for the remembrance of me," and it is called by many Christians "our sacrifice of praise and thanksgiving" after the traditional language of the rite. Pentecost—which cannot be separated from the Great Commission—is that harvest that follows giving God the glory. That happens in churches, at weddings, on battlefields, and anywhere and *any-when* in which God is given glory; for the giving of glory to God is both the essence of worship and what makes it so attractive. These three: baptism, communing with one another in the name of the Lord, and the pursuit of God's harvest, are what establish the boundaries of our humanity.

Mankind alone is capable of entering into relationships that are voluntary, reciprocal, and developmental. Greek rooted philosophers think the essence is in our ability to make language and to think and plan ahead, but anthropologists and students of animal behavior have shown that animals do these things to a much higher degree than was thought when I was a boy—although I always knew that a cat could make a plan and a dog could ask to come in or go out. Anthropologists think the heart of humanity is in our use of tools, but otters use rocks to get at and open their food; orangutans use sticks even to fight their wars. Poets and psychologists—not to mention the producers of Star Trek—think the center of humanity is in the deep feelings we harbor. Yet, anyone who gets into the woods—or his or her own backyard—or sees an octopus change color at an aquarium, knows that emotion is not unique to human beings.

But the voluntary choice of an association, the willing abandonment of prerogative—real or imagined—that is best symbolized in confessing Jesus with the lips, believing Him in the heart, and acting on that confession through baptism—is unique to Adam and his progeny. Animals will congregate, and even mate, but they do not choose from among alternatives when they do this. Choice, coupled with commitment when we take a job, make a friend, or enter into marriage, is something only we are capable of, and it is the reason that God was able to walk with Adam in the cool of the evening.

Reciprocity is what is created when one person responds to another, not necessarily with an equal and opposite reaction, but with a chosen behavior that restores balance, completes a transaction, escalates or ends a conflict, or simply expresses gratitude. (Dog bites dog who in turn bites back, for instance.) If you steal my dog, I might forgive you, negotiate with you for his return, sue you, or call the police, but it is unlikely that I will simply steal your dog to get even. Reciprocity is what we share in the communion, whatever form or tradition it may reflect, as we remember what God did for us in the greatest spiritual battle of all time, responding with our praise and thanksgiving—and the sacrifice of the time it takes to worship in this way.

Pentecost symbolizes, in all ways, the developmental dimension that is unique to human beings. Development is what the whole complex of participation in escalating outbursts of His glory, trading our own sense of reasonable time for His journey-from-Galilee-to-Jerusalem sense of time, and a commitment to warfare by honor are all about. Animals are what they are; their personalities and potentialities are up front from the day of their birth. But we are each very different—hopefully better—human beings 20 years into marriage, career, and walk with God. Our ability to morph and grow is expressed in the Great Commission's mandate to teach one another to observe all that He has done and said; in His promise that we will do greater things than these in His name; and in the very fact that the Pentecost outpouring gave a glimpse, only in retrospect, of what it would be like to take the message to Samaria and all the world, and the many faithful adaptations that would become necessary as we grow into the fullness of the stature of Christ.

None of us, save Jesus, has attained full humanity yet. But our capacity for voluntary, reciprocal, and developmental relationships is what makes covenant possible for and in us alone of the many species God has created. Worship is, of course, the very essence of the covenant we have with God, in which He gives us abundant life and we promise to put Him first in our lives. But faithfulness to covenant relation is what the war between God and the enemy has been about since the apple in the Garden. Worship and praise are the ways we put God on the throne, alongside loving our neighbors just because we honor God when we do this, and so these become the reciprocal methods of dethroning the enemy. Worship then becomes the ultimate act of spiritual warfare.

No Substitute for Ministry

The sacrifice of Isaac is an ultimate act of both worship and ministry. Moses' departure from the burning bush on the road to Egypt ranks just as high. Scripture permits no substitution of the one for the other.

God has called Abraham to return the gift he waited a century to obtain. God promised Isaac to Abraham as a feature of their covenant together. Abraham has not always been completely faithful—there are the incidents with Hagar and Ishmael—but this time he does not hesitate. God has asked for obedience and service before Him, and Abraham does not even question the obvious fact that this God who prides Himself on being the only God who does not require human sacrifice now requires a human sacrifice. When Abraham reaches the place God has shown him, he tells the servants to wait. "Stay here with the donkey while I and the boy go over

there. We will worship and then we will come back to you"
(Gen. 22:5).

God tells His people over and over again from one end of
the Bible to the other that He is not interested in sacrifice for its
own sake. He wants the sacrifice of a broken and contrite heart;
He wants justice and mercy to roll like a mighty river; He wants
worship in spirit and in truth; He wants the widows and orphans to be warmed and well fed. Our worship is not purposed
to make us comfortable, but to do the work of the Father as
Jesus does when He heals on the Sabbath as quickly as He will
preach and pray on the Sabbath. "To obey is better than sacrifice," God says in First Samuel 15:22—not that obedience is a
substitute for sacrifice, but is actually its highest form.

And so Abraham obeys what seems to make no sense, just
as Peter obeys the call to kill and eat the forbidden animals
seen in his vision of Acts 10. Abraham will later remember
that God is the One who provides and that He only appears
to contradict Himself from time to time. Peter will recall at
some point that Jesus declared all foods clean way back in
Mark 7. But Abraham will only discover the ram that God has
provided for the sacrifice by taking Isaac and going to the
place of sacrifice, just as Peter will only recognize God's blessing on the Gentiles after he enters the centurion's home in
the aftermath of his mind-blowing vision. God has received
the obedience He wanted, and the men are prepared for the
next step in their respective journeys because they did not attempt to separate worship from the obedience that informs
all ministry.

Moses' situation is not so unlike Abraham's. He is out
shepherding when he sees a bush in flames that will not be

quenched. Spontaneous combustion in the desert is not so odd; unquenchable flame is something else. When Moses sees that he is in the presence of the Living God, he is properly awed and behaves accordingly. That is to say, he removes his sandals and worships. When the dialogue gets around to going off to Egypt to rescue the people whose cries the Lord has heard, it gets a little more complicated for Moses. True, he made an attempt at rescue before leaving the country and joining the family of Jethro, but it was an impulse and the fruit was not good. Now the Lord wants him to go back to the land of his disgrace and carry out a sustained rescue operation—with no leeway given for the vagaries of poor impulse control.

Even Captain Nemo of the submarine Nautilus understands that individual acts of heroism are of little value in isolation. He tells Professor Arronax that good must build upon itself in order to become strong. God is calling Moses to high stakes discipline, and Moses gives Him an argument, unlike Abraham. He does commit to the mission, eventually, and proves to be more consistently faithful than even Abraham once he starts. But the point of it all is in Exodus 3:12, "And God said, 'I will be with you. And this will be the sign to you that it is I who have sent you. When you have brought the people out of Egypt, you will worship God on this mountain." In other words, the cycle of worship and obedience to the ministry call and back to worship is laid out in the very beginning of the history of the people of God as a people.

The people of Yahweh need constant reminders—just as we do today. In Isaiah 58 the prophet thunders that they fast without really fasting and humble themselves for a show—and then wonder why God is not impressed. But what really

stokes the prophetic fireball is the total disregard for the authentic fast of Yahweh in which the chains of injustice are
loosed, the naked clothed, and the hungry fed. Isaiah says
that God will hear the prayers when the yoke of oppression
and the pointing finger of gossip are loosened. He calls the
people to spend themselves on behalf of the poor and then
come to worship. It changes little by Jesus' day; He calls on
the Pharisees and other leaders to tithe justice and kindness—without neglecting the other goods from which the
first fruits are to go to God—because in truth the God who
has given it all in the Person of His Son wants it all in the person of our obligation of ourselves (see Matt. 23:23).

Apparently we still don't have it. James devotes plenty of
ink in his epistle to the obligation for ministry to authenticate
worship. "If anyone considers himself religious and yet does not
keep a tight rein on his tongue he deceives himself and his
religion is worthless. Religion that God our Father accepts as
pure and faultless is this: to look after orphans and widows in
their distress and to keep oneself from being polluted by the
world" (James 1:26-27). He must not think he's hit it hard
enough; he devotes almost half of the second chapter to an
exhortation about action speaking louder than words. We may
deceive ourselves into believing that prayer for revival and
transformation is more important than taking a bag of groceries
to a poor family, and we may reverse the deception as well. The
reality is that God wants it all before He will call it worship that
is of value in the war for which He has recruited us.

The message of Amos and Hosea is that worship instead
of justice and mercy is just another form of idolatry—short-
cutting to God—and Joel calls for worship as the response
to disaster, which is brought about by justice and idolatry

(see Amos 5:21-24; Hosea 6:6; Joel 1:14; 2:12-17). The call is for worship in its fullness, with the inclusion of repentance for the errors and neglects that made way for disaster, because authentic worship enthrones the Lord and makes way for the coming of His Kingdom down that straight highway in the desert for which Isaiah also pleads. In Bible times victorious kings would return to their thrones only after their people had constructed a new roadway for them to travel in triumph. If we would be agents of transformation in our communities, we need to be leaders of the kind of corporate repentance that builds that highway of praise, thanksgiving, and obedience.

That means—among other things—that we include prayer for our brothers and sisters who are sick or sad or desperate in the service alongside an opportunity for them to be prayed for in front of God and everybody, whatever style of prayer we may favor. It means—if we belong to a church that serves communion regularly—we send the meal out to sick and shut-in members with people trained and commissioned for that kind of ministry. And it means we do not do our caring for the poor in a corner.

I mentioned a miracle in an earlier chapter in which 38 prime rib roasts were miraculously increased to about 60 when the workers were faithful in their generosity and extravagant in their prayer on the day that about 50 percent more people showed up for Christmas Dinner than were expected. The occasion was the annual meal put on by so many churches for the poor, and this is always a good and pleasing thing to God. But the difference in the church that saw the miracle is that, for them, the use of paper plates is out of the question. Volunteers bring their best crystal and china for the table they agree to host. Others wait on each table as though it were for a reservation at the most exclusive restaurant in the city. Still, others drive the buses that go to bring the people to dinner and take them home. And the invisible ones are the ones in the prayer room throughout the feast as they seek God's face for every one of the honored guests. When we set the table for God in this way, it should be no great surprise that He personally shows up.

Ministry on the Sabbath is one of the ongoing controversies between Jesus and the religious leaders of His culture. Jesus is a Sabbath keeper, not a Sabbath breaker; the controversy develops from the failure of these leaders to detect the connection between worship that includes ministry and worship that limits itself to acts of piety alone. In Matthew 12:11-13, He asks if any of them would fail to rescue a sheep that has fallen into a pit on the Sabbath—which is specifically permitted in Torah—before He proceeds to heal a man with a withered hand in the synagogue. Another such healing is recounted in John 5, and Jesus' response to the accusers is a simple, "My Father is always at His work to this very day, and I, too, am working" (John 5:17). He later adds "I tell you the truth, the Son can do nothing by Himself; He can do only what He sees His Father doing, because whatever the Father does the Son also does" (John 5:19). They completely miss the point that if we are made in the image of God, we are made for His imitation as well—and at all times.

We need our rest, and it is for this reason that God has commanded us to take it. Jesus frequently leads the band of disciples into the hills for times of retreat and rest in prayer and worship. But He seeks passionately to get it across to us that the best rest in the world is in placing our full attention on

God and joining Him in what He is doing. This is the essence of worship as warfare; it is worship in spirit and in truth.

As a pastor I am often called upon to visit the sick on the Sabbath. One time I brought communion to Iris late on a Sabbath morning as she lay dying from lung cancer. When I arrived she was in restraints because she had become delirious and combative during the night. When I arrived I spoke to her as she thrashed about in the bed; I said, "Iris, it's Father Jim, and I want you to know that I am here and that Jesus is here." She immediately relaxed, took a deep and peaceful breath, and went home to be with Jesus. I will always be glad that I was there with this little one, and that it was a Sabbath day.

Warring in worship draws us into that bed depicted in Luke 11:5-13—the one holding the uncountable multitude in intimate fellowship with the Father, Son, and Spirit—but also one in which everyone is ready at all times to jump up and answer the door for any who may have found themselves outside and needy.

WHEN SUBMISSION MEETS PROVISION

The paradox is that while God's provision for the unfolding and implementing of His Will and His Kingdom is unlimited, there is simply no way to do His Will outside of our abject dependency on His Spirit operating in us. Even Jesus is unable to minister the Kingdom in the absence of that faithful submission which draws the Spirit. Mark 6:5-6 reports, "He could not do any miracles there, except lay His hands on a few sick people and heal them. And He was amazed at their lack of faith," in His hometown of Nazareth. Faithful submission is what marks the centurion who calls on Jesus to heal his servant from a distance in Matthew 8 and Cornelius—that other centurion—who begs Peter to come and minister the Gospel in Acts 10 following Peter's vision of the animals on the cloth. It is this submission that opens us to the exercise of the always-available authority of the unarmed man. When the submission, which is ours, meets the provision, which is His, beef roasts tend to multiply, demonic spirits in sand mandalas are scattered in the wind, and Christians begin to impact their communities in the power of the Spirit.

PrayNorthState is one of several prayer ministries making a monthly visit to the state of California's capitol in Sacramento. The land on which the capitol is located was a donation from the Roman Catholic Church in California in the 19th century, and we have had the privilege of honoring their leaders during some of our visits. As we protocoled the Catholic leaders— engaging warfare by honor—so we protocol authorities from the state government. In our case we work with a number of Christians who happen to be elected members of the state assembly or senate and who are willing to arrange the use of a hearing or committee room inside the building. We bring interdenominational teams, ranging in size from half a dozen to as many as two-dozen; we exercise the weapons of our warfare in terms of blessing, forgiveness, and communing in the name of the Lord; and we worship Him in song, prayer, and the speaking of portions of His Word over the state and her government. We include prayer warriors from Sacramento itself (students from the state university come when they can), the greater Redding and Chico areas, some of the tiny communities near the Oregon border, and from the Los Angeles basin in our gatherings. We come as a cross-section of the state as much as of the Body.

Our theory is simple enough. Jesus won all power and authority on the cross He bore in Jerusalem 2,000 years ago; yet He still says to all men and women, "Behold, I stand at the door and knock" (Rev. 3:20 KJV). California demonstrates her original dedication to Christ in the plethora of Christian place names that dot her maps—from Los Angeles to San Jose and San Francisco and San Diego—to the naming of her capitol city and river after the Supper of the Lord and His presence in the midst of us when we celebrate it. In imitation of Him we knock on every door we can find; when we are admitted we address worship as warfare to Him, but we do not assert prerogative. Like the King Himself, we stand on privilege and promise alone.

California has earned the reputation in some Christian circles of holding an anti-family and anti-business atmosphere in a legislative and regulatory death grip. Certainly since the regular prayer visits of Aglow, the Governor's Prayer Team, National Day of Prayer affiliates, and our own ministry (among others) began, there have been significant pieces of hostile-to-families legislation that have been defeated or vetoed. Redefinitions of marriage, assisted suicide authority, and restrictions on parental rights to discipline and educate children as they see fit have died. Restrictions on commerce and attempts at tracking the movements of citizens have been eased or eliminated. There is no way to document a connection with the prayer movement, and the truth is that similar measures continue to be passed and signed into law. But there has been significant and demonstrable fruit—and the encouragement through this fruit to keep waiting on the Lord in worship.

When we first began these prayer visits some years ago, we were struck by the stuffiness of the atmosphere inside the capitol. It was as though someone had drawn most of the oxygen from the building for the first year. Yet, more and more as we offer to God the sweet fragrance of simple and heartfelt worship we—and newcomers to our group—comment that the air is noticeably freshened. We pray and prophesy over the ones who join us and send them back refreshed and re-energized for their ministries on campus and in the cities from which they come. The most spectacular changes we see in the capitol are in the faces of the staffers who come for prayer and do the daily legwork for their legislative employers. We get calls and e-mails frequently from these hardworking albeit unsung officials telling us of the changes in their own lives as we pray for those who keep the machinery of state government in their care.

One aid told me that when we first began asking his help, he thought we were certifiable nutcases; he said that after the first year the fruit of the Spirit, evidenced in his own sense of peace and hope, was too overwhelming to attribute to anything other than God's influence on his life mediated through our presence. Another aid has begun praying with authority for her colleagues on both sides of the aisle and reports at least one healing from a life-threatening cancer in the brother of one of the aides from the other political party. The cancer had been ruled untreatable by the man's doctors. We understand the miracle as a sacramental outburst—we praise God for His healing of a man and the reconciliation He brings between two representatives of opposing political viewpoints—as we await the unfolding of His promise to claim our state and her government.

Annual visits to the Battlefield of Culloden in Scotland yield tremendous fruit of this type. This Celtic equivalent of the Little Bighorn in our own culture was the site of a 1746 massacre of Scottish Highlanders and the death of the dream of Scots' independence from England. Intercessors from each of the regions of Scotland make periodic visits to pray for revival and transformation in that land; until recently all reported an overwhelming sense of confusion over the battlefield rendering any sort of insightful prayer a virtual impossibility. (Diana and I were struck by this confusion on our own first visit in 2005.) The strategy has been to keep worshiping there until breakthrough would come, and on our return in 2006, we saw that the sense of confusion was gone.

On that same occasion, we had a prophetic word to honor the ancient enemies of our clan—we are descendants of Grahams, and the Campbells are heirs of a long enmity with our people among others. In obedience we went to the mass grave of those Campbells who fought in the service of the English invaders in 1746. We knelt at the headstone and prayed blessings on our ancient enemies and on all of their descendants. We anointed the stone with oil and watched as the generous serving we had poured out was literally sucked into the stone. We praised the Lord in our awe and reflected that if the very stones were that thirsty for healing and forgiveness the thirst in the heart of the people of Scotland—scattered all over the world in the aftermath of their failed war against their English overlords—must be of biblical proportions.

We returned the following year—for our God is a God of duration and waiting upon His purposes—and this time the prophetic word was to come with representation of the English who fought at Culloden. All of our efforts to construct a team of Americans and Scots—of Scottish and English descent—were frustrated as one after another of those committed to the journey were forced by circumstances to drop out. Only when we arrived at the home of our hosts did we discover that the man of the house was a direct descendant of the English soldiers who fought at Culloden. Not only did he exhibit this descent, his family had remained in the Highlands to serve the conquered people after the battle. Although completely unfamiliar with the concepts of prophetic activity that we teach, he accompanied us to the battlefield as his way of honoring his foreign guests. Once there he began to prophesy Luke 9:60 as we worshiped, "Let the dead bury their own dead, but you go and proclaim the Kingdom of God." On a day when renovations of the site were underway, to make sure the memory of the bloodshed would always be fresh in minds and hearts, there could have been no more appropriate word from the Lord.

Later we discovered that the Osprey or Sea Eagle—as symbolic of the Central Scottish Highlands as the Bald Eagle is for us in the United States and extinct there for many past decades—had returned to the Highlands in the form of one mating in the same year the confusion over Culloden had lifted. The eagles are now everywhere in the land, and they are but one sign, along with the paired buck deer cited in an earlier chapter, that God is in the land and on the move. The warfare of worship is paving a straight highway for Him in the desert of hearts that thirst for Him.

A commitment to unrelenting worship is a commitment to protocol the Lord our God. It is what the disciples do when Jesus calls them to cast their net on the other side of the boat in Luke 5:1-11. He is standing on the shore of Lake Gennesaret when He notices the discouragement of Simon and his co-workers after a night of no catch. He enters the boat and asks Simon to put away from the land a short distance so that He can teach from that vantage point. But while He is teaching He asks Simon to put the nets over the side one more time. It is clear from the text that the fishermen—who are expert enough at their craft to have acquired a small fleet of boats—have no more expectation of success now than I had when I prayed for Kaifafa in Fiji. "But because you say so, I will let down the nets," says Simon nonetheless (Luke 5:5). They are—of course—overwhelmed when the catch is so enormous it threatens to break the nets and sink two of the boats. Although he has not been worshiping up to now—he was, after all, a man at work— Simon now falls to his knees before this Lord he had not recognized before. But Jesus lifts him and tells him that as he worships he should also plan to escalate into catching men and women from now on. We can infer that Simon's obedience in casting the net was the beginning of true worship in his life, as surely as it is the beginning of mission in the great pentecostal movement, which is shaped by the Great Commission.

Mission in the name of the Lord requires treating those He loves as we would treat Him. The apostle John's first letter is filled almost entirely with the exhortation to love our brothers and sisters as well as the repeated assertion that this agape love for one another is the prime symptom that we are in love with God. He goes so far in John 4:20-21 as to say, "If anyone says, 'I love God,' yet hates [rejects] his brother he is a liar. For anyone who does not love his brother, whom he has seen, cannot love God, whom he has not seen. And He has given us this command: Whoever loves God must also love his brother." But it is Luke 10:1-9 that shapes this commandment for us.

Jesus has sent 72 of His disciples out in the same way He sent the first 12 earlier—into the towns and villages where He has not yet appeared. As in Luke 9 He tells them to take nothing of their own; their resource is the Spirit that He has placed on them for ministry in His Name. He instructs them to bless each home they enter—without regard to what they think the householders deserve. He assures them that their peace will rest there if the inhabitants are prepared to receive it; if it returns, the people have self-selected out of the Kingdom. He tells them to hang out with the people in His instruction to stay where they are welcomed and to eat what they are given; Jesus earned His reputation as a glutton and wine-bibber by simply being with people and having no agenda other than loving on the folks His Father created through His Word. He further instructs them to heal the sick—that is, to meet the needs of the people they encounter as the Spirit of God enables. Finally they are to confess the faith that is in them—as we are to do in mission whether the location is Fiji or Fresno.

We bless, hang out, meet needs, and bear witness—in that order—because we are to earn the right to be heard before we give them something they need to hear. This is what Jesus does when He stands on privilege instead of on the prerogative He won in the act of creation and again on the cross, and we need to imitate Him—whether in prayer at a capitol built on land donated by a branch of the Body of Christ, sharing coffee with a neighbor who does not yet know our Master, or reading the Bible out loud over a city after first securing a permit from city officials. Sleeping where they sleep, doing what they do, and eating what they eat—so long as it is not specifically forbidden in Scripture—is the way we earn the right to be heard. All too often Christians think they can justify whatever rude or highhanded behavior they like because of some imagined moral superiority over their audience—like the man I knew who wore paper towels in his ears at his place of business to demonstrate his disgust for the rock music that blared from the speakers in his company cafeteria; thinking himself a paragon of integrity, he earned for himself only a reputation for weirdness. But when we prostrate ourselves before the Lord as a lifestyle—which is the original meaning of worship in most any language we might speak it—we see more and more the wisdom and the glory of this authority of the unarmed man that He practices at all times.

God demonstrated the truth of this authority one night with Navy Seals on a rescue mission. The team of eight Seals entered a building in which 30 or more hostages had been held by terrorists for a long enough timeframe that captivity and helplessly waiting for death were the only realities they knew. The Seals had taken out the guards, but a speedy exit to the extraction point was the only hope of ongoing life for them as well as for their charges. The hostages were huddled on the concrete floor in the fetal position and a seemingly comatose state of lethargy; the team leader, bristling with weapons, could not even get their attention as he pleaded with them to get up and follow him, explaining that carrying them out was beyond the capacity of his team.

Finally he laid his own body on the ground, assumed the fetal position, and spoke to the man who seemed as much leader of the hostages as anyone else. "I am here to rescue you. But you must all stand and follow me out of the building so that we can be picked up." When the man saw this big bristling commando in the same position of submission, his leaden veil of despair fell away. He stood up and helped get the others to their feet. It was not the incredible firepower carried by the Seals that saved the day; it was the quick thinking of their leader who so identified with the people he had come to save that they were able to identify with him.

Worship—understood paradoxically as an end in itself just as the burning bush of Exodus was a place of meeting with the Lord of Heaven and earth—and as a launching pad into ministry in Egypt from which the ministers will return with the harvest and the knowledge that they have never ceased to worship before the walls of Jericho come tumbling down—enables the developmental change in our DNA through which we progress from being people called to humanity to becoming authentic human beings in the image of the Living God. In this setting our submission meets His provision, and the Kingdom on earth as it is in Heaven is to be the inexorable result.

A HOUSE OF PRAYER FOR ALL NATIONS

In Mark 10 we are taken through a series of episodes with sacrifice as the unitary theme of many dimensions. First, there is the rich young man who wants desperately to follow Jesus—but not desperately enough to let go of the possessions through which he thinks he controls the events of his life (see Mark 10:17-23). Unwilling to prostrate himself before Jesus through sacrifice of the prerogative of wealth, he goes away saddened but unbowed. It is amazing how often we choose worship leaders based on their gifts and talents instead of on their demonstrated self-abasement before God. The same earthly math is applied in the choice of virtually all leaders in the Church—we wonder why transformation does not come to our communities—and the disciples are astounded when Jesus permits this man to depart. The Kingdom will not come on his watch.

Later in the chapter, James and John approach Jesus with their request to sit on His right and on His left when He comes into His Kingdom. (The scene would remind any teenager of calling shotgun as he enters his friend's car.) He replies that not even He has the option of choosing his shotguns in the Kingdom—and He does not seem to resent the fact—but He assures them that they will drink the cup of suffering prepared for His friends and Him before the glory begins. When the other ten hear of the attempted grab for power and prestige, they are furious; Jesus calls all of them together to remind them once again that God's thoughts and ways of looking at things are not ours. He offers them another chance to begin to look at things through God's eyes. (See Mark 10:35-45.)

> *You know that those who are regarded as rulers of the Gentiles lord it over them, and their high officials exercise authority over them. Not so with you. Instead, whoever wants to become great among you must be your servant, and whoever wants to be first must be slave of all. For even the Son of Man did not come to be served, but to serve, and to give His life as a ransom for many* (Mark 10:42-45).

Truth is that God enters the world in order to restore the structure of sacrifice on which it is based.

We are taught in our schools (sacred and secular) that nature is grounded in a concept called natural selection—we often express it as the survival of the fittest. While natural

selection does indeed take place in both nature and culture—
the big dog defeats his rivals and becomes the head of the pack,
while the biggest elk becomes the leader of the herd in the
same way—a look at the very foundations of nature reveals that
this is one of the biggest whoppers the devil ever told. Every
species of animal—from spiders to salmon—endures only
because parents sacrifice some or all of their lives to see to it
that their young are fed and protected from predators—from
the mammalian mother who gives the milk from her body, to
the bird who draws the eagle away from her nest by offering
herself as prey. (Were this not so, there would be no survival for
any species beyond a single generation.) The white blood cells
in our human bodies—each of which has an independent
existence of its own—launch themselves in a massive kamikaze
attack on any microbes that invade our bodies through breaks
in the skin or ingestion or any other means; they absorb the
invaders and wink themselves out of existence that we might
live in health and happiness. And our cultures proclaim, even in
our fallen and grubbing-for-supremacy mindset, that it is
always the hero who sacrifices himself or herself for the
community who is responsible for the well-being of that
community. We proclaim it because our created existence is
grounded in the concept of sacrifice-enabling survival.

Jesus' insistence on servant leadership in Mark 10—and
throughout the Gospels in both statement and demonstration—is about His intended restoration of authentic nature
through His sacrifice of self. He seeks true and spiritual worship as the bookends of that process when talking with the
woman at the well; she responds to His leading by returning
at once to her village, risking what little reputation she may
still possess on her challenge to "Come, see a man who told

me everything I ever did. Could this be the Christ?" (see John 4:7-26;39-42).

We are taught to think of the triumphal entry into Jerusalem on the donkey as a moment of dramatic self-assertion for the Lord because it is shown that the people shouted their *hosannas* and laid their branches in His path. But the prophecy He fulfills is Zechariah 9:9, "Rejoice greatly, O Daughter of Zion! Shout, Daughter of Jerusalem! See, your King comes to you, righteous and having salvation, gentle and riding on a donkey." A donkey for a mount, of course, is a mark of humility; many versions of the Bible use words like *humble* and *lowly* in place of *gentle* in the prophetic verse. This King is as unlike Nebuchadnezzar of Babylon and Xerxes of Persia, as Peter the fisherman and Paul the tent maker are unlike bishops with their coach-and-four-horses or the great leaders of denominations and television ministries with their entourage. No wonder the weapons we are assigned, when Paul talks of the weapons not of this world (although they are not named there) for demolishing the strongholds of the enemy, are those such as blessing, forgiveness, and the sharing of bread and wine in the name of the One who shared them in Emmaus on the first Easter evening (see 2 Cor. 10:3-5).

God is enthroned on the praises of His people while the enemy is enthroned on the sin and the shortcuts of the people of God. This is why God never judges a city or a nation on the basis of the evil it may express, but only in terms of the righteousness that is present or lacking within it. (Sodom would have been spared, according to Genesis 18, if but ten righteous men had been found there.) He is not interested in the shadow of a nation that has been stolen, but rather in the restoration of His Kingdom. That Kingdom is established by

His work and confirmed and consecrated in our worship and repentance before the resurrected Word of God incarnate.

All of this came together in my mind as we ministered in a Glasgow, Scotland church on a recent mission trip to the land of my ancestral home. It is a part of the Scots' psyche to believe so thoroughly in the Calvinist doctrine of human depravity that it is difficult for them to imagine a God who is actually in love with them and who joys over them. This congregation was no exception to the rule; they believed that God was doing wonderful things in many lands, but they were pretty sure He was not going to do them in the midst of such reprobates as themselves. They were happy to thank God for not sending them all to hell; they would ask little of Him beyond a bare salvation. As I preached of the heroic and prophetic signs we were seeing in their nation with our own eyes, the message was politely received; but there was little in the way of response. Until Heather came forward for prayer, that is.

Heather was born and had lived in the congregation for all of her 40-plus years. She had been born without hearing in one ear, and the hearing in the other was disappearing fast—in her increasing desperation, she asked the pastoral couple from the states to pray for her. We prayed alongside two Scots intercessors from the congregation for about 20 minutes and saw some reported improvement but nothing dramatic. I sent Diana and the Scots to the back with Heather so that they could keep praying and the worship could continue. They prayed for another 20-or-so minutes until the service was interrupted by Heather's shriek, "It's so loud! The music is so loud!"

The worship was not really all that loud; it was simply that she had never before heard it at full volume and in stereo. The Lord restored her hearing in the context of worship, and the escalation is that a cross-section of her congregation now knows that the miracle is real—she was born there—and that God intends to perform His wonders in their midst as well as in the midst of others. They cannot stop talking about it, and they cannot any longer escape the call of God on their lives to become not just people who worship but people of worship. Such a transformation features unlimited expectations of God and of themselves.

Worship is not intended to be so much something we do, as it is to be someone we become over time. If we view worship as primary, as escalating, and as framing our existence, we soon come to see that whatever shapes our worship, likewise shapes our lives. At the same time we can say just as truly that whatever has no place in worship—such as aggression and self-importance—has no real place in mission either. Praise God, we are made for authentic worship and authentic mission—against which the gates of hell are falling down as the army of God rides in on the donkeys He provides.

Worship is the way we corporately become that house of prayer for all nations that is described in Isaiah 56:1-8 and cited by Jesus in Mark 11:17.

Endnote

1. Lt. Carey H. Cash, *A Table In The Presence* (Nashville, TN: Thomas Nelson, 2004).

Chapter 11

REPENTANCE—THE BEGINNING

OF THE GOOD NEWS

It was my privilege to be one member of a focus group invited to view a rough cut of Mel Gibson's *The Passion of the Christ* in late 2003. I was especially struck by the flashback of the woman taken in adultery—one of many flashbacks shown as Jesus hung on the cross for our sins. The really striking feature of the scene as it unfolded in front of me was the complete lack of dialogue—the words of John 8 were unspoken as we watched Jesus draw a line in the sand that was straight and deep. When He stood the men with the stones looked at the ground and—one by one—began to let the stones fall from their hands onto the ground at their feet. They turned away and wandered off.

Actually there was one feature that was even more strik-ing—to me. Although no words were spoken on the screen, I distinctly heard the voice of my Savior saying—to these men and to me—"You have three options. You can throw your stones at this sinful woman; she deserves it and you have caught her red-handed. Or you can reflect that you are just as full of sin yourselves—in that case let he who is without sin among you cast the first stone. Or you can see that I stand with this sinner who needs me. You can cross the line I have drawn and stand with me and this sinful person. You can be where I am." (See John 8:3-11.)

As anyone who reads the Word knows, the men did not throw their stones. They knew the truth of what Jesus said, and they dropped their stones and went away. But they did not go the extra step and cross over to where Jesus stands with the one He has forgiven and told to go and sin no more. They pulled away from their sinful decision to stand as judge and jury over one who was no farther from the Kingdom than they, but they did not accept the invitation to step into abundant life.

Jesus didn't say it, but He could have added, "I'm not asking you to stand with this sinner; I am inviting you to stand with me. But I am standing with the sinner, and you have to decide whether to stand with me and include her, or stay where you are and reject both of us. I came to seek and to save—and to stand with—the lost." He could have added that, or He could just remind us that we have the Law and the Prophets and they surely testify to what He is doing on His side of that line in the sand.

Anyway we frame it, the men contented themselves with sliding no deeper into the sin in which they live as long as they reject the radical call of Christ into the larger life of the Kingdom. Accepting that call would require an equally radical repentance—turning away—from the edifice of respectability they have built on what they consider their adherence to their own invented standards of behavior. The have—in a variation of what every one of us does in our commitment to the bondage of original sin—substituted 613 laws and regulations for engagement with the living God and the abundant life His Son and Spirit have come to bring. In this incident they turn away from Him and return to their homes—no doubt resenting the challenge He offers and they reject. The good news is that He keeps renewing the offer.

The call to repentance is not a prelude to the Good News—it is the outset of it.

THE BEGINNING OF THE GOOD NEWS

Mark 1 begins with:

> *The beginning of the gospel about Jesus Christ, the Son of God. It is written in Isaiah the prophet: "I will send my messenger ahead of you, who will prepare your way"—"a voice of one calling in the desert, 'Prepare the way for the Lord, make straight paths for Him.'" And so John came, baptizing in the desert region and preaching a baptism of repentance for the forgiveness of sins* (Mark 1:1-4).

The first verse says it all. Mark offers the briefest narrative of the ministry of John the Baptist, although it includes the essential elements. We hear that he is only paving the way for a much more powerful figure who will come after. We see John calling the people of Israel—now Judea—to make a straight path or highway in the desert for our God and King and thus fulfill the word spoken by Isaiah. We hear the wonderful challenge to bear fruit that is consistent with repentance. But the best news is what we hear in that first verse—this challenge to repentance is not a preparation for the Gospel—it is the Gospel!

There have always been twin borders of that pathway in the desert. They are the ministries of prayer and worship from a humbled heart and service from a humbled life that is re-dedicated to following the pillar of cloud by day and the pillar of fire by night. The fruit never seems to be properly expressed in the gaudiness of ceremonialism that is empty of heartfelt need of salvation, and it is never present in activities that are designed to impress God with our devotion.

Second Chronicles 7:14 sums up the one when God says, "If my people, who are called by my name, will humble themselves and pray and seek My face and turn from their wicked ways, then will I hear from heaven and will forgive their sin and will heal their land." God delivers this oracle at the dedication of the temple in Jerusalem—an impressive enough occasion and one He does not scorn. But His real concern is always and obviously for the attitude of hearts turned over to Him, not just bodies in a kneeling position. As we established back in Chapter 5, the wicked things we do are symptoms of the worship we give to our substitutes for God—whether idols we build or habits of mind that refuse to join Jesus beside an adulterous woman because we cannot bear to think we too commit adultery and need His forgiveness and healing as much as do those we consider beneath us; in authentic humility we will turn toward Him and away from them.

When John the Baptist declares—in the more elaborate accounts given in Matthew and Luke—that the Lord can make true children of Abraham from the very stones on which we walk and when Jesus later speaks of turning hearts of stone to hearts of flesh, they do not seek to insult so much as to remind that it is God's creative act that provides citizens of the Kingdom. But they point out that God will act only when we ask—as though we mean it—and so the fruit of His creation becomes also the fruit of repentance.

Micah summarizes the other border of that desert highway in his proclamation, "He has showed you, O man, what is good. And what does the Lord require of you? To act justly and to love mercy and to walk humbly with your God" (Micah 6:7-9). If we would partner with the Lord in the unfolding of His Kingdom in our midst, He is not looking for great programs or impressive scholarship—although these things certainly have their place. He is looking for us to visit the sick and the imprisoned, to comfort the lonely, and to stand with the abused and afflicted. He is longing for us to pray with the authority He has given us in His Son and by His Spirit—whether or not we get instant gratification for our trouble. He is expecting us to treat one another the way He treats us.

Zechariah expresses the same truth even more forcefully in the eighth chapter of his prophetic book and just after the promise of a harvest that will be both envy and blessing for the nations who have looked scornfully on Israel. "'These are the things you are to do: Speak the truth to each other, and render true and sound judgment in your courts; do not plot evil against your neighbor, and do not love to swear falsely. I hate all this,' declares the Lord" (Zech. 8:16-17). The Jews have returned penniless from exile and come home to a ruined land. They have no prospects for self-improvement, and that is exactly where the Lord who makes His strength perfect in our weakness can always do His best work. Those same Jews returned to their land at the close of World War II—men and women without a place of their own and scorned by all the world—and Israel is today the fulfillment of that ancient promise uttered by Zechariah. None of this is rocket science, despite our best efforts to codify and analyze and place it under a microscope so that we might understand and claim grace as our own creation. When we repent enough to permit Him to re-create our hearts, the fruit is in treating one another the way He treats us—and all other things become possible when and if we seek first His Kingdom.

But repentance is the prerequisite. Jesus pleads with His own people in Matthew 13 when He speaks of the fulfillment of Isaiah's prophecy in Him:

> *You will be ever hearing but never understanding; you will be seeing but never perceiving. For this people's heart has become calloused; they hardly hear with their ears, and they have closed their eyes. Otherwise they might see with their eyes, hear with their ears, understand with their hearts and turn, and I would heal them* (Matthew 13:14-15).

The leaders to whom Jesus speaks believe that they have already repented, as do so many Christians today, because they have acknowledged the lordship of God over their lives. But repentance is not a one-time event. It is a process; otherwise why would Jesus indulge so many developmental images in Matthew 13 alone—from the parable of the sower to those of the mustard seed, the leaven in the loaf, and even the one about wheat and weeds growing together in the same field—a common enough sight in Judea and in any farmer's field of our time. The process Jesus has in mind is a progression of little lettings-go that can be so small as to resemble the invisible growth of one day in a mustard seed or a blade of grass. They can also be as dramatic as the issue of a new baby from the birth canal or the sudden outgrowing of Mr. Chun's leg on that morning in Fiji. The point is that our God is a God of duration—which translates into human terms like faithfulness—and He wants us to image Him in prayer and in service—accepting no substitutes and taking no shortcuts.

God's call to a lifestyle of repentance can be answered in the middle of disaster and in the midst of comfort—although the disaster calls are often easier for the simple reason that what God wants us to let go has already been ripped from our hands.

CONVENTIONAL AND UNCONVENTIONAL NEEDINESS

Steve has enjoyed a long career of leadership over many ministries in our region. He is a well-known icon of caring for children, the poor, and people who have suffered devastating losses at the hands of criminals and just plain horrific accidents. He was recently caught stealing from his current ministry venture, pled no contest to the charges, and was sentenced to a well-deserved term in state prison for what he did. What exactly did he do?

He took a shortcut to God. He led himself to believe that if he took small amounts for what seemed like necessities at the time it would do no harm because he planned to pay it back anyway. Some of the funds were used for ministry purposes, like going on a short-term mission to Africa to lend support to ministries there—when his fund-raising efforts did not bring in the needed money on time he saw a shortcut and walked it. Some of it went to pay for a badly needed vacation for his family that he had planned for years. He got a really good deal on the trip and decided not to wait until he could afford it. It was just another walk on a shortcut. Some went to pay for a wedding for people he loved—he took the shortcut rather than let them down. He held onto the altar of the leaven of Herod, and when it collapsed under him, the devastation was more paralyzing than the blow to Kaifafa in Fiji. The fruit of idolatry always is.

The good news is that Steve is making no excuses for himself. He is coming to grips with his idolatry and turning away from it. He has made a plan for restitution of what he stole after he completes his prison term. Most important of all, he is clinging to the Lord in prison like he never clung to Him before. That is repentance.

Steve has partnered with dozens of pastors and civic and political leaders over the years. He is a well-known figure in the church he attended until his arrest. Not one of these leaders remembered the statement Jesus makes in Matthew 25 that when we visit those who are sick or in prison we visit Jesus Himself. They bow at the altar of the leaven of the Pharisees—

satisfied that they have not committed adultery with their position and unwilling to risk whatever it is they believe would be at risk if they put down their daytimers and their blueprints for the next program or the next building project long enough to reach out to a brother who knows he does not deserve their care but who very much needs it. The need is enough for Jesus, but not for some of His own.

Clete grew up in a church I connected with for some years. (He was long gone by the time I became involved.) Over the years of his youth, he compromised his values for the thrill of the moment in an escalating pattern that began with a beer in middle school and progressed to stealing a little cash and smoking a little weed in high school. Just prior to his 21st birthday, he and a friend decided to rob a local derelict who had just gotten his welfare check; Clete and his friend needed to get money for drugs. They promised him drugs for the money, took him outside of the town where they lived, and killed him. Clete swore he never intended to harm the man; the situation just got out of hand, and the altar of Herod came crashing down on top of him too.

The pastor who had known Clete all of his life called me when the arrest was announced. He said he had spent all of the energy he could on Clete; now that he was retired, Clete and his problems belonged to me. He filled me in as much as he could in a phone conversation about a young man I had never before heard of. I went to see him in the county jail at once and found there a broken young man. He confessed his deep need of someone much bigger than himself and accepted Jesus as His Lord on the spot. He entered into abundant life and the peace passing understanding in the same moment.

One of the best ways to determine the authenticity of a so-called jailhouse conversion is in whether the inmate then begins to ask favors and intervention from the pastor. Clete asked nothing from me but prayer and instruction in the faith he had waltzed around for two decades but never before embraced. He told me later that—although he would rather be free on the outside—he would not trade the freedom he had on the inside for a return to even the risk of his former lifestyle. He pled guilty to all of the counts against him although; after two weeks of prayer, he believed the Lord was not giving him permission to testify against the partner who actually killed the victim. He received a sentence that was several years longer for his non-cooperation with prosecutors but said he believed it was the right decision; his partner was subsequently convicted and given a life sentence, and the last time I heard from Clete, he had led more than 30 inmates to the Lord and was struggling with his commitment to the Lord to quit smoking. That too is repentance—with a few bumps in the road.

Clete always remembered his former pastor as a friend and role model—even when he dismissed what the pastor tried to teach him. When Clete was broken, he did not hold the pastor's absence against him, but the pastor did forget Jesus' command to bear one another's burdens and thus fulfill His law. Like the Pharisees before him, he was convinced that his adherence to the law—he would have gone to visit Clete when he was pastor of the church—was all that God would ask of him. He missed the thrill of leading a bona fide prodigal home to his Abba. This prodigal would lead many more home when the Spirit had strengthened him; the old pastor missed out on that joy as well.

Hugh was an outlaw biker, a drug dealer, and one of the most miserably addicted men he had ever encountered. He always carried a nine millimeter pistol with him, and nobody messed with him—that would be a seriously life-threatening mistake. He imagined the leaven of Herod bowing to him. Yet as dangerous as Hugh was, and as capable of taking whatever he wanted and using it in any way that might please him at the moment, he only longed for the promised peace of death. One night he rented a motel room, cleaned and loaded his gun, laid it on a table, and got ready to end his life. As he walked to the table to pick up the gun, he saw the Gideon Bible that is placed in so many hotel and motel rooms. He became enraged, threw the book down on the floor, and shot it with his gun. He then collapsed sobbing onto the bed. Later that night he begged the Lord Jesus to set him free, and that is exactly what Jesus did.

Today Hugh leads the regional incarnation of one of the most successful recovery ministries in history. He is happily married and one of the gentlest men I have ever met. He thinks it the most unimaginable miracle that God does anything worthwhile with such a one as he—and he revels in the reality that the Lord is constantly on the lookout for just such a one as he. He considers his repentance to be a process in which he will be fully invested for the rest of his life. That is major league repentance.

Hugh is welcomed to speak in some of the churches of our region while others prefer he not get too close because of the unsavory-looking characters he hangs out with. He was asked to vacate the church that had given him office space for a time because some of the members were frightened of the people they saw coming onto their campus to visit Hugh and his workers. God has provided Hugh with offices much more spacious and comfortable than what he had to give up. He cannot believe the favor God and his new landlord have shown him. The congregation that asked him to leave cannot know how their adherence to the leaven of the Pharisees has robbed them of the opportunity to learn that mercy is better than sacrifice.

All of these people are compromised in their faith—some on conventional altars and some on altars not so conventional. The difference is only between what God says about faithfulness and what our cultural consensus says, for that consensus establishes conventions within which we try to live. We understand that stealing and murdering and drug dealing cannot be tolerated because they threaten the health of our culture—and so they do. But God understands that turning our backs on the people who need a hand that they clearly do not deserve threatens the health of the Kingdom as surely as do the other compromises. People of any kind of compromise need to recognize that repentance is not just something we do when we renounce a former way of life and receive Jesus' offer of abundant life in exchange for our prior sins. It is a process that begins at that point and continues at least until we stand before the throne in the Presence of the King who is clothed in Majesty.

Wherever Holy Spirit transformation has come upon a community or a nation, it begins with people who recognize their bankruptcy before the Lord and enter into a process of progressive repentance. Sometimes these people are recognized leaders when the process begins. Sometimes they become recognized as leaders because they have visibly entered into that process and the fruits have become evident in their lives and in the lives of the people around them who have followed their lead. It is a process that is as crucial in our corporate life as in our personal existence.

When Jackson Senyonga and others in the Church in Uganda became heartbroken over the poverty—spiritual and material—of their nation, he was just another pastor of a few dozen Africans with little hope. Today his church numbers in the thousands, and his nation has astounded the world as the infection rate from AIDS has been cut in half. When church leaders like Poate Mata in Fiji reflected on their own impotence to heal the ethnic and cultural rifts that triggered a bloody coup there in 2000, they soon realized that their own intolerance of each other was the principal culprit. They began to join together in all night prayer vigils—not ignoring but rejoicing in the fact that God had made so many different styles and concepts to glorify Him and still remain within the confines of His written record called the Bible. They continued their corporate repentance with acts of contrition and apology to the families of missionaries they had murdered and cannibalized in the 19th century—they did not take refuge behind the bromide that it was all so long ago or that it was covered by the Blood. Time heals only when Jesus steps into it, and the Blood covers only what we surrender to it.

Fiji and Uganda continue to experience poverty and political instability. (Fiji experienced another coup in 2006, and the leaders on both sides claim to be following Jesus in what they have done.) This means only that the process of repentance in these nations is not finished—and neither is the glory that God means to unleash there. Their advantage over the rest of us is that they have fewer and fewer conventions behind which to stand and excuse themselves. They know that the call to repentance—the opportunity to turn away from the best they can do to the best that God can do with people willing to lay down their lives and progressively take on His life—is the beginning of the Good News of Jesus Christ. They joy in it.

TWO VISIONS

God has given me two visions over the past decade, both dealing with His call on the Church—first—to engage in a progressive repentance that abandons any pretense of an earned righteousness. Ironically enough, both came in the same weekly gathering of pastors for prayer in my city, although they were given some years apart.

In the first vision I found myself standing on a beach from which the water had been drawn back. (I did not know at the time that this means a tsunami is coming.) The newly uncovered shingle was a mass of sand and rocks, shells and marine plants, all jumbled together. There were many beachgoers on the shore, and I somehow knew that all of them were Christians. As soon as they saw their beach so dramatically increased, they ran onto the newly dry land and began to bring order out of the chaos they found there. Small groups clustered in various parts of the beach and busied themselves in cooperative efforts to arrange the sea shells and rocks and other things they found in well thought out patterns of great beauty. They were doing this for the glory and pleasure of God, but they were not watching to see what God was doing.

As I looked up I saw the water that had pulled back rising into a hundred foot wall of coming destruction. It was a tsunami and it was poised to fall with all of its crushing weight right on the groups of people so busily arranging the orderly patterns on the beach. My heart froze at the magnitude of the danger, until I looked again and saw Jesus surfing the great wave.

In the vision I called to Jesus, "You can't let the wave fall on these good people. Their plan is to help you; they're arranging all that stuff for your pleasure." He answered that they didn't care at all what He wanted; their only care was to do what they wanted to do. He said, "If they cared about me they would be looking at me." I saw that He was dealing objects into the wave, like a dealer would deal cards. When I looked closer, I saw that He was dealing people into the wave; when they were dealt they had a surfboard and were surfing the wave with Him. He said, "These are the ones who care enough about their life in me to keep letting go of their own life. They keep letting go of whatever I am not doing at the moment. They keep their eyes on me and what I do they do— and you can see they do it as well as I do."

I tried one more time. "But Jesus, you are a God of order and not of chaos. If this wave falls there will be nothing but chaos all over that beach—not to mention the bodies of the dead." He answered, "The dead are going to have to bury their own dead. Do you think for one minute I cannot make every drop fall exactly where I want it to? My plans include a tsunami; their plans are about arranging shells on a beach. They are going to have to choose, as these have chosen. Or not."

I have real-time experience of a congregation that failed the test of the tsunami, although the consequence was nowhere near as dramatic as what the vision threatened— yet. The church was filled with the Holy Spirit, and the signs

and wonders that associated with the Holy Spirit revival of
the 1960s and '70s were typical faire for them. Healings and
prophetic words came often, and they loved to tell each
other of the goodness and the graciousness of the Lord. They
had designated a couple as their congregational evangelists—
they passed out tracts at a park each week—and they gave 10
percent of the church's income to support missionaries
whether they could afford it or not at any given time. When
they received a new young pastor, they began to do serious
outreach into the community, concentrating their efforts on
helping the homeless with food vouchers and referrals to various social service agencies both sacred and secular. This small
congregation made it their business to do in the community
something larger churches were not doing—what they called
their Resource Center became the go-to place for anyone
coming into town who did not know how to get help for their
particular needs. But—when the new pastor began preaching
that they were each called to be Great Commission Christians—when he attempted to teach and exhort them to be out
sharing their personal witness with everyone they might
meet—there was resistance.

It was a time when small groups were popular and the
congregation formed home fellowships for prayer, ministry
to one another, and worship in a more personalized setting.
The young pastor told each of the groups that their purpose
was to disciple the new and old members who would catch
fire because of the witnessing and the signs and wonders God
would provide. He told them they were to meet together
until they had grown to a certain number of old and new
members; then they were to split so that the personal intimacy of a small family grouping could be maintained while

new groups were planted. But—they flatly refused to split when the time came because they would miss their old friends too much. The youth group was growing, and the youth leaders approached the pastor with a request—which he refused—to take only the oldest and most trusted members on a series of special outings; the rationale was that when they had achieved a sufficient level of intimacy they would be better able to minister to those on the fringes of the group. Although they continued to faithfully serve the homeless through their Resource Center, some members became nervous when some of the homeless began attending services, and others felt that some rules should be established to allay those concerns. The pastor kept exhorting them to focus on their duty to be a church of witnesses outside the church walls; they did not heed his calls, although they loved him too much to hold it against him. Eventually the Lord pulled him to another posting. Over the years that church has remained a small and affectionate body. The gifts of the Spirit have been pretty much withdrawn because when we become a church of mere words and not of the Word, He does not waste His power in our midst. I was associated with this church for a time, and God taught me something during my time with them. He taught me that a Christian who does not take all his marching orders from the Great Commission needs to ask himself if he is really a faithful Christian. He taught me that such Christians and their churches need to seriously turn about—repent—and seek the face of the Lord instead of the face in the mirror if they would enter into real life.

The second vision came some years after the first. In this one I found myself riding on the back of a bay horse. We were galloping over a verdant plain in late springtime and the wind was rushing through my hair; the power of the animal and the freshness of the air were intoxicating. Then I saw Jesus some distance ahead; He was riding a white horse, and I urged my mount to go faster in hopes of catching up with Him. We did begin to gain on Him—He was making no effort to get ahead—and I noticed that the closer I got to Him the more the color of my horse changed to the same color as His.

This was amazing to me—and even more exciting than the first blush of knowing I was riding the same fields as Jesus. I began to experiment—if I dropped back, my horse reassumed its normal bay color, but if I began to catch up again, the color would gradually change to white as I came closer and closer. I grew tired of playing games with colors and got serious about catching Jesus; I lowered my head to minimize wind resistance and spoke to my horse with all of the joy I felt as we approached. When I did finally pull even with my Lord, He turned and smiled; He had obviously been waiting for me to come up even with Him. But then my playfulness returned, and I spurred my mount (although my feet were bare) to pass Him—and another amazing thing happened—as I pulled away from Him, the color of my horse returned to bay. When I saw this I marveled for a moment before making sure I stayed even with him—not slipping in front and not falling behind—for the rest of the ride.

I had not known it was possible to get out in front of God until this vision was given to me. It is possible, and there are consequences.

My own denomination—which is known to many Americans only as "that church that makes gay people into bishops"—was not always a byword for departure from biblical orthodoxy. She was born in an evangelistic outburst accompanied by all of the signs and wonders we associate with apostolic times in the fifth and sixth century British Isles. Her spiritual roots are in characters like Patrick and Columba—the one kidnapped by Irish pirates, miraculously freed and returned to his people, only to be told by the Lord that He had been preparing Patrick in captivity to bring the Gospel to the Irish. Columba was exiled from Ireland after fighting one too many duels; with a dozen companions he crossed the Irish Sea in a bull hide boat, and God did miracles through their hands that included raising the dead and supernaturally opening the gates of fortresses after the warlord promised that he would listen to their witness only if just such a thing should happen. They both lived a life of constant repentance as no circumstance of their lives ever permitted a moment of complacency.

Patrick was the son of wealthy Christians who never gave a thought to God until God became his only companion in the sheepfold where he lived as a slave—much like Jake De-Shazer. Columba was so invested in being a warrior that he would never have given the time of day to a God of peace until his warrior status was ripped out of his hands—much like Fuchida Mitsuo. When God made His strength perfect in their helplessness, they began a journey of turning progressively toward Him that would last the rest of their lives and carry them through countless dangers in which they were completely clueless and without resource—except for what the Spirit gave and explained. Men and women who followed in their spiritual footsteps brought the Gospel to the Americas and to the African continent, not to mention the Pacific Islands. But a serious disconnect rocked them during the 1860s in the United States.

A revival broke out in the Episcopal Church during that time, and it was concentrated among semi-literate dock workers and such. Many coming to know the Lord were unable to read the books given by mission workers seeking to disciple them. Pastors began introducing visual aids that had not been a part of this branch of the Church for centuries—colored stoles, candles on altars, and even the use of incense in worship. The desire was to illustrate the majesty of a God who yet was passionate about coming amongst His people, and these people could relate to the visible actions and accouterments of the ceremonials. The restorations of these practices disturbed some in leadership; they looked too much like practices still in use in the Roman Catholic Church, and the alarm was raised that Rome was seeking to pull the Protestant brethren back into "popish" bondage. Denominational leaders killed the revival, and the American Episcopal Church has never again been a force for revival. It has become a church of internal focus—on liturgy and social programs.

While some of these have real merit and do serve the needs of real people, reality is that once the Body takes its eye from Jesus on His horse—from the establishment of His Kingdom—it is only a matter of time until doctrinal aberration becomes the defining feature of that branch of the Body. The horsemen fell behind Jesus when they killed the revival. In their presumed enlightenment concerning human sexuality and in their claim to paths to God other than Jesus, they have pulled way out in front of Him—riding paths He would never take. Today the Episcopalian leaders are mired in litigation, attempting to force congregations to choose between orthodoxy and loss of their property should they leave, while those who have broken away are re-discovering the Great Commission as their reason for being.

But by some accounts the Church has lost two thirds of her membership in the meantime. There are serious consequences when we fail to follow on the one hand and try to lead our Lord on the other.

Other denominations are facing the same quandary, albeit over differing circumstances. One mainline denomination I know was born of the Second Great Awakening in North America; their missionaries conquered the frontier for Jesus with no resources beyond a Bible, a horse, and the Holy Spirit. In later years they put their mission focus on eradicating drinking—because it was a very real scourge of death and disability to thousands. They were instrumental in securing national prohibition—with the unintended consequence of unleashing the worst era of organized crime in our history, the subsequent failure of prohibition, and a plague of substance abuse more pervasive today than it was then. They never recovered their mission focus and today content themselves with lobbying for social reforms based on dubious science. The fire has gone out for them; they too are dying.

At least one denomination born of early 20th century revival movements that featured resurgence of signs and wonders now defines itself in terms of specific manifestations of certain of those gifts—and tends to ignore the others. Another group so fears those same signs and wonders that leaders must pledge they don't believe in miracles today before they may teach; yet another is so consumed with preventing women from taking a teaching or leadership post in their congregations that they too have forgotten their Great Commission identity. None of these bodies are growing, despite the fact that they still profess to be people of the Great Commission. When Christians major in the minors, no good for the Kingdom ever comes from it.

At least one national ministry that claims to exist solely for the spread of the faith of Christ crucified instructs evangelists that unless new converts have been brought to believe they have transgressed the Ten Commandments before coming to faith their conversion cannot be accepted as genuine. This obsession with legality is a far cry from the Lord who began conversation with a notorious sinner like Zacchaeus (see Luke 19) with a simple invitation to come down from a tree and join Him for lunch. If Paul taught us anything, it is that the Law is indeed the Law—but it is not the point of focus in Christ.

Corporate repentance—returning focus to where Jesus is heading and at the pace He is moving—is the only hope for the restoration of corporate health and vitality.

It is no different when the subject is a city or region instead of a denomination. There was strong sentiment in a California city to invite the Billy Graham organization to hold a massive crusade a few years ago. I participated in meetings with a representative of that organization and key local pastors. The rep made it clear that Graham was very interested in coming to the city; he made it equally clear that his people were not interested in simply holding a crusade and then going home. The gathered church in that city would be expected to spend the next two years pulling together for pastoring the coming harvest. The gathered leaders would have to shelve their pet projects and devote their congregational lives to preparing for this harvest event. After much reflection they decided they were not willing to shelve their projects for two years and march to the same drummer. The crusade was abandoned—and the Body in that city is less united than it has been in a number of years. The leaders view one another with affection; they simply have no common frame of reference or focus. They chose not to repent as a process.

In a city closer to home the leaders of several large evangelical churches decided to hold a crusade featuring an evangelist of lesser fame than Billy Graham but—they calculated—more likely to appeal to the demographics of their population. I attended the kick-off luncheon and made note of who signed up to volunteer time and energy. One of the few rules of preparing the ground in a city for transformation is to permit the leadership to self-select—those with the fire in the belly are the ones who emerge as leaders—but that is not how these pastors went about their business. They began a series of luncheon appointments with the key people—the best people—they had chosen in an effort to gain their support; they never spoke to a single volunteer from the original luncheon. Within a few weeks talk of the crusade had died out; the chosen persons had not gotten hot, and the passion quickly cooled. I recalled the tsunami vision and felt a deep grief for them.

PARABLES OF REPENTANCE

Matthew 25 consists solely of three parables of the Kingdom. The parables of the ten virgins, the talents, and the sheep and goats are worth yet another look. These stories of Jesus are not usually thought of as parables of repentance, but in the sense that concept is used in this chapter, there is nothing else that they are about. They address three things that fallen human beings are less than likely to do.

We shy from committing intimate engagement—which partakes of that voluntary relation that specially fits us to live in covenant and is one of the distinguishing characteristics of authentic human being. The whole point of the parable of the ten virgins is that they are assigned to wait for the coming of the bridegroom. They are expected to remain awake through the night and to discipline themselves to have enough oil so they will not waste precious time that could be spent with the bridegroom looking to buy oil. They—and we—are asked to be accountable to the groom and his needs, taking the attitude that meeting his needs will affect the meeting of their own; seeking first his kingdom and glory will result in the securing of all other things that they might need.

But the very first sin in the Garden of Eden was the refusal of relation. Adam and Eve ate the knowledge of good and evil when the opportunity was to learn of these things while walking with the Lord Himself. When God called him on it, Adam again rejected engagement when he said it was the woman God gave Him who made him sin. Until we make repentance a lifestyle—receiving from God the wherewithal to become human on a daily basis—we will be poor stewards of the Kingdom, and we should not be surprised that divorce and estrangement from family is as common among Christians as it is with those outside the Body. On the other hand, when we choose to lay aside our life, one decision after another, Jesus says we will find that real life awaits us.

The crux of the parable of the talents is in two men willing to risk for the Kingdom—to invest in it—compared to the stark refusal of the third to bear any risk. The parable is addressed to our capacity for reciprocity—another mark of the authentic humanity we receive from the One who made us. The master has given each servant some money while He makes a journey. Every man wants to see his property produce; Jesus' listeners would take this much for granted. When the master gives to the servants he invests in their courage, devotion, and skill. He is overjoyed to find the first two have in turn invested—reciprocated his confidence in them—and are the richer for it. He is disgusted with the man who did not reciprocate—who did nothing but sit on the gift.

Reciprocity is a pre-requisite for the cooperative venture— the First Corinthians 12 world—that is envisioned in the Kingdom of God and the prophetic community God is creating so that His Kingdom can unfold within its boundaries. Risk is intrinsic to reciprocity—we don't know how our response to initiative will be received because we have abandoned the option of a knee-jerk equal and opposite reaction. We have denied ourselves the comfort of engaging with laws and rules that cover every situation we can imagine—a comfort the Pharisees made into an idol and received Jesus' scorn for their trouble. Truthfully, God is so invested in the concept of investment in the Kingdom for its own sake that I believe— although I can't prove it from Scripture—that the master would be just as joyful if the men who invested his gifts in good faith lost the whole amount. He wants to know that they are riding beside Him, that they are willing to surf that 100-foot wave as long as He is in it with them.

Refusal to risk—to invest what might be lost, in order to gain what is of greater (even eternal) value, is a default position for people playing at humanity. It was the sin of David when he had Uriah murdered in his lust for Bathsheba; for when Nathan the prophet upbraids him in Second Samuel 12, he quotes God saying He has given David all he could want and would give more if asked—but David trusted his own cleverness instead of the Lord's goodness. It was the sin of the pastors who refused to shelve their plans for two years for the sake of a harvest of souls, and it was the sin of the leaders who relied on their own estimation of who was best qualified to back a crusade in the other city instead of taking a chance on people who volunteered themselves but were not the cronies of the local big guns. We tend to become willing to risk all on the Kingdom and its King only when we have stripped—or been stripped of —over time all our buffers against it. That is why Jesus says, "Blessed are the poor in spirit, for theirs is the Kingdom of Heaven" (Matt. 5:3).

The parable of the sheep and goats hinges on a developing relationship with Jesus, the third thing we find impossible to do without first embracing a lifestyle of repentance, and the third leg of a three-legged stool of authentic human being. The only conceivable explanation for the shared ignorance of sheep and goats of having served or failed to serve Jesus is that the former have become so accustomed to behaving as Jesus does that they do it as second nature. (The goats are hanging back from any kind of relation, waiting for the dramatic moment to impress the Lord with their holiness.) That can only come about as a development—an escalation—of the fruit of hanging out with someone. The parable illustrates the statement of Richard Foster, cited in an earlier chapter, that in real prayer we begin to think God's thoughts after Him. This does not come about as the result of one Herculean effort at imitation; it is the fruit of repeated efforts to do what we see Him doing as He does what He sees the Father doing. But it requires a lifestyle of repentance; as long as we think we cannot be bothered with what we consider trivia—like a man in prison or an addict struggling to find both dignity and sobriety—we will never discover what and whom Jesus finds important.

In Mark 11:17 Jesus says, "My house will be called a house of prayer for all nations." Even this statement cannot be understood apart from a commitment to a lifetime of repentance—and the joy that comes from it. The concept of a house of prayer for the nations presupposes an understanding of the prayers lofted from that house as being corporate, desperate, and evangelistic.

Jesus quotes Isaiah 56 when He identifies His Father's house of prayer for all nations. The first eight verses of that chapter are all about the Kingdom including any who keep the Lord's Sabbath—from all of the nations. In Acts 17:26-27, God says through Paul's mouth, "From one man He made every nation of men, that they should inhabit the whole earth…God did this so that men would seek Him and perhaps reach out for Him and find Him, though He is not far from each one of us." The Jews had no concept of a private relationship with God—it was always corporate to them—and neither should we. But Jesus, who maintains that He has sheep from many folds and that He is bringing them home, goes far beyond Jewish parochialism to declare that the temple of His Spirit is for all and all on an equal footing of love and acceptance. What He promises to us we should surely give to each other. The house of prayer is a place of gathering—of community in Him.

This house of prayer must be a place of desperate seeking of the Lord—for only then does our seeking become the wholehearted surrender it is intended to be. That desperation must be born of a lively sense of personal bankruptcy before the Lord. What would drive an Isaiah to cry out that he is ruined, that he is a man of unclean lips, and that he lives amongst the unclean—a thing He knows because he has seen the Lord (see Isa. 6)? What would move a Paul to admit that he is the last of all the apostles and "one abnormally born" (the Greek word used in First Corinthians 12:8 literally means "as an abortion") and to hold everything he has as rubbish or loss (see Phil. 3)—if not that very lively sense of bankruptcy and the desperation that comes with such an admission? If we see them as icons of faithfulness, then we need to imitate them as they imitate Jesus. The Jesus we imitate—let's remember—is the Jesus who cried out to His Abba from the cross, "Why have you forsaken me" (see Matt. 27:46; Mark 15:34). The prayers of those desperate for a touch from God are the ones He cannot resist.

Finally, this house of prayer must be a place of evangelistic prayer. It must be such a place because only then can we hope to live there in the image of the Living God.

Reality is that everything God does is for the primary purpose of His revelation of Himself. When He reveals Himself in the parting of the Red Sea, it is a most public manifestation, and even when He reveals Himself privately to Moses at the burning bush, it is for the purpose of sending an emissary to Egypt so that He might be revealed to Hebrew and Egyptian alike. Whenever Jesus does a miracle, it is always in the presence of at least the disciples, and usually it is before a crowd—as when He feeds the multitudes. In the Book of

Ezekiel alone, God says—more than 60 times—that He does this or says this so that the people will know that He is the Sovereign Lord. If His primary purpose is to reveal Himself, then the primary purpose of our prayer and our service must be to reveal Him to others by revealing Him in ourselves. Only then can we claim to be living in the image in which He creates us.

Parables of repentance come in historical events as well as in the pages of the Scriptures. The Battle of Culloden—fought in 1746 between Scottish Highlanders and a combination of British forces and the Scots who aligned with them—sounded the death knell for Scottish independence from Britain and for the culture that proclaimed that independence. The battle was a massacre of the Highlanders and the aftermath of pillage and death made the battle seem almost tame by comparison. Over the next century the Highlanders were first stripped of their language and their ways; they were eventually forced off of their very lands in the notorious Highland Clearances of the early 19th century. They were scattered to the four winds as surely as were the Jews following the A.D. 70 destruction of their city and their temple. They lost that battle because they insisted on using outmoded tactics—clans charging as independent infantry wielding broadswords over broken ground and into the muzzles of artillery—it was their stubborn adherence to what had worked before that sealed their doom. But in the horrific aftermath of the debacle, something changed.

The Scots realized it was their failure to repent—to see if there might be a new thing God was doing in their midst—that had cost them everything. In their scattering they became as committed to innovation and flexible creativity as they had once clung to whatever they had because it was what they had. Over the past two centuries, Scots have contributed innovations in medicine, the arts, engineering, political thought and action, and missionary fervor far out of proportion to their numbers. Now it is people of Scottish descent—dispersed to many nations and often with little memory or awareness of the land of their fathers—who are increasingly headed back to the homeland to lend a hand as God wills to the revival and transformation of the land from which they were forced. For them the process of repentance has only just begun—and they joy in the opportunity.

Meanwhile, in my own city there is an ongoing opportunity to engage this process with the outcome still in doubt. I mentioned a prophecy over the city back in Chapter 1 that concerns the downtown mall in Redding. The prophetic word was that the mall—which has been the biggest political football in the city since the commercial heart of the city moved to an area known as Dana Drive—was meant by God to become a center of ministry and service rather than the restored center of commerce about which so many continue to dream and strategize. It was later made clear that the mall stands within a couple of blocks from what was once the heart of prostitution in Redding. Since prostitution is a perversion of the gift of service, the Lord determined to redeem the downtown by installing service that honors Him to replace the service that mocks the men and women He creates.

At the time the prophetic word was uttered the mall was already between one half and two thirds devoted to service concerns of various kinds. With the opening of a new college of nursing that dedication is between 75 and 80 percent, and Christians are opening businesses in the near vicinity that continue the process of re-setting the atmosphere. But the city fathers have turned a deaf ear to prophetic voices about the mall; they and the downtown developers are still seeking ways to renew the commercial vitality of the mall. Their approach is in sharp contrast to the fathers of Fairbanks, Alaska, during the '90s.

When the Fairbanks fathers realized that the core of their downtown was so depressed that established companies like Montgomery Ward could not make a go of it, they called a roundtable meeting of leaders from every conceivable sphere of influence. My friend, Suuqinna, was asked to represent native and spiritual concerns. There came a point in the meeting when someone suggested asking the man of God what he thought ought to be done. Suuqinna asked his own question, "What is the history of the downtown?" The mayor responded with what everyone already knew—during the Alaska Gold Rush days the downtown had been a four square block brothel. Suuqinna told them that sexual sin is one of the four big polluters of the land from a biblical standpoint. (The others are idolatry, covenant breaking, and the shedding of innocent blood.) He said that the land was polluted and nothing would thrive there until it had been cleansed. He suggested a gathering of Christians to walk and pray and bless and repent. The mayor broke into the ensuing uproar with a simple declaration, "I don't care if I am the only one to show up; next Saturday I will be on the street praying. We've got nothing to lose, and I say the man is making sense."

The following Saturday morning, representatives from 28 local churches showed up for the walk. They spent four hours praising the Lord, blessing the city, repenting in identification with their forebears for the sin on the land, and exercising their John 21:19-23 authority to forgive the sins they encounter. God moved into the space that had been cleared for Him—as surely as Jesus occupied the space in the Jerusalem temple where once the money changers had clamored for attention.

Diana and I made our first visit to Fairbanks in 2001. We know that there is nothing magical about prayer so that we might automatically receive whatever we desire in its wake. But today the downtown of Fairbanks is a site of new construction and new life. Businesses are struggling for success—as they do everywhere and at all times—but they are making it. New construction was a common and vital sight when we visited. New life was everywhere in evidence; there was hope and a future alongside God's promise to prosper. The prayer of a man or group of men offered in bold humility is not magical—it is miraculous—and God is not slow to respond to honest repentance. My prayer for everyone reading these words is that they will begin to ask not, "How can we make our city what we want it to be?" but rather, "How can we turn our city over to God and participate in its becoming what He wants it to be?"

Repentance, as a lifestyle, is the path to transformation. It is an opportunity to step across that line Jesus draws in the sand so that we stand with Him and His. It is the beginning of the good news of Jesus Christ for individuals and for their communities, and certainly for the Body that is encompassed by the heart of the living God.

Chapter 12

⌒

ON EARTH AS IT IS IN HEAVEN

Diana and I went to Mindanao, the Philippines, in September 2006. In the city of Koronadal, it was our privilege to lead a pastors' conference for training in the kinds of prophetic acts with impact we see in California. One hundred and fifty pastors came in from preaching stations in the mountains and cities of that region for the three-day conference. Many hiked jungle trails down steep mountainsides to get to flooded rivers choked with mud and debris. Once they found a way across they still had to hitch a ride with whatever transport they could find into the city, and finally to the compound where we waited to share with them a Kingdom already in their midst.

These men and women risk their lives for their Lord each time they stand to preach. Insurgent bands roam the mountains where they speak the Good News from structures of bamboo not much larger than an American bedroom; the insurgents—some Marxist and some Muslim—share a hatred for Christians. (Our host pastor patrolled the compound—unarmed—each night until about 4 a.m. so that if they came for the Americans we would have some warning. Knowing we were under God's protection, Pastor Amado exercised the authority of the un-armed man.) For them it goes with the territory to trust the Lord to get them across a flooded river.

The rain was both hard and relentless as we waited for the pastors to come in; they looked like drowned rats as they strag-gled and struggled in on the first night. They carried home-grown vegetables in their backpacks, along with their clothing; our hosts could provide rice and the meat of the eight pigs that they were given a year earlier to raise for this occasion. As the first few came into the compound, I asked the Lord silently if we should pray for the rain to stop as we had done in Fiji. He said, "No, just begin the teaching." As we worshiped and shared stories of the Lord, about two hours into the evening, I asked again if we should not pray with authority for the rain to stop as we had done in Fiji. Again, He answered with a "no," but this time I asked Him why.

He said, "I want to honor their sacrifice." He was so fiercely proud of what His people offered to Him in their trek down the water-slicked slopes of the mountain that He would not dream of demeaning the gift by stopping the rain—and thus declaring the sacrifice unnecessary. When I shared that word with the pastors, their tears of astonishment that the Lord of the universe would so honor them, blended with the rain on the roof. When we shared the Supper of the Lord two nights later, the rain came to a crescendo on the tin roof for a full minute as we raised our portion of bread and said, "Let us eat in the name of the Lord Jesus." He gave another 60-second crescendo when we raised our glasses and said, "Let us drink in the name of the Lord Jesus Christ."

On the first night of the conference, we prayed for healing in those who were sick or injured—as we would normally do—asking some of the Filipino leaders to assist us. But, while they were perfectly happy to translate for us, they did not lay their hands on and pray for their friends; they left that entirely to Diana and me, and everyone who came for prayer was healed. The next night, we stood on the platform and prayed for the leaders, telling them we would not pray for the sick that night—only the locals could do that—and again everyone who came was immediately healed. After the meeting our hostess told us, through her tears, that no one had ever trusted them as completely as we did. "But if God so trusted them," we said to her, "how could we not?"

This time on Mindanao is the first time in our ministry when every person prayed for was fully and instantly healed of whatever issue he or she brought to the platform. It was the same when we returned to Davao City and preached in one of the churches before returning to California. This is what God has promised through His Son when He says that the dead shall be raised and the lepers cured in the Kingdom—without exception. What we saw was a sacramental outburst of the Kingdom of God in that kind of fullness. It was not the only Kingdom outburst we saw on the trip.

Over our first ten days in Mindanao we participated in the Sixth World Christian Gathering on Indigenous Peoples. The gathering was held at a resort hotel and native people from all over the world—nearly 600 strong—came together to worship God, share what He has planted in all of our cultures, and struggle to become the people He has called us to be. It was at just such a gathering in Sweden (see Chapter 6) that I was called upon to bring a word about repentance—even for the victims of oppression—as the path in the desert that leads to Holy Spirit transformation of communities and nations. The response from the gathered in that time was overwhelming. We spent the next four hours repenting to one another for the many ways in which we had betrayed each other through the behavior of our ancestors. We later danced and sang in the joy of the Lord as we were restored to the fellowship and embrace of Kingdom intimacy depicted in Luke 11 when the house-holder says that His children are all with Him in bed (see Luke 11:7). But many of the world leaders of the indigenous move-ment were not present in Sweden. And the spirit of division and victimization, crying out for the other to repent and give justice, came with them to Davao City. The gathering was ten days of joyful fellowship in the Lord, punctuated by struggle with and against that spirit. And it is in that very struggle that another sacramental outburst of the Kingdom came about.

Diana and I brought no prophetic word with us to Davao. We came only to be with—and worship with—people we love. But as the days passed in the midst of our friends, who have been historically dishonored by people who look like us, we felt the Lord more and more pressing in on us to give our testimony as the descendants of Scottish Highlanders. Our people too were rounded up, cast off of the land in which God placed us, and butchered or exiled so that our conquerors and oppressors could graze their sheep where our children once played and our ancestors sang anthems to the Lord. My personal testimony includes history of Pacific Islanders—people of color—who stole my own inheritance after I befriended them. It includes God's question to me, "Will you live in the bitterness of the injustice or will you forgive and receive Me as your cup and your portion on earth as it is in Heaven?"

The question now was whether we were called to impose ourselves on the platform from which we were not scheduled to speak. Was our testimony pivotal enough for God's purpose in the gathering that we should go to the leadership committee—despite the conviction we brought to Davao that we were not called this year to the role we had accepted in Sweden? We wrestled in prayer the whole night until the Lord broke through just before dawn with singing.

It took Him that whole sleepless night to pry me loose from focus on the question to focus on Him. It took the whole night for me to begin to hear Him singing the old praise song chorus, "You're all I want; you're all I've ever needed. You're all I want; show me that you are near." He then showed me that the European contingent would be making the cultural presentation that evening. I could go to my friend, Hakon, and ask for Diana and me to be included with their group; this would also provide an easy confirmation that we had indeed heard from the Lord—if Hakon was OK with including the two Americans in the European presentation of indigenous culture.

And for any who are wondering about hearing the Lord sing praise songs to the very people who should be singing to

Him—of course all praise and glory is for God alone. He has earned it and He alone deserves it; He gave those words to a worship leader named Kelly Carpenter that they might be dedicated to Him in the song, Draw Me Close. But how many know that He has never required anything of us that He does not first give to us? He loves us enough to sing to us for eternity; what is an entitlement for Him is His gift to us. He is always singing to each and every one of us; when our focus is on Him we can begin to hear Him.

When I entered the breakfast room, I saw Hakon on the other side and went toward him. Before I could say a word, he grasped me in a bear hug and asked me if Diana and I would be willing to be part of their cultural presentation that evening. The Lord had spoken to him about it when he woke up that morning.

We gave our testimony that evening. I was dressed in the tribal regalia of my Scottish clan—regalia I wore for the first time on coming to this gathering. In what we had to say, we included the struggle to forgive those who had stolen from us personally alongside those who stole from our ancestors. We shared how our struggle was a daily one; but we spoke our unshakable conviction that there could be but one final outcome—on earth as it is in Heaven. Our testimony added controversy to the struggle in the leadership councils and in the hearts of everyone present for the gathering. The fruit was that, over the next three days, more than 40 people singled us out to tell us how they had been set free when we spoke of our struggle—and of God's insistent love.

There was other dramatic fruit of God's unrelenting love manifesting in the struggle to become His people inside the skin in which He chooses to ferment His Spirit in each of us. Monte Ohia, founder of the World Christian Gathering on Indigenous Peoples, led a workshop on reconciliation each afternoon. One day he told of how the Lord called him to begin to gather his own Maori people of New Zealand into a community of pride in the Lord and joy in the culture He gave them. He first held 50 meetings around the country in which he called on his people to repent of the idolatry and cruelties they had practiced before and since the coming of the white invaders of their land. Only then, he had said, could they begin to seriously seek the Lord and claim His justice for their children. After sharing this story, Ohia asked if there were any representatives of a tribe present who needed to ask forgiveness of others who might also be present. A Filipino man in the back stood and came to the front.

He told of being from a tribe that lived in the mountains of Luzon—the island on which the capitol city of Manila is located. He confessed that his tribe still hunted human heads today and that as a young man he had taken heads from a neighboring tribe to present as a gift to his bride for a token of his ability to provide for her. He said that he had given that up when he received Christ, but he had never asked forgiveness from the people he had injured. He wanted to beg that forgiveness now.

Two men from the tribe he had wounded came forward; their struggle was evident even in the way they walked to the front of the room. They accepted his repentance and shook his hand, but God had only just begun to work His miracles in them. When we saw them the next day—after what must have been a night of talk and prayer for the three of them— they were lounging together and draping their arms around each other, as Filipino men do with their friends. This was just as much a sacramental outburst of the Kingdom in its fullness as was the healing of all the prayed-for in Koronadal.

It is not much of a stretch to see God's hand and gladness in the events of Koronadal. Of course, He would be the prime mover in healing nearly 200 people and leaving no one to wonder when his time would come. It would be just like Him to be so pleased with the sacrifice those pastors made when they risked death just to come and hear a word from the Lord that He would orchestrate the rain into crescendo when they ate and drank in His Name. And surely He would honor the struggle of His people back in Davao City to be people of repentance at the same time that they continue to seek justice in a world that denies any wrong has been done to them. But is this very struggle also a manifestation of the Kingdom—and the prophetic community that both proclaims and embodies it?

Jesus provides one of the most enigmatic visions of His Kingdom in Matthew 13:24-29. In it God has planted a wheat crop while the enemy has planted weeds that look just like the wheat. The King tells His servants—who want to uproot the weeds before they damage the good crop—to let them grow together for a while. By their fruit they will be known; the reckoning will take place at the harvest—not before. To act sooner would be to risk uprooting the wrong plants, and God's well-known will is that none should perish. It is for this reason that He calls us to continue to work out our own salvation "with fear and trembling" in Philippians 2:12. Kingdom life is a process. Consequently, the struggle we undertake between the encrustations on our hearts, the healing in His wings—and the occasional caress from His talons—is also a manifestation of His

Kingdom in our midst. This is so that we will engage with Him each time, and with one another, despite the risk and the pain of the encounter.

God is absolutely committed to the provision of healing, life-giving, and restoration that He promises in Matthew 11. In that Kingdom vision all live, all live in health, and all live in light of the Good News. But He is just as committed to loving us without measure while we seek His face in the middle of our struggles, as He promises in Matthew 13. It is another of those paradoxes that provoke a whoop of delight from our God and King on earth as He has set it in Heaven —another way He comes across to set free in Heaven what we turn loose on earth and vice versa (see Matt. 18:18). And in this season of unusual miracles, if we are paying attention to Him and not to our conception of Him, it is always possible to see more of His wonders where we live than wherever we go—as we have seen in Northern California. It all comes about through the process of radical engagement with Him and with each other.

A KINGDOM OF RADICAL ENGAGEMENT

Two of the central enigmas of Scripture are found in Genesis 2:20-25 and Proverbs 29:18. They are as emblematic as they are enigmatic of the nature and shape of the Kingdom of God, but we seldom think of them in the context of the Kingdom.

Letting the last be first calls for a look at the famous verse out of Proverbs that the King James translates as, "Without a vision the people perish" (Prov. 29:18 KJV). In more contemporary translations it is usually more like the New International's "Where there is no revelation the people cast off restraint," but the Hebrew word we translate as "vision" or "revelation" is *chazon* (see Prov. 29:18). It means *visage* or *face*. The Word of God—found in the very depths of the Old Testament—is that in order to live and live abundantly we must look God in the face. His Kingdom is one of radical engagement with the King.

Some will say, "But doesn't God always say in the Old Testament that if we try to look Him in the face we will surely die?" He surely does say that in Exodus 33:20, and He repeats it three verses later. But the context is that the children of Israel have just been worshiping the golden calf while Moses and God were communing on Mount Sinai. The Covenant has not yet been sealed in the blood of the Israelite's foreskins—will not be for another generation, until they are in the land of Canaan. It is only common sense that we not look into the unimaginable candle power of the light of the face of God when we are unprepared for the fullness of that light on the one hand and just back from mucking about in the darkness of sin on the other. The pupils of our eyes, spiritual and physical alike, are max-extended and mini-equipped at this point.

Even though the belief was common in ancient times that to look in the face of Yahweh was to incite death, Genesis 32:30 reads, "So Jacob called the place Peniel, saying, 'It is because I saw God face to face, and yet my life was spared.'" God comes down onto the mountain in smoke and fire to speak directly to the people in Exodus 19 and 20—before the episode of idolatry with the golden calf. Whether they saw Him clearly through the smoke of His passing in flame or not, it is clearly His intention to be seen by the people He loves. Proverbs 29:18 simply points out that—once the pre-requisites have been satisfied—the goal was always to look God in the face. It is the most radical engagement imaginable, and the giving of the Law and the Prophecies are only the paving stones of a road to that engagement in which He trumpets, "I will be their God and they will be my people" (Heb. 8:10).

The prerequisites are finally and ultimately fulfilled in the coming of Jesus who is called Christ. In John 14:9 He says to His disciples, who are fearful that they will not recognize the Father when He comes, "Anyone who has seen me has seen the Father," and again in John 14:11, "Believe me when I say that I am in the Father and the Father is in Me." If we have seen one, we have seen the other—and the seeing is full-on, as in eyeball to eyeball. The encounter is the fulfillment of all that God meant and intended when He told David and then Jeremiah that He had known them in the womb before they were born (see Ps. 139:13; Jer. 1:5). It is all that He meant when He caused John the Baptist to reciprocate—knowing Jesus from within his mother's womb as that engagement is depicted in Luke 1:41.

That call to citizenship in a Kingdom in which none take offense at Jesus is a corporate call sent out to billions of individuals to come and live in the prophetic community that looks at and is looked upon by the face of God. We caught a glimpse of that community in the Philippines. We caught it in the people God healed and honored and in the people who wrestled with their own impediments to living in a community with their restored friends and their redeemed enemies in the same big bed.

In the Old Testament those paving stones are ripped up as often as they are laid down. When Adam and Eve betray God by eating the fruit instead of waiting on Him for whatever knowledge they need, they disengage from Him in favor of a life without reference to Him. (Jesus passes the test they failed in Matthew 4 and Luke 4; the devil tempts Him to do the things He knows He was sent to do—but Jesus refuses to do His life's work without reference to His Father.) They disengage from one another when God comes looking for them in the garden. Instead of accepting responsibility for what they have done, Adam says that the woman God gave him made him disobey that same God. "The woman made me do it, and you gave her to me so it is everybody's fault but mine," could easily have been the words out of the first man's mouth. (See Genesis 3:1-13.)

Reality is that we are going to have to look God in the face, and we are going to have to be holy people in order to do it without destroying ourselves in the process. That puts us between a rock and a hard place, leaving us dependent on Him who requires holiness to make us holy. It is the Rock doing the heavy lifting, but the hard place is that we are called to participate by engaging, as best we can, whenever we can. The Old and New Testaments are the stories of that escalating process, and they tell us that we will come to engage with God through one another and, as we engage with Him, we will engage just as radically with one another.

The Genesis 2 passage is the one in which God says it is not a good idea for the man to be alone. We translate what He says as, "But for Adam no suitable helper was found," within the kingdom of animals that Adam has just finished naming (see Gen. 2:20). Actually the Hebrew word ezer has nothing to do with being a helper or helpmate, although people in intimate relation can certainly be expected to help each other in a multitude of ways. We could say that the concept is all about helping—so long as we understand that the helping is both equal and reciprocal between the two of them. The word, at its most literal, means something like, "one who can look Him in the face." We could not ask for a more descriptive term for the kind of intimate and radical engagement God intends for His people with one another, as surely as He means it for and with Himself.

What does it mean to engage one another as we engage God? Jesus says it plainly when He summarizes the whole Law between loving God and loving the neighbor as we love ourselves in Matthew 22:39; He says the same thing a moment earlier to the rich young man in Matthew 19:19, calling him to honor his parents and love his neighbor as he loves himself. But we are not talking about affection or even semi-sacrificial kindness here. The Bible uses the word *agapao* in these and in a cavalcade of other New Testament verses throughout the Gospels and the Epistles. The word means to pour out—to turn ourselves inside out for the other, if we will. And it is this kind of radical engagement that is offered to Adam and Eve in The Garden and commanded of the disciples on their way to another garden—Gethsemane—in John 13:34. Jesus repeats the command to pour themselves out for one another as He is about to pour Himself out for them in John 15:12, and Paul gives it to us, yet again, in Ephesians 5:2 as "and live a life of love, just as Christ loved us and gave Himself up for us as a fragrant offering and sacrifice to God."

Most of the time this kind of loving does not reach to the ultimate sacrifice. It is spelled out plainly enough in the Old Testament when God tells the returning exiles to prepare for a bumper harvest in Zechariah 8:16-17. "These are the things you are to do: Speak the truth to each other and render true and sound judgment in your courts; do not plot evil against your neighbor and do not love to swear falsely…." It gets even more basic in Micah 6:8 when He says, "And what does the Lord require of you? To act justly and to love mercy and to walk humbly with your God." These kinds of simple behaviors lead to more than good harvests of wheat; they produce what the Lord calls a true Sabbath in Isaiah 56 when He equates the keeping of that Sabbath with the maintenance of justice and the prevention of (ourselves) doing evil (see Isa. 56:1-2). In Isaiah 58, God says He will be impressed with fasting when the people fast from injustice, set others free, and share their food with the hungry (see Isa. 58:3-8).

In the New Testament, the same spelling out takes place in seemingly non-major league arenas like how we treat children when important events and persons are underway and present. "Let the children come to me and do not hinder them," says Jesus in Mark 10:14. About the Mosaic provision for divorce, Jesus tells the Pharisees, "It was because your hearts were hard that Moses wrote you this law" (Mark 10:5). We can read, "Because you disengaged from the woman I gave you, it will be as you will it." He goes on to say that marriage is of the very fabric of creation, that "God made them male and female. For this reason a man will leave his father and mother and be united to his wife, and the two will become one flesh. So they are no longer two, but one" (Mark 10:7-8).

Jesus points out that the only real exception Moses made back in Deuteronomy 24 is for adultery. It was never at the whim of the husband—as the Pharisees were teaching in the first century—and it was only permitted because, in cases of adultery, the covenant is effectively broken and the parties might as well admit it if they must. Moses acknowledged it as a tragic occasion in a desperately fallen world but never as an option for life in the Kingdom of God.

Paul calls on his flock to be truthful and forgiving at all costs in Ephesians 4, just like the prophets before him. And he exhorts men and women in marriage to submit to one another out of reverence for Christ in the next chapter. His explicit division of the submission of husbands to wives and wives to husbands is just that—a differentiation of role in the mutual engagement through submission to which both are called. Because it is a covenant, it only works when both are engaged in faithfulness. And because the marriage relation is a model for the Church, and thus the prophetic community, it only works when we see ourselves in the First Corinthians 12 model for that community.

"So if we want to see God come in a Gospel of power and not of mere words, all we have to do is treat each other the way He treats us?" we ask. Yes, that is all there is to preparing the ground for the transformation of our communities into the Kingdom of God. It is not as easy as it is simple; any who think that it is should talk to the rich young man who came before Jesus in Matthew 19—or the leaders who failed to visit Steve and Clete in prison (see Chapter 10) or who don't want Hugh coming around their churches with his biker and ex-addict friends. But that really is all there is to it.

That means we of the charismatic stream of the River of God need to focus more on our treatment of one another than on the quest for new and better miracles. If we do that, we will see the real miracles and there will be no shortage of high voltage Holy Spirit activity in our midst; it will begin with the unusual and proceed to the unimaginable.

We of the evangelical stream, uncomfortable with all the talk about miracles and power encounters on every book shelf and television screen, should not get too comfortable with what I am saying. If we really seek justice like a river and think of all people as more important than we are (see Rom. 12:10)—and not necessarily just those in sync with our favorite doctrinal formulations—we will soon have more miracles around us than we can count, and it will have nothing to do with whether we speak in tongues or not.

And those of us coming from the liturgical stream can take pride for only an instant in having symbolized it all in our ceremonials for centuries. God is planning to smoke us with the supremely confrontational question: when you perform your rituals, where is your heart? If we are worshiping Him and serving one another, we too will find that the things we offer to God are filled with the power of God to a degree we have never conceived and will never comprehend. Just ask the demons and their servants who will not come onto land (see Chapter 3) where the Lord has set His table on their altar and addressed the bloodguilt on the land with His blood in the community of Forest Ranch, on the beach in Fiji, or on the bluff over Moo' Kini.

Of course, when we step across that line to join Jesus and the sinful woman the way I saw it in *The Passion of the Christ*, we achieve both kinds of engagement in the same stroke—just the way our God and Christ seems to want it. We become Barnabas people—just the apostolic model for which God is calling in this generation. His ministry epitomizes the engagement that is the theme of every page of this book.

A BARNABAS GENERATION

The first mention we have of the apostle Barnabas comes in Acts 4:36-37. "Joseph, a Levite from Cypress, whom the apostles called Barnabas (which means Son of Encouragement), sold a field he owned and brought the money and put it at the apostles' feet." In Barnabas, are all of the elements of that Matthew 25 vision of the Kingdom citizen brought together and on display inside the bold humility of this man? Even in this first little vignette we find a man who by definition—being a Levite—is praying and dynamically waiting on the Lord and who by conviction—being a disciple—has escalated that praying and waiting into Kingdom living. He has sold what he had for an investment in the Kingdom and has laid the proceeds at the apostles' feet for the benefit of the poor as they might decide—acting like one of the sheep instead one of the goats. If we would be agents of Kingdom transformation in our communities, we must set ourselves to become Barnabas people.

The next Barnabas sighting comes in Acts 9 when he meets Saul—who will become Paul—and brings him to the apostles (see Acts 9:26-27). This is as risky as it is self-effacing; he could have adopted a wait-and-see attitude or even sought to mentor the newbie himself, but he brings him in, offers encouragement, and stands aside to cover the proceedings in prayer. By Acts 11 he is on mission assignment in Antioch—encouraging the new converts there and realizing that the work is more than he can handle by himself. Rather than seeking his own glory, he sends for the rookie, Saul, and they share the work until things stabilize in the city. By Acts 13 things are copasetic in Antioch, and the community delivers a composite word of prophecy (Barnabas is one of the speakers) to the effect that

Paul and Barnabas are to be set apart and sent on a new mission. In Salamis and Pisidian Antioch he permits the more fiery and articulate Paul to do most of the speaking while he flies high prayer cover for the mission. (See Acts 13:1-12.) In Acts 14 they have moved on to Iconium, and Barnabas is doing more of the speaking, although he is still flying high cover (see Acts 14). Acts 15 finds them back in Jerusalem—referring the controversy about new converts keeping the Jewish Law back to the Apostolic Council (of which Barnabas is a member) for decision as the Holy Spirit leads. After that decision is handed down as another composite revelation—"It seemed good to the Holy Spirit and to us..." (Acts 15:28)—Barnabas attempts to broker reconciliation between Paul and John Mark, which leaves their friendship in tatters (see Acts 15). This reference, to yet another sacrifice of his comfort and security for the sake of the Kingdom, is the last we hear of this son of encouragement in the Bible.

The core of the character of Barnabas is not in his standing back from time to time from the center of attention, although that kind of humility is more than pleasing to the Lord when it is His will. Nor is it in the boldness with which he stands forward when he is called to do that. It is in the bold humility through which he works out his salvation in fear and trembling. In Acts 9 he takes a chance on the man who claims Christ after a career of persecuting Christians; yet he is humble enough to place him in more authoritative hands for vetting (see Acts 9). In Acts 11 he hits the bricks and leads the mission in Antioch; yet he is happy to call for and accept help when that is needed. In the various cities he visits with Paul, he speaks when he has a word and prays when others have it. And in the Apostolic Council and its aftermath, he does what he hears God calling him to do—no more and no less. He acts in ways appropriate to his character and calling—and to the unfolding character and call of God—because his eye is always on His Lord and never on himself. He knows and appreciates that his is one very essential role in the prophetic community envisioned in First Corinthians 12—but it is still just one role.

Our God is a God of escalation, duration, and honor. Barnabas is at all times a man paying prayerful attention to God and what He is doing—waiting for that Bridegroom on full alert—and faithfully pursuing the escalating reality of an unfolding Kingdom. That puts him in the spirit of the watchful virgins. He is an investor in the Kingdom who is in it for the long haul, from donating the proceeds of that field to leaving his life and profession in Jerusalem to go wherever and for whatever duration he is sent. That aligns him with the men given the five and the two talents. He is a man who understands that none of us transcend the basics of the faith once delivered to the saints, and he practices those basic acts of agape all the days of his life. That places him squarely in the camp of the sheep—not the goats—and finds him standing across the line where Jesus and the sinful woman are waiting to welcome.

God is calling for a generation of believers who are so impressed with Him that we notice a water glass whose level does not fall even while we are listening to a very impressive speaker sharing with us the Word of God—and capable of noticing a gas tank that stays full even when we are on our way to deliver the Word of God. He wants us to be as excited about the unusual miracles for which we did not ask as we are about the ones for which we begged and exhorted—and He wants us to pay attention to the implicit teaching in these miracles so that we can participate in their escalation. He wants a generation that is committed to the ministry of the earthworm—giving ourselves without reservation to tasks as simple as aerating soil, digesting and distributing Kingdom nutrients, and encouraging strong roots systems as both disciples and disciplers operating on God's timeframe rather than our own. And He seeks a generation that never forgets to feed the hungry, clothe the naked, and visit the sick and imprisoned— as though these things were at least as important as the next fresh revelation—or doctrinal formulation. As one man I know likes to say, "If it ain't practical, it ain't prophetic."

As a pre-believer at San Diego State University I consumed the novels of Herman Hesse, a writer almost as popular as J.R.R. Tolkein in the late '60s. *Siddhartha* is a fictionalized life of the man named Siddhartha Gautama—and better known to the world as the Buddha. At a pivotal moment in the story Siddhartha is asked by a spiritual master to give an account of his accomplishments in pursuit of enlightenment. He answers that he can think and he can wait and he can fast.[1]

As a Christian, I remained intrigued with a life that valued thought, patience, and the ability to do without—even though I knew that Jesus was somehow calling me to a higher existence than this, one which is so often equated with the Christian ideal by people who truly understand neither. One day the Lord showed me that, as His follower, I am invited to become a person of prayer, worship, and sharing. The personhood to which Jesus calls us is as different from the nirvana (oblivion) to which the Buddha calls his followers as life in a community of the integrated ones is different from a state of complete isolation.

To be one of internally generated thought, patience, and self-denial—as humbling and unpretentious as these qualities might be—is to embody a self-contained life not unlike that of Captain Nemo. But prayer invites dialogue and engagement with the One who makes us; it is way beyond mere contemplation and analysis. Worship includes sacrifice and implies the devotion of self to that same One who gifts us with our self. It takes us from waiting to waiting upon and from sharing amounts to the giving of life for the sake of the Life-giver. This is exactly what Jesus says must be done if we would find life in Him. There is no reason for the process ever to end, because the fruit just gets better.

All faiths, save one, are about things to know. Christianity is about a Person to know and—through engagement—persons to become. Does the Christian faith require thought, patience, and the self-denial symbolized in the concept of fasting? The answer is yes, but the answer transcends a simple yes as much as it transcends human comprehension and ability. It is impossible to engage as God calls for engagement in terms of our own resources—we squandered those resources in The Garden and in each of our histories of betrayal and disengagement; and they were never sufficient anyway. He leaves open the path He left to the father of the demonized boy in Mark 9:24—"I do believe; help me overcome my unbelief." It is the same path He opens to Peter—who betrayed Him by desertion as surely as did Judas—asking in John 21, "Simon son of John, do you truly love me" (John 21:15-16).

Christians looking for the Kingdom, as Jews once looked for the Messiah, are offered a lifetime of repentance that escalates, investment that endures, and performance of the basics that are the heart of honoring one another as God honors us and sacrifices Himself for us before asking the analogous sacrifice of us. This really is all there is to it.

LIVING INSIDE A MIRACLE

In *Living As Ambassadors of Relationships* I told the story of what God has been doing in Diana for the past several years. He has been systematically—as He understands the term—restoring her to a level of health for which she was created but has never before experienced. Among other things her fibromyalgia is history. Her spinal curvature is slowly resolving. By way of signposts and challenges to her faith—sacramental outbursts in series—He has been healing her food allergies in the reverse order in which she acquired them. One day in prayer, when He declared His intention to heal all of her, Diana asked the Lord why He does not just do it in one great and miraculous outburst of His power. He replied with His own question, "Would you rather have a miracle or live inside one?" When He put it that way, her answer was a no-brainer. She happily offers to Him the sacrifice of praise and proclamation at each stage of the healing journey on which He has her walking with Him.

It is God's will and plan that we should live with Him inside an unfolding miracle. This is the shape of the Kingdom, on earth as it is in Heaven. This is the place and purpose of the prophetic community.

We were called to fly high prayer cover over a convention in Fresno, California, not long ago. A district—we call them dioceses in my denomination—was planning to amend its constitution to permit a declaration of independence from the national Episcopalian body that has engaged in multiple forms of apostasy over a lengthy span of time. Independence would permit them to re-align with another jurisdiction within the Anglican Communion that is committed, not only to biblical orthodoxy, but to that Great Commission identity without which even so-called correct belief is useless to the Kingdom. There was high anxiety on the part of diocesan leaders as to whether they would achieve the two-thirds majority of voting delegates in both clergy and lay orders to amend the constitution. (They knew that opponents would engage in political maneuvers to confuse and frustrate; they also knew that the clergy were being asked to risk their pensions and their ministerial credentials.) As we so often do, we brought in an interdenominational team at the bishop's invitation. We were there to pray blessing on all concerned, release whatever prophetic words the Lord might give, and pray with focus into those words that they might be glorious for the Lord in their fulfillment.

The convention was to run from Friday morning to Saturday afternoon with the crucial vote planned for Saturday morning. We arrived on Thursday afternoon to walk and pray over the grounds and inside the buildings where the activities would take place. We blessed the people and the proceedings, asked and offered forgiveness for those who had sinned or would sin—on either side of the controversy—and shared the Lord's Supper with a special focus on healing and restoration of the mission of this branch in this place. The Lord provided a composite revelation in which three prophetic themes emerged from the prayer and worship we engaged.

The first word was simply, "Release the Spirit of worship," over the convention with special reference to the passage in

Second Chronicles 20 in which King Jehoshaphat sends the praise band out ahead of the military force that is defending Jerusalem (see 2 Chron. 20:21-22). The word was that if our focus was on worshiping God, He would be free within that invitation to deal with the political realities far more dynamically than the delegates could do it. (A visiting bishop, preaching Saturday morning and with no input from us, chose to preach on this text for a most dramatic confirmation.) The second word was, "Choose this day whom you will serve," and we were supernaturally directed to Joshua 24:15, in which those words appear. Finally, the Lord had directed us to Mark 2 and the paralytic who is healed of his paralysis as a sign that Jesus indeed has authority to forgive sin. The word was, "Rise, take up your pallet and walk; the time of paralysis is past" (see Mark 2:9). This last word was yet another confirmation that the Lord requires more of His people than mere correct belief or legalistic adherence to scriptural mandates on our behavior. He wants us partnering with Him to usher—deacon—His Kingdom on earth.

Two other prophetic words made bookends for these focal points of prayers. The first came as we blessed and anointed the bishop himself; one of us spoke a vision in which the bishop played badminton against an unseen but formidable opponent. The Lord called the bishop to accept both His timing and shaping for his play. In the vision the bishop watched as the Lord guided the shuttlecock to its perfected resting place—just before he levitated the bishop over the net into the same spot! Diana then shared that, as she watched the same vision, the Lord showed her many arrows aimed at the bishop; the Lord turned the arrows to chaff and blew them back at the archers. Some of the chaff stung the faces of the archers they hit while other bits of chaff turned into warm breezes that caressed the faces of the archers they encountered. She interpreted this to mean that as we prayed some in the convention who were planning to vote against independence would change their minds.

The other bookend came at the prayer and praise service that night when one of our team spoke the Word of the Lord, "Relax. I've got a lot more riding on this than you do." We all had a good laugh—and relaxed our own tension—at this one.

There was much confusion and frustration in the wake of political moves designed to that end on Friday. We kept praying in agreement with the words we had been given and encouraging even the most frustrated to keep their eyes on the Lord and their focus on worship in the chaos. The convention itself was sprocketed by worship services before and within it; quiet but spontaneous expressions of worship dotted the floor even during business sessions. By Saturday morning the confusion had disappeared, and it was clear from body language and the lack of will for prolonged debate that a corporate choice was being made about whom to serve in that diocese. Exhortations from platform and floor microphones were more and more about moving forward into a new dawn of mission and less and less about holding to a halcyon history.

All the while, God continued to pour out His composite revelation into the crucible of human decision; at one point a speaker rose to the floor microphone to read from Revelation 2 about God's commendation of the Ephesian Church for their devotion to orthodoxy and to their authentic apostles. At the same time, He chides them for abandoning their first love of the Lord Himself and His mission imperative. The leader of a visiting delegation later approached me to share that four of his people watched slack-jawed as the speaker spoke—they had received the same passage at the same moment.

The final vote was more than 80 percent of the clergy and 90 percent of the laity seeking resurrection through realignment. (It was obvious that a number of delegates had changed their minds during the convention—as Diana prophesied.) The three prophetic frames for the gathering—the spirit of worship, the choice of service, and the picking up of the pallet—were visibly and dynamically expressed on the floor of the convention as delegates sought and responded to the Spirit of the living God.

At least as important was the gracious manner in which the bishop expressed his love and support for the dissidents— promising to welcome them if they remained in the diocese or let them go in peace and without penalty if they chose to remain attached to the national church. Yet, readers need to know this story because it is a sacramentally-outbursting example of living inside a miracle on a corporate scale.

More than a decade ago, a prophetic team from the Kansas City International House of Prayer encountered a crowd of Anglicans praying for their denomination's national convention in Philadelphia. The bishop of the Fresno-based diocese was among those who received their prophetic word. The prophetic team referred the Anglican intercessors to a number of verses from Haggai 2 and Isaiah 62. They proclaimed God's promise to permit the death of this denomination so that He could resurrect it—even making her a kind of first fruits for the Body of Christ in the United States. What we witnessed—as participants and as observers—was not just American history or even

Church history in the making, but the unfolding of a chapter of salvation history.

To date, the declaration spoken in Philadelphia in 1997 can be seen coming true, phoneme by phoneme and syllable by syllable, as faithful Anglicans seek God's face and rely on His promise that we cannot fail to find Him when we seek Him with all of our hearts. The mandate of a Faithworks Coalition is being daily perfected in the strength of a God who cannot ignore our weakness. (Remember, they have trouble funding a secretarial position, but they can and do—in Him—cut welfare rolls in half and build transitional housing complexes.) The favor on the Jesus Culture is spreading that ministry all over the world and deepening its impact on the streets and campuses of our community. The destiny of a ministry like Carenet Pregnancy Centers to become a full-service medical facility featuring prayer is manifesting one day at a time; and whether you are the next Roger Ralston, the next Sharre Littrell, or the next unnamed volunteer—without whose kindness to a client or prayer for a miracle, the process cannot continue—God is honoring His servants and calling us friends. The ground for transformation of a community is being plowed and planted through prophetic acts with impact like Paah-ho-ammi and the annual speaking of God's Word over the city.

What is the difference between living inside these macro miracles and the micro one in which God has placed Diana for the healing of her body? Not a jot or a tittle.

If you are praying for your own denomination's resurrection, for your community, for a generational revival, or for whatever dimension of the whole Kingdom that God has laid on your heart—and especially if the pace is so slow it would embarrass a tortoise—grow not weary in well-doing. There are sacramental outbursts and unusual miracles coming forth all around you. His will is that you seek His face until you can see these things for yourself—and hear as He sings His songs to you. Then, He wants you to notice the teaching that is implicit in each budding intervention into our world so that you and others with whom you pray can sow into them and watch them escalate—for our God is a God of escalation.

If you have been serving the Lord in that quarter of the vineyard in which He placed you a long time ago, recognize that in these outbursts of His glory are the sound of a trumpet declaring His impending return. (Just remember that we don't know what words like "impending" mean to Him.) He is a God of duration—a God who says that the ones who endure to the end are the ones who are saved; His presence in any day makes it a special day because any day spent in His courts is better than a thousand spent anywhere else (see Ps. 84:10).

It is our privilege as much as our obligation to honor one another in His Name; when we do that, we honor Him. But we also get to participate in the honor He heaps on His own as He names us His good and faithful servants. There is no privilege greater than washing the feet of those He has set apart—the word is *saints*—because when we do this, we get to wash His feet, or so He says. That privilege is ours when we treat one another as though they were more important than we are—whether that means praying for and serving the saints or trusting them in their vocation to serve the Kingdom and us.

We are—each of us—called and privileged to a life of progressive repentance, investment in the Kingdom, and repetition of the basics of the Kingdom life. We are invited to do the scariest and most excitingly wonderful thing anyone has ever done—to become so radically engaged with the Lord our God and with the people who are called by His name as to take our place within the prophetic community of the Body of Christ. We have had our Davids and our Peters and our Pauls—and we may well have them again. But we are offered the chance of a lifetime today to become a Body of Barnabas people. That is the model of First Corinthians 12. That is how it will be on earth as it is in Heaven in this day.

He says, "You're all I want; you're all I've ever needed. You're all I want; show me that you are near."

Endnote

1. Hermann Hesse, *Siddhartha* (New York: Bantam Books, 1971), 64.

ABOUT THE AUTHOR

Jim Wilson taught for over a decade in California public schools before being called into the ministry. He graduated from Seabury-Western Theological Seminary in 1985 and pastored congregations for 16 years. From that vantage point, he has seen and celebrated the work of God's Holy Spirit in charismatic, evangelical, and mainline bodies with equal awe and enthusiasm. He and his wife, Diana, launched PrayNorthState in February 2001, making it their full-time ministry in June of that year.

Jim teaches on personal evangelism, congregational development, leadership, spiritual giftings, and the simple majesty of God's creation. His focus has been on community transformation and reconciliation since 1996. His ministry crosses denominational and cultural barriers as he shares the wonder of God's call to the Body of Christ to become a genuinely cooperative Body. He has written more than 300 articles for newspapers and periodicals, and his first book, *Living As Ambassadors of Relationships*, was published by Destiny Image Publishers. He hosts popular weekly radio and television programs and ministers across the United States and in multiple nations from Northern Europe to the Pacific Rim and Asia.

Since 2001 Jim has offered a series of weekend training events designed to teach the principles of prayer evangelism, warfare by honor, and prophetic acts with impact as they provide opportunities to practice these principles. He and Diana have established Prayer Vanguard—praying teams that prepare and pave for transformation—in nearly 20 Northern California communities. Jim leads an interdenominational team of intercessors who come alongside communities, churches, and ministries seeking the Kingdom of God and His blessing anywhere in the state of California.

Jim and Diana share a passion to seed 10,000 intercessors across Northern California—praying for their neighbors, their communities, and God's Kingdom harvest. They believe that God is on the move in equal parts of prophetic and pragmatic events for community transformation. Their passion—and their ministry—is PrayNorthState.

CONTACT THE AUTHOR

PRAY**N**ORTHSTATE

The Rev. James and Diana Wilson

P.O. Box 493743
Redding, CA 96049-3743

Phone: 530-941-3470

E-mail: praynorthstate@charter.net
Website: www.praynorthstate.org

Additional copies of this book and other
book titles from DESTINY IMAGE are
available at your local bookstore.

Call toll-free: 1-800-722-6774.

Send a request for a catalog to:

Destiny Image Publishers, Inc.

P.O. Box 310
Shippensburg, PA 17257-0310

"Speaking to the Purposes of God for this
Generation and for the Generations to Come."

For a complete list of our titles,
visit us at www.destinyimage.com.